Shug Jordan

SHUG

The Life and Times of Auburn's
RALPH 'SHUG' JORDAN

Rich Donnell

OWL BAY
Publishers

Owl Bay Publishers
P.O. Box 6461
Montgomery, AL 36106

Owl Bay books are available at special discounts for bulk purchases
for sales promotions, premiums, fund-raising, or educational use.

Design by Randall Williams

Manufactured in the United States of America.

LIBRARY OF CONGRESS CATALOGING-IN-PUBLICATION DATA

    Donnell, Rich
      Shug : the life and times of Auburn's Ralph 'Shug'
Jordan / Rich Donnell.
          p. cm.
    ISBN 0-9638568-0-4
    1. Jordan, Ralph.   2. Football coaches--United
States--Biography.
    3. Auburn University. I. Title.
    GV939.J66D66 1993
    796.332'07'092--DC20
    [B]
                        93-11974
                           CIP

For May, Sarah, and Jay

His life was gentle, and the elements

So mixed in him that Nature might stand up

And say to all the world, 'This was a man!'

–William Shakespeare

Contents

• • • • • • • • •

Acknowledgments

My interest in writing a biography of James Ralph "Shug" Jordan dates back to September 1979, when as a young sportswriter I interviewed Jordan at length in his office in Memorial Coliseum on the Auburn University campus. This was just ten months before he died.

Besides his long reign as head football coach at my alma mater and my lifelong admiration of the man, what appealed to me was the range of Jordan's association with college football, from his playing days in the late 1920s to his final years as head coach in the mid-1970s. Jordan played college football when Knute Rockne reached his peak as the head coach at Notre Dame, and in fact Jordan played at Auburn under former Rockne players Chet Wynne and Roger Kiley. Jordan's coaching career began as the Great Depression tired out, rolled along until World War II, moved into the 1950s era of crew cuts, flat tops and conservative tight-T running attacks, sailed into the turbulent 1960s and the onslaught of the passing game, and vaulted into the age of specialization and the emergence of the black football player in the Southeastern Conference. Jordan had a reputation as a conservative coach, but the record shows that he adjusted with the times and continued to field successful teams year after year.

In 1985, five years after Jordan's death, I wrote an article for *Alabama Magazine* about Jordan. It was during the research and interview process for this story that I began to appreciate the true depth of the man. I learned among other things that he was a war hero. I suspected a biography would be forthcoming.

Projects like this book require encouragement and two memorable moments spurred me forward. One was when Vince Dooley, the former Georgia head football coach and current athletic director, came to Montgomery in 1989 to promote his autobiography, *Dooley's Dawgs*. Following a dinner at which Dooley was the guest speaker, I approached him and presented my idea for the biography. Dooley responded with conviction that he felt the book needed to be done. Dooley's support of this book, and his deep respect and love for his former coach, is reflected in his foreword to this volume.

The second moment occurred in early 1992 during a conversation with David Housel, sports information director at Auburn. I was weighing whether to make the ultimate plunge into the project — which at that time had no backing of a publisher — when Housel stated, "I think one needs to be written and I can't think of a better man to write it than you." These were tremendously uplifting words from a veteran Auburn man and the best sports information director in the country.

As my hours of research accumulated, luck came my way when George Littleton of Owl Bay Publishers caught wind of the project. Littleton, an Auburn native and great admirer of Shug Jordan, enthusiastically endorsed the biography and we were off. Littleton's Auburn background was crucial in helping me understand Jordan's love for the loveliest village and his role as a member of the community.

Of course the book could not have been written without the cooperation of the people who knew Shug Jordan best. I considered Kenny Howard, head trainer for all of Jordan's teams, to be an interview of paramount importance. I called Howard before I called anyone else. Had Howard said he wasn't interested in talking with me, I would have had second thoughts about continuing the project. But Howard took to the idea and provided valuable commentary on Jordan's life and character. So did Buck Bradberry, former Jordan assistant and former head of the Auburn Alumni Association; so did

Gene Lorendo, who assisted Jordan for all of his twenty-five years as head coach; so did George Atkins, former Jordan player and for sixteen years a line coach under Jordan. I relied on these four men again and again.

I am very grateful to Ralph Jordan Jr., the only son of Shug Jordan. He supported the project wholeheartedly and discussed even the most personal aspects of his father's life and death.

I am also grateful to the many other players and coaches I interviewed. They, too, were greatly supportive of the book. If nothing else comes across in this biography, I hope readers sense the warm and lasting relationships Jordan established with so many of his players and coaches. I should add that many of these interviews were conducted with football heroes of mine. Was I nervous when I talked with the likes of Tucker Frederickson, Pat Sullivan and Terry Beasley? You bet I was.

Two very touching conversations will forever stay with me. One was with Don Fuell, the quarterback who was at the center of Auburn's three-year probation from 1958-1960. Fuell told me about the day the SEC kicked him out of the conference and placed Auburn on probation: he received the jarring news and went up to his hotel room and cried. Likewise, a full thirty-five years later, Fuell broke down as we discussed those events over the phone.

Neither will I forget J.D. Bush, a football teammate of Jordan's from 1929-1931, unashamedly crying as he remembered his final visit with Jordan shortly before his old friend died.

A required exercise in the creation of this book was reading and studying the material already "out there." David Housel's two books, *Saturdays To Remember* and *from the desk of david housel...*, *A Collection Of Auburn Stories*, and Clyde Bolton's *War Eagle, The Story of Auburn Football*, grew ragged from my continued use. I also benefited from the material published last year as part of the celebration of 100 years of Auburn football. A little-known book, *National Champions*, written by Jim Koger, provided amazing insight into the early years of college football.

Auburn University Photographic Services manager Les King —

who became the University's chief photographer the same year Shug Jordan became its head coach — was invaluable in bringing the book to life. My only regret is that I was unable to incorporate more of the magnificent material Mr. King made available to me.

The Southeastern Conference Football Guide and various Auburn football media guides served as my key references for statistics and records. I should add here that for the sake of brevity and clarity I used only the Associated Press All-SEC teams when naming Auburn players honored as all-conference; and used only the Associated Press college football poll, once it came into existence, in my references to national rankings. My preference for the Associated Press was tied purely to Auburn's national championship in 1957 as awarded by the Associated Press. When naming All-Americans I did not limit myself to the AP team, but named Auburn players who had made first team on any of numerous All-American teams, as is also done by the SEC football guide.

While I quickly came to realize that much had been written about Shug Jordan and Auburn football, I also recognized that much of what had been written could be elaborated on, and much had yet to come into focus.

Shug Jordan was a great man. I hope this book helps explain why, and that it fills what I perceived as a great gap on the shelf of the college football library.

Rich Donnell

Foreword
• • • • • • • • •

By VINCENT J. DOOLEY

During a very difficult time in the history of Auburn University, Coach Ralph "Shug" Jordan returned in 1951 to his alma mater as the head football coach. Auburn, known then as A.P.I., Alabama Polytechnic Institute, like many agricultural and mechanical schools in the Deep South, historically represented the long-suffering people of the state who struggled against the power of the big city and the more affluent state universities. Auburn's plight was made worse during that era since the football team, which normally could serve as a unifying source and point of pride, was regarded as one of the worst in the country. The Tigers, also known at that time as the Plainsmen, went almost a decade without a winning season. This long drought was culminated in 1950 prior to Coach Jordan's arrival when the team suffered the ultimate humiliation by losing every game!

After an extensive national search, Auburn decided to put its future in the hands of an Auburn alumnus for the first time in the school's history. Coach Jordan had impressed a majority of the committee members by saying, "If you can't put your faith in an Auburn man, who can you put your faith in?"

From that moment in 1951, and for the next quarter of a century, Coach Jordan truly became the symbol of the Auburn spirit. He became the model of what Auburn was, is, and aspires to be. He provided leadership to a university that desperately needed leadership, particularly at the grass roots level.

"Shug," as he was affectionately known, revitalized the football team and made the Tigers a winner. He taught the Auburn people to feel good about themselves, and he became their main point of pride. The people shouted "War Eagle!" with a conviction and a devotion unheard of in the past. He challenged them to stand tall and believe in themselves and reminded them that being an Auburn person was something that was very special indeed. He lifted their spirits and made them feel like first-class citizens, and then when he thought they had erred, he chastised them and reminded them that "Auburn people don't act that way."

His life and leadership affected a whole generation of Auburn people and indirectly affected others. I, perhaps more than many, was directly influenced by him for a lifetime. For twelve years I was part of his program as a player and a coach, and from him I developed the basis for a coaching philosophy that I took with me to Georgia — a philosophy that emphasized well-conditioned, disciplined football teams that believed in themselves and the university they represented. The influence went beyond the football field, and is best explained in his "7 D's of Success." In addition to discipline, Coach Jordan preached "Desire, Determination, Dedication, Dependability, Desperation and "Damn it anyway!" (a common expression used when it was necessary to make a tough decision). I also learned that one can be both a tough disciplinarian and a compassionate gentleman, and that one should have an appreciation of history as he so often referred to the way things had been done "down through the years."

History will record that Coach Jordan not only related to the larger world of Auburn University and beyond its playing fields, but he was also one of the heroes of the Deep South in its struggles to maintain the best of its culture and way of life, and at the same time, to be progressive in a fast-moving, changing world.

The influence Coach Jordan had on my life and my career dramatically flashed before me in a few short seconds while walking across the playing field in 1975 in Sanford Stadium in Athens, Georgia, to shake his hand as a rival coach for the last time. We had competed against each other the previous eleven years, and since he had announced his retirement prior to the season this moment would end our rivalry. As I approached him and saw his countenance, my happiness as the winning coach was immediately tempered. I quickly reflected on this grand and wonderful man who, during the previous twenty-five years, had coached me, given me my first job, and then become a tough competitor when I became coach of the Georgia Bulldogs. In his truest genteel style, this warm gentleman extended his hand, congratulated me, and gave me that special Coach Jordan smile. As always, he was most gracious in a difficult time, and I knew it was particularly tough on him that year since his last season as a coach had gone so poorly.

All of those thoughts flashed before me during that short walk to the middle of the field. I was never a person to show great outward emotion, perhaps because he also influenced me that way. But at that moment, I became very emotional, and I embraced Coach Jordan expressing my deep appreciation, respect, and love for this gentleman coach.

It was the final salute to my coach and to the man who not only had a profound effect on my life, but also on the lives of a generation of Auburn people. He left us all a legacy that will be passed on to future generations of Auburn people, and all people in general, "down through the years."

SHUG

1

"A dark day when we left"
●●●●●●●●●●●●●●●●●●●●●●●●●●●●

Things were bad for Shug Jordan at Auburn following World War II.

Carl Voyles, Auburn's head football coach and athletic director, didn't like having Jordan and a handful of other returning war veterans around. The way Voyles saw it, only by law had they been allowed to return to Auburn to fill the positions they had held before the war. During the war years Voyles had hired his own staff and he was going to make it tough on the ones who came back.

"Voyles wanted to show people that we weren't cooperating with him," said Elmer Salter, who had been director of athletic publicity at Auburn before entering the service. "We weren't trusted. He did everything he could to make us want to leave."

Voyles would drive around Auburn at night to see if any of the "outcast" members of the staff were visiting each other. In Voyles's mind, such visits indicated that they were conspiring against him. It got so bad that the "outcasts" were reluctant to be seen together.

"I remember several times getting in my car with Shug and heading for the woods towards Notasulga and Loachapoka, just so we could talk and see what the situation was without anybody seeing us," Salter said. "To talk among ourselves we had to find some secret ways."

Elmer Salter and Shug Jordan sneaking out of Auburn so they could talk?

These were pure Auburn men. Between them, they had already accumulated almost thirty years at Auburn *before* World War II.

Salter graduated from Auburn in 1928 and became Auburn's first director of athletic publicity in 1929. He held the position until he entered the service in 1942.

One of Salter's claims to fame was closing the deal on Auburn's participation in the Rhumba Bowl in Havana, Cuba, which was played on New Year's Day, 1937. Salter arrived in Cuba ahead of the team and only at the last hour — when he collected a final payment of $7,500, as promised for Auburn's participation — did he send word back that the team could catch the train for Tampa, where it would board a ship for Cuba. The game was part of a sports festival that also featured gold medalist track star Jesse Owens racing against a horse. (The race ended prematurely when the horse cut across the infield.) Auburn tied Villanova 7-7.

Salter first heard of Jordan through his brother, Gerald Salter, who taught at Selma High School in Selma, Alabama. Gerald told Elmer that Auburn had an outstanding freshman athlete who had graduated from Selma High, and that Elmer should look him up. The rest, as they say, is history.

Jordan played football, basketball and baseball every year at Auburn, beginning as a freshman in 1928. In his senior year, Jordan established himself as the school's best all-around athlete when he started at center on the football team, excelled for the third straight year as a forward on the basketball team, and pitched for the baseball team. Dozens of Auburn newspaper articles during Jordan's playing career carried Elmer Salter's byline.

After graduating in 1932, Jordan joined Auburn's staff as an assistant freshman football coach. The next year he became head freshman coach. Salter and Jordan roomed together in 1933 along with Jimmy Hitchcock, who in the previous year had run, passed and kicked Auburn to an undefeated season. Hitchcock became Auburn's first All-American. After Hitchcock graduated, he assisted Jordan with the freshman team. The roommates lived at a boarding house run by Fob James's grandmother. James was a star running back on Jordan's early Auburn teams in the 1950s; he was elected governor of Alabama in 1978.

Jordan remained head freshman football coach for five years and then joined head varsity coach Jack Meagher's staff as an assistant line coach. Jordan also coached the varsity basketball team and the freshman baseball team. Salter traveled with Jordan in the three-car caravan that transported the basketball squads until Jordan entered the Army in early 1942.

Such were the backgrounds of Elmer Salter and Shug Jordan, who were sneaking out of Auburn so they could talk.

Jordan understood that a head coach wanted his own staff, but he didn't appreciate the cold shoulder. His thoughts honed in on his career and future. He had a wife and two daughters to support. He was thirty-five years old. He loved Auburn, and had hoped his future would be there. But it hadn't worked out that way.

"We were just not accepted as part of the coaching staff," Jordan said. "I knew we had to move on. I had no idea that I would ever come back to Auburn, and, indeed, it was a dark day for the Jordan family when we left."

Auburn University, in the summer of 1946, had run off its favorite son: James Ralph "Shug" Jordan.

2

"I've never known a better man"
●●●●●●●●●●●●●●●●●●●●●●●●●●●●●●●●●●

Jeff Beard, Auburn's athletic director from 1951 to 1972, and one of the men most responsible for hiring Jordan as head coach in 1951, marveled at Jordan's record and career. Few coaches in the history of college football can match Jordan's accomplishments. But Beard also said of his close friend Shug: "His record doesn't speak for him as a man."

During his twenty-five years as head football coach at Auburn, Shug Jordan's Tigers won 176 games, lost eighty-three and tied six. His 1957 team won Auburn's only national championship with a 10-0 record. The 1957 squad also won Auburn's first Southeastern Conference title. Thirteen times, Jordan's teams finished in the Associated Press top twenty, seven times in the top ten, and four times in the top five. They appeared in twelve bowl games, and NCAA probation cost them at least four more appearances. Jordan's teams produced a Heisman Trophy winner in 1971 in quarterback Pat Sullivan, and an Outland Trophy winner in 1958 — guard Zeke Smith — for the nation's best interior lineman. Twenty-two players made first-team All-American during the Jordan era. Of his twenty-five Auburn teams, twenty-two had winning records.

Beard's comment about Jordan — that even his sterling record didn't match the greatness of the man — was not meant to minimize Jordan's numbers on the field or the honors he achieved. Certainly 176 victories, which places Jordan high on the all-time win list ahead of such greats as General Bob Neyland, Wallace Wade and Bobby

Dodd, are not to be understated; nor are Jordan's four SEC Coach of the Year awards (1953, 1957 and 1972, as given by the Associated Press; and 1963 by United Press International).

Beard was saying that Jordan the man was bigger than the game — that the makeup of Jordan's character impacted his peers and players long after the final horn had sounded. The National Football Foundation Hall of Fame recognized this when it inducted Jordan posthumously in 1982. Auburn fans endorsed this in 1992 when they voted Jordan as the head coach on Auburn's 100-year team. Jordan, as a player, assistant coach and head coach, participated in thirty-nine of those 100 years.

Jordan's players felt his impact all along. They remember Jordan as a son remembers his father. Their deep affection for Jordan right down the line — whether they played for him in 1951 or 1975, whether they were city-slick from Atlanta or country-fried from Fayette — is unfailing. This can't be said of many college football coaches.

"Until he died, I never saw him when he didn't ask about my mother," said Lloyd Nix, who quarterbacked Jordan's 1957 national champions.

Buck Bradberry, who played at the University of Georgia when Jordan was an assistant coach there, and coached under Jordan at Auburn from 1951-1965, said, "Coach Jordan coached by making his players and assistants feel good about themselves. The way he did it, it was almost like his personality itself demanded respect, because he was so respectful of you."

"He was a humanitarian," Beard said. "He understood other people's problems."

Following is a portion of a letter that David Langner wrote to Jimmie McDowell, executive director of the National Football Foundation Hall of Fame, in recommending Jordan's induction in 1982. Langner played defensive back under Jordan from 1971-1973. He became forever etched in Auburn football history when he ran two fourth-quarter blocked punts for touchdowns in Auburn's 17-16 win over Alabama in 1972. Langner's letter offers a glimpse at Jordan's relationship with many of his players.

"Mr. McDowell, there's no way I can tell you what Coach Jordan meant to me as a football player and as a person. All of us were his boys. It didn't make any difference if we played or if we sat on the bench, he loved us and cared for us as individuals and each of us knew it and loved him.

"I was fortunate enough to experience some success on the football field. I couldn't handle it and I did some things I'm not particularly proud of doing. I didn't want to see Coach Jordan because I knew I had not lived up to what he expected of me. From talking with other people, I knew he had kept up with me and still cared about me.

"When my first child was born, I knew it was time to put my life back together. Coach Jordan was the first person I went to see. He helped me back in school and helped me get a graduate assistant's position.

"Everything I am and everything I hope to be, I owe to him ... because he loved and cared about me as a person."

Jordan's wife Evelyn said, "At one time more than 95 percent of the players who played four years for him earned their degrees from Auburn. He was so proud when our players went on to become doctors, lawyers, educators and successful people in their chosen field. He felt like the things learned on the football field, qualities like leadership, courage, dedication and discipline, were qualities that would help the players later in life. It's hard for boys to do more than play football, but he always told them it would be worth the effort."

Thirty-eight Auburn players made the academic All-SEC team in Jordan's years as head coach. Among them were Fob James, Jimmy Phillips, Lloyd Nix, Zeke Smith, Jackie Burkett, Ed Dyas, Bill Cody, Buddy McClinton, Pat Sullivan, and Mike Neel. Six players — Phillips, Burkett, Dyas, Cody, McClinton, and linebacker Bobby Davis — made academic All-American.

If Jordan found out one of his players had skipped class, he made them run.

Gusty Yearout, a first-team All-SEC linebacker in 1967, became a successful attorney in Birmingham. He had planned since high school to attend law school, but after his final season as an Auburn player he wanted to become a coach instead. That Yearout was named academic All-SEC for his grades in pre-law was not lost on Jordan.

"I went to Coach Jordan and asked him if he would let me be a graduate assistant," Yearout recalled. "He said he thought I wanted to go to law school. I said I wanted to try coaching for a year or two and that if I didn't like it I'd go to law school."

Jordan's reply shaped Yearout's future.

"I'll tell you what," Jordan advised. "You go to law school and if you don't like that, then come back and I'll give you a job. This business appears to be real glamorous and wonderful, but it's a difficult business and it's not a business that can be a secure profession like being a lawyer. But if you go to law school and don't like it, I'll give you a job."

"That always made me respect him and have an understanding of him," said Yearout.

Jordan had much the same influence on his assistant coaches. They remember him for the great amount of responsibility he gave. They remember his fairness. They remember him for making them feel a part of the Auburn program, which is why so many of them stayed with him for so long. Ten coaches worked at his side for ten years or more.

"I've never known a better man," said George Atkins, offensive line coach for sixteen years, from 1956-1971.

Shug Jordan was a gentleman. That's usually what those who knew him best say first about him. He was a man of his word. He was polished, well-mannered, social, and scholarly. He fraternized well with the university faculty. He remembered people's first names. He spoke slowly and eloquently, with an endearing drawl. It was easy for him to speak totally from the heart in front of two-hundred people.

"He was a very literate coach," said Caroline Draughon, a Selma High classmate of Jordan's and wife of the late Auburn University president Ralph Draughon. "He spoke beautifully. He never said 'git.' He read a great deal. He lived quietly when he could. But he was always very gracious to entertain and work with the faculty and alumni."

Jordan's excellent sense of humor served him well from his early days on the road recruiting players and seeking alumni support to his later years when his speeches became much sought-after. When something tickled him, his voice rose a notch until it disappeared into a big smile and a hearty chuckle.

Jordan had the ability to make light of a situation. Before World War II, Elmer Salter and Jordan ate lunch in Sewanee, Tennessee, before a basketball game there. It was a Friday. Jordan was Catholic. The menu didn't mention fish. Salter brought it to the coach's attention.

Jordan replied, "I'm Episcopalian today."

In fact, Jordan loved good, old-fashioned Southern country cooking at the lunch-hour: meat loaf, pork chops, butterbeans, tomatoes, fried corn, cornbread, a plate of barbecue and corn-on-the-cob. He poured on the salt. He would occasionally go on a diet and proudly announce to his family that he had dropped ten pounds, but he never stayed away from country cooking for long.

Jordan's knack for putting a moment into a lighter and proper perspective carried into the most intense football games. He could rise above the game and for a second or two not take it too seriously. Many Auburn fans at Legion Field in Birmingham booed when Jordan sent in Gardner Jett to attempt a 42-yard field goal with under ten minutes remaining in the 1972 Alabama game. The Tide led 16-0 and Auburn's offense had made its best drive of the day.

With the boos resounding, Jordan glanced behind him at head trainer Kenny Howard. Jordan smiled and, with a quick glance up into the stands, said, "They don't think we're gonna win, do they?"

It was serious business, but it was still a game. Jett made the field goal to cut the lead to 16-3. Auburn went on to win, thanks to two blocked punts, 17-16.

When the play on the field was going well, Jordan was not such a perfectionist that he couldn't make light of a mistake. In 1957, the year of the national title, Auburn played its fifth game of the season in Houston. Auburn jumped out to a 22-0 lead and was knocking on the goal line again with time running out in the first half. Jordan sent his quarterback, Lloyd Nix, and two star ends, Red Phillips and Jerry Wilson, back into the game with the simple instruction "to get it in the end zone." Nix promptly threw an interception that was returned eighty-nine yards for a Houston touchdown.

Jordan confronted Nix as he returned to the sidelines, grabbed him by the shoulder pads and stared the quarterback right in the eye. "Dammit, Lloyd, I meant *our* end zone," Jordan said.

Jordan's gentlemanly nature did not mean he was above bearing a grudge, getting in a rage, being tough or spitting out a cuss word. Mike Neel, linebacker from 1970-1972, and an assistant under Jordan, said Jordan possessed both a great sense of humor and an extremely tough, almost mean streak. An acquaintance of Jordan said he could be "one stubborn Irishman." When intense, his face would grow hard. His left hand would tug on his left ear lobe.

He was not one to make the sports pages every day because of his criticism of an issue, but when the matter moved him to speak, Jordan hit hard. In May 1958, the SEC executive committee and SEC commissioner ruled in agreement with an earlier finding of the NCAA council that Auburn committed infractions involving the recruitment of Guntersville High School quarterback Don Fuell. The ruling slapped Auburn, which had bitterly contested the charges, with a three-year penalty and kicked Fuell, who had played his freshman year at Auburn, out of the conference.

Jordan responded: "The Southeastern Conference missed a great opportunity to grow up and become a real conference today. The commissioner missed a great opportunity to grow up and be a real commissioner."

"No doubt he was fiery," said Phil Gargis, quarterback for Jordan's last two teams in 1974 and 1975. "Yes, he was a calm person, a Southern gentleman, but you cross him and he had fire in him."

"You did not want to bring his wrath down on you," said Jack Thornton, who was an All-American tackle in 1965. "The stadium steps were awfully high."

While it can be stated that men such as Jordan and Knute Rockne were greater than the game, their personalities hinged on football. As others have found in their search for Rockne's character, the search for Jordan's character weaves its way into how he coached football. Two areas in which he excelled were discipline and inspiration.

"I have always had a profound respect for discipline," Jordan said. "That has to be number one on the list. If you don't have a well-disciplined organization, army, business, school or team, I don't think you can amount to anything. Some coaches can have great recruiting years, great personnel, great material and not win. And I think the fundamental reason is because they're not disciplined. Some people, some coaches, some military teachers can take inferior personnel and win because of discipline."

Discipline was indeed number one on Jordan's "7-D's Of Success," a paper he wrote and publicized. His "7-D's" were: Discipline, Desire to Excel, Determination, Dedication, Dependability, Desperation, and Damn It Anyway, the latter meaning that when all else had failed a man had to plow ahead on guts and instinct.

He stated, "It has often been said, and rightly so, that football would not be worth the sacrifice it demands of players if it were not for the lessons it teaches its participants about life."

On discipline, Jordan wrote, "Any successful person must learn to discipline himself before he can discipline others, and before he can learn to discipline himself, he must learn to accept discipline from others. Football teaches discipline in training obviously, but, by applying a set of rules to govern play, football lets a man discover how he will react in a given situation and what he can and can't do. This tells a man where his breaking point is."

The foundations of discipline, Jordan believed, were the basic, written, concrete team rules, and the line he drew in his players' minds that they should not cross.

The most serious disciplinary action Jordan ever took involving a player was the dismissal from the team, following spring practice in 1957, of that fall's probable starting quarterback along with a leading fullback candidate. As a result, Lloyd Nix started at quarterback and Billy Atkins started at fullback. They spearheaded Auburn's drive to the national title. Jordan felt this act of discipline brought the team together and sparked its drive to the crown.

Jordan's disciplinary actions relating to rule-breaking were compassionate but firm. They usually occurred behind closed doors. He would sometimes give a player a second chance. He often agonized over disciplinary actions. But if the player stepped out of line again, discipline would come like the snap of a finger. And it was final.

Quarterback Pat Sullivan, at the request of his teammates, once visited Jordan's office to plead with him to reverse a decision to suspend a player from the team. Before Sullivan opened his mouth, Jordan gestured with his left hand for Sullivan to stop.

"I know what you want, but I'm not letting him back on," Jordan said of the suspended player. "I had to do something to shock him in order to wake him up."

If there was a problem with a player, Jordan might ask for the opinions of his assistant coaches during a staff meeting. He would start with the coach beside him and move around the table. When they all had spoken, Jordan would say, "Gentlemen, I've listened to all of you and you all have good ideas, but here's how it's going to be."

A player in the late 1960s attempted to pass several bad checks. It was not the first disciplinary incident involving the player. Jordan asked the assistants their opinions and most commented that the boy had received and blown enough chances and should be dismissed from the squad. Offensive line coach George Atkins, sensing that Jordan might be in a forgiving mood, pointed out the boy's successful development as a winning player and that Auburn needed winners in its program. Atkins offered to make the boy work off his debt through some rigorous rock-clearing labor at Atkins's lake house. Jordan said he would go along with Atkins, but emphasized, "If he steps out of line again, I'll be talking to you. You better keep his ass straight."

The player went on to a great career at Auburn.

Matters of a less-serious nature, given that he liked what he heard from the player, could draw forth some of Jordan's wit. In 1973, Jordan called freshman quarterback Phil Gargis on the carpet because he heard Gargis had been fighting in public.

"Phillip, you're the quarterback, I'm the coach," Jordan said. "We have to be honest with each other. Tell me what happened."

Gargis told his side of the story: he had been in a fight, but he hadn't started the confrontation. The feisty Gargis felt he had been harassed beyond what a man should have to endure.

"I got a call that you used brass knuckles," Jordan said, with his back to Gargis.

"No sir, I did not," Gargis replied.

Jordan turned back around toward Gargis. "Did you whip his ass good?" he asked.

"Yes sir," Gargis replied.

Gargis, reflecting on the incident, recalled, "If it was a situation where you were protecting your honor, your pride, Coach Jordan understood."

Jordan felt that poor behavior on the players' part, and the same was true for the assistant coaches, reflected poorly on him and the team, but more importantly reflected poorly on Auburn University.

"Auburn people don't do that," Jordan would say. Or, "That's not the Auburn way." He even criticized the student body on occasion for inappropriate behavior.

Jordan's love for Auburn University, his devotion to it, was the backbone of his character and his methods.

Jordan would relate how during his military service overseas in World War II he frequently encountered a special bond when he ran into Auburn grads; how it lifted him up. This was a man with a strong sense of duty, honor and integrity; a man who always tried to do the right thing for the young men who had been placed in his charge. He did it with Auburn in mind.

Just as Rockne cannot be separated from Notre Dame, Jordan cannot be separated from Auburn. After all, Jordan graduated from Auburn and then coached there for thirty-five years. He only left Auburn twice — once because of the war, and once because he wasn't welcome when he returned from the war. Jordan was a friend of the community. People could touch him. He chose to die in Auburn.

Jordan was an Auburn man through and through, both on and off the field. He expected the same commitment from his players and coaches. If they strayed, they paid the price, sometimes a dear one.

One of his assistants, in a bid for more control, began bad-mouthing another coach to the Auburn alumni. Word of it got back to Jordan. When the assistant came to Jordan and asked to be promoted, Jordan said it wasn't a good idea. When the assistant said that Jordan either had to promote him or he would leave the staff, Jordan replied, "We're sure going to miss you."

Innate in Jordan's discipline, in addition to obeying the rules, was a steadfast, fundamental work ethic on the practice field. An assistant coach described the mid-week practice sessions as "some heavy knocking, some hard-ass work." Jordan always emphasized getting the work in, or bemoaned his squad falling behind due to injury or weather. He would fret over a season-opening game when the opponent had played a week earlier and had a week of work under its belt.

Jordan appreciated it when his players put out their best effort. It made him almost gleeful. Of his defense's effort during one fall practice, Jordan bellowed, "I want to tell you they stood up on their hind legs today and let them have it, went after the offense, went after their throats!"

But if practice didn't go well and the work ethic wasn't there, Jordan's spirit sagged. "I sometimes forget it, but it's been a fight ever since I've known it, a fight with the individuals, fight with the offense, fight with the defense or fight with something every day to get a job done," he said.

Even in victory, if the team failed to put forth the effort, Jordan could become downright nasty. Throughout his career Jordan held Sunday morning workouts, mainly to see if any nagging injuries needed medical attention, but also to get the players up out of bed. After a brief period of loosening up, the team would take it to the showers. But after a narrow victory over a weak opponent in the mid-1960s, Jordan's Sunday morning "sermon" invited the players to line up at the goal line and run 100-yard sprints for two hours. When the preaching was over, few players were left standing. Most were throwing up.

Be they superstars or third-teamers, the players who appreciated Jordan's rules and stuck it out on the practice field discovered brotherhood and manhood, and enjoyed a lasting friendship with Jordan. The experience of running on to the field and playing football before sixty-thousand people was icing on the cake.

Once Jordan had his players' respect, had their attention, had a ready ear, he could inspire and motivate them as well as any coach in the history of the game. His expertise in inspiration is not as well known as his self-proclaimed propensity for discipline. His style ranged from scholarly to fiery, from compassionate to intimidating. His method might be a few simple words delivered on the practice field in the middle of the week.

Jordan constantly zeroed in on the right moment to do something or say something that would boost his team's morale and sharpen its competitive edge.

Once, following several extremely hot consecutive days of pre-season practice, Jordan had head trainer Kenny Howard call the players together in the training room before the afternoon workout. The players reported in their pads. The room was like a tomb. The players sat staring at the floor, waiting for the word to go out and knock heads under the scorching sun. Then Howard, at Jordan's instruction, announced they would go out in just shorts and helmets.

"I want to tell you they darn nigh tore down this six-million dollar coliseum," Jordan said. "And you know, we can think of all the psychology in the world and little cute things we can say to the squad to lift them up, but I want to tell you something and you can put it down in your notebook: There's nothing like a rainy day, or if you can't have a rainy day, there's nothing like a day in shorts and t-shirts."

College football tradition links many great coaches with the halftime talk. Jordan had his moments there, but he wasn't one to rip apart the locker room. The situation of the game determined his message, and he could be especially anxious if he felt his team was playing below its capabilities against a sub-par opponent.

He would pound his left fist into his right palm and say, "You're dead, there's no enthusiasm, you've got to have enthusiasm to play this game." He'd pause a moment and drop his head, giving the players time to think. "Hell!" he'd suddenly bark. "You can't even make love without enthusiasm!" The players would roar and crash onto the field, the weight of the world lifted from their shoulders.

If the team was struggling against a strong opponent, Jordan's message was more motivational. If the team was playing well, he dwelt on the positives.

Jordan's players seem to best remember the speeches he made on the Friday before Saturday's game. Here the team knelt around him on the field following a short workout. He frequently drew from history, in which he was extremely well read. Many of his talks referenced World War II. Jordan was a great admirer of General George Patton. He quoted from Winston Churchill's war speech in the House of Commons — "Never in the field of human conflict was so much owed by so many to so few." He referred to the Normandy invasion and the Battle of the Bulge. "You felt like you were on the battlefield," said Rusty Deen, defensive end from 1972-1974. Jordan quoted from the Bible, and in particular *Ecclesiastes*. He recited Shakespeare.

"Coach Jordan was a great student of history," said Kenny Howard. "This was part of his coaching makeup all the way through."

"It's as clear to me as yesterday, when we were able to come back and beat Alabama," recalled Pat Sullivan of Jordan's Friday talk preceding the 1970 game. "We had lost a lot of people. We were like a M.A.S.H. unit. After the workout, Coach Jordan called us up in the south end zone of Legion Field. He talked about the history of the American people, like in World War II, when Japan bombed Pearl Harbor; that it would have been easy for the American people to quit, but it wasn't the American way. Someone always rose to the occasion."

Auburn, surprise-attacked by Alabama, fell behind 17-0 before rising to the win, 33-28.

Jordan's messages also recalled historical feats of great courage against overwhelming and even impossible odds. There was something to be said for courage in defeat, something to be said for men who dug in and battled to their inevitable end. He referred to Custer's Last Stand, when General George Armstrong Custer's Seventh Cavalry was overrun by Sitting Bull, Crazy Horse and several Indian tribes at the Battle of Little Bighorn in Montana in 1876. He often cited Alfred Tennyson's poem "The Charge of the Light Brigade." Tennyson wrote it shortly after reading an account of a battle during the Crimean War in 1854. Because of a confusion in orders, six-hundred British cavalrymen had charged entrenched batteries of Russian artillery. The blunder cost most of the horsemen their lives. The poem glorified the charging riders for their adherence to duty. Jordan loved it.

> Cannon to the left of them,
> Cannon in front of them,
>   Volleyed and thundered;
> Stormed at with shot and shell,
> Boldly they rode and well,
> Into the jaws of Death,
> Into the mouth of hell
>   Rode the six hundred.

Jordan also became a student of the Civil War. He could describe in depth the great battles and knew much about the Confederate generals and the strategies they employed.

Jordan knew something about charging into the heat of battle fire from his experiences in World War II. He participated in four major invasions as an Army engineer, including Normandy, where shrapnel pierced him as he attacked the beach.

"Men, I know we're getting ready to break up, and you'll be going to a movie tonight and having a good time," Jordan told his team on the field one Friday. "But when you get back in your room tonight and lie down, talk to that Man upstairs, try to ask him to help you tomorrow. When they were about to let us off the landing craft, you better believe we were all on our hands and knees. And this is going to be a war tomorrow."

Jordan once surprised the freshman team as they sat on the bus waiting to leave for Tuscaloosa to play the Tide frosh. Jordan boarded just as the driver started to close the doors. The bus grew silent. "Men, there's one thing we don't teach at Auburn and that's hate," Jordan said. "But you've got to have a little to go to battle."

There were days when Jordan relied purely on his instincts, such as the Friday before the Tennessee game in 1972. The players, who would later be tagged "The Amazin's," were about to board the buses at Sewell Hall in Auburn for the ride to Legion Field. It was Auburn's third game of the season. Tennessee was ranked fourth nationally while Auburn, coming off the Sullivan-to-Beasley era, had been picked near the bottom of the conference and had performed sluggishly in a 14-7 win against tiny Chattanooga. Jordan called the team back into the dining hall. He chewed them out.

"I see in some of your eyes getting on the bus that you don't think we can win," he stated. "I don't care if it's just eleven of you who get on the bus, but those eleven better know we're going up there to win. Not maybe we can win, but going up there to win!"

Auburn won, 10-6, and went on to finish the season with a 10-1 record and ranked fifth nationally.

If Auburn fans in the Jordan years thought a good pre-season ranking was a curse for the Tigers, they're in good company because Jordan once mentioned the scenario himself. After a disappointing season-opening loss late in his career, and having entered the game ranked seventh in the nation, Jordan said, "You ask yourself the question, and I really don't have the answer to it: Do we ever do well at Auburn when we're riding high? It seems like we operate best from the underdog position."

Indeed, assuming the role of the underdog motivated Jordan.

"The underdog! That's the name of the game, that's Americana if you will," Jordan said. "People are for the underdogs and underdogs can rise up and knock off the mighty. That's happened all the way back in history. The Roman Empire disintegrated and people picked them apart. And on top of that, why heck, David and Goliath, let's go back to the Bible. I guess David was about a forty-point underdog in that match. But Goliath ended up on his backside. So you see, anything can happen. I've been with the high elation of upset victory and in the depths of despair after being a heavy favorite and getting the stuffing kicked out of us. But I'll have to concede, that's what makes the American game of football the finest, most colorful, the greatest game in the United States if not the world."

Jordan loved to win this great game he so adored, yet he could leave a loss behind him on the field better than most. And in the final days of his life he would question the increasing pressure to win at any cost.

3

"Don't wait to be a great man"
●●●●●●●●●●●●●●●●●●●●●●●●●●●●●●●●●●●

Everyone remembers the famous Selma-to-Montgomery civil rights march in the 1960s. Almost forgotten now is Shug Jordan's not-so-famous 1920s march from Montgomery to Selma. But Sol Tepper, a boyhood pal and teammate of Jordan's during their Selma High days, never forgot their long walk home. Tepper made it, too, along with a couple of other buddies.

Jordan, Tepper and friends had hitchhiked from Selma to Montgomery to see the University of Alabama play at Cramton Bowl. The Tide usually played one game a year in Montgomery and the boys didn't miss it. This was during Alabama's Rose Bowl era, featuring backs Johnny Mack Brown, Pooley Hubert and Red Barnes. The boys would either sneak into the game or, if they waited outside the gate long enough, somebody would give them tickets.

Usually they had a pre-arranged ride back, but one game ran extra long and they missed their ride. In the minds of energetic high school boys, a missed ride provided a good excuse to make the fifty-odd-mile trek home on foot. It became a challenge, in fact.

"We always went out of our way to get a lot of exercise," said Tepper. "We didn't think anything of playing four straight games of basketball and then running four or five miles."

They started out on their journey-by-foot before dark, passing wagons along the way. But the autumn night turned frigid, midnight passed, and two-thirds of the way home the weary lads sought rest and relief from a biting wind. In Benton, about fifteen miles from

Selma, they came upon a stack of plywood sheets piled in front of a country store. They snatched several panels, leaned them together to form a rough shelter, and huddled inside. But the cold wind continued to whip, and after a few bone-rattling, teeth-chattering minutes they agreed that they would keep warmer by walking. They started again toward Selma.

"We walked all the way back, fifty-five miles," Tepper said. "We got home just before sun-up. The food tasted pretty good when we got there."

"Later on, Shug said it always gave him the shivers when he passed by that place where the plywood was," Tepper said.

Selma, Alabama, before the First World War, before the arrival of the boll weevil, was a thriving city. It was built on a level sandy plateau that ran back from a steep soapstone bluff rising from the rippling waters of the Alabama River. By 1910, population had increased to fourteen thousand, a 50 percent jump since the turn of the century. Selma was the largest cotton market in central Alabama, handling 125,000 bales annually. Selma maintained two cotton compresses, four large cotton warehouses, and four cottonseed oil mills. It also had a brick plant, an iron foundry and machine shop, an ice plant, four dairies, ten wholesale grocery houses, wood products operations feeding on area forests, and six banks supported by ample capital.

A newspaper article at the time described Selma with paved streets, lawns shaded by massive live oaks, perfect sewerage and a dozen miles of electric city street railway.

"Selma is blessed with a mild climate, no sunstrokes in the summer, no blizzards in the winter, and the lowest death rate in the state," the Chamber of Commerce proclaimed.

Selma was also a major railroad town. Eight lines radiated from the city like the spokes of a wheel. The Southern Railroad owned five lines, Louisville & Nashville operated two lines and Western of Alabama accounted for the remaining line.

James Ralph Jordan was born here on September 25, 1910, the son of a career railroad man. His father, James Harry Jordan, and mother, Katherine Agnes Darby, had married in Selma on February 17, 1909. They met when Harry Jordan lived at a boarding house owned by Katherine Darby's mother, Mary Elizabeth Dietz Darby, a German immigrant, who had married William Elliot Darby, an Irish immigrant. William Darby operated an inn and a general store before dying in 1898. His passing prompted his wife to open the boarding house.

Harry Jordan left the coal mining town of Benson, West Virginia, at the turn of the century and came to Selma. In 1902, he began a forty-year career with Southern Railroad as a fireman.

William Lapsley, known as "Billy" when he and Shug Jordan were close friends in high school, recalled of Harry Jordan, "He was a pleasant, good man, a strong man. They had a good, happy house."

Jordan's buddy Tepper remembered that Mr. Jordan "was a quiet man, gentle spoken, about like Shug was. He didn't have too much to say unless he was spoken to."

Tepper said that Mr. Jordan had a blue scar on his face from a train wreck; coal dust getting into the cut caused the unusual coloration.

Mr. Jordan was a member of the Fireman's Union. Several high school pals of young Shug, including Tepper, joined the national guard and tried to get Shug to do the same. But because the guard was routinely called on when the railroad union went on strike, Shug refused to join, not wanting to risk an encounter with his father.

"When I was growing up, most everybody in Selma worked for the railroad," said Mrs. Dorothy Neill Moore, who was in high school with Jordan. "That's where the money in Selma came from."

Mrs. Moore also recalled what may be the oldest known Shug Jordan story.

"When I was five years old, my mother gave me a birthday party. Shug was a year younger than me. His mother, Katie Darby, was walking him to the party with my present. He got to a certain distance and he balked. He wouldn't come. So she had to take him home and then she came back to the party by herself with the gift. It was an ivory-colored fan with a chain that I could hang around my neck. Katie was a very sweet person. I just always loved her."

It is unknown whether this was an early indication of Jordan's shyness around girls, or that he could be headstrong when he wanted, and the idea of bringing a fan to a little girl's birthday party didn't agree with him.

Katie Jordan called her oldest son "Rally," which caused him to wince. Attracted by the Irish makeup of his mother's family, Jordan traveled to Ireland several times during his life. Katie Jordan was a talker and story-teller and certainly much of her son's communications skill came from her.

Jordan attended Sacred Heart Academy, a private Catholic elementary school. When Jordan, who was a southpaw, began to write left-handed, the sisters at the school rapped him on the knuckles so he would write right-handed. As a result, Jordan became ambidextrous and possessed dazzling handwriting skills. He could write with both hands at the same time. Starting with the letter "n" he could write his last name backward with his right hand while writing his first name forward with his left hand. He could also write words in mirror-image.

Harry Jordan's railroad work moved him and his family for a brief period to the Whatley-Allen area, which is southeast of Grove Hill, below Selma in Clarke County. Jordan finished grammar school there.

"I saw a basketball team for the first time," Jordan said. "I remember some of the kids said I would never be able to play basketball because I was left-handed."

Jordan recalled having to take a test at the Amity Church to see if he was ready to move from grammar school to high school. He passed it and the family moved back to Selma, onto Furniss Street. A second son had by then been born, Ned, who was seven years younger than Shug. Harry Jordan continued to work for the railroad. The family wasn't rich, but a railroad job was a steady one, even through the Great Depression of the late 1920s and early 1930s.

By 1923, the year Jordan began ninth grade at Selma High

School, the city was rebounding from the devastating effects of the boll weevil. The pest reached the state in 1914 and by 1917 the cotton market in Dallas County had dwindled to fourteen-thousand bales. Farmers switched to soybeans, cattle and timber production. The Selma Chamber of Commerce referred to the area as the "Clover Belt," trying to promote the rich prairie soil for growing crops other than cotton. Selma adjusted and the years immediately following World War I were prosperous. A sign at the city limits proclaimed Selma as the fastest-growing town in Alabama. The Selma Country Club opened in 1924. A new YMCA was built in 1925.

Several years earlier, in 1919, a twenty-year-old man named Paul Grist had moved from Atlanta to Selma to become physical education director of the YMCA. Jordan would forever refer to Grist as "my first coach." Grist was instrumental in getting the new Y facility built.

Roswell Falkenberry, many years the editor and publisher of *The Selma Times-Journal* newspaper, said, "All of us owe a lot to Paul Grist because he brought us all up. Shug and me and all the kids just worshipped him. He was a good Christian man. You either did right when you were around him or he straightened you out in a hurry."

Mrs. Roswell Falkenberry, a Selma historian, said of Grist, "He was a sincere Christian, he taught good sportsmanship, he was a sterling sort of man. He made the boys feel good about themselves, gave them ideals. He insisted on discipline and hard work."

Her description of Grist is almost identical to that later used to depict Jordan himself. Grist became General Secretary of the Selma Y in 1934.

The Y became a second home to boys like Jordan, Lapsley and Tepper. "The YMCA was *the* place," said Lapsley. "Everybody — Catholics, Jews, Protestants — went to the YMCA."

Tepper remembered that he and Jordan served as counselors for Grist at the Y's Camp Fremont.

Grist's church basketball league especially attracted the boys. Jordan said that because his Catholic church didn't have a team, he often slipped into the Presbyterian or Baptist Sunday schools so he could play on their teams.

Grist, who outlived Jordan by two years, said of his former pupil, "I told him, 'Son, don't wait to be a great man, be a great boy.' Shug was a great boy. He became a great man."

Grist said he saw in Jordan from the beginning the possibility of a great athlete. And later on, reflecting on Jordan's play in the Y leagues, in high school and college, Grist said, "Ralph Jordan was the Pete Maravich of his day. It was unbelievable what he could do on a basketball court."

But before Jordan could display his athletic prowess, there was the matter of a nickname, and how Ralph Jordan came to be called "Shug." Many stories have surfaced through the years concerning the nickname, but the truth is that Jordan's classmate, Billy Lapsley, gave it to him when they first met in high school. Sol Tepper remembered the exact moment.

"We were all shaking hands and meeting each other down at the Selma High School gym the first day of high school," Tepper recalled. "Billy Lapsley says to Jordan, 'Where are you from?' Jordan says, 'I've been living in Whatley.' And Lapsley says, 'Oh, down there where the sugar cane grows. We're going to call you Sugar Cane. We're going to call you Shug.' Billy Lapsley has the honor of giving Shug his nickname."

Lapsley acknowledged that he pinned the nickname on the future Hall of Famer. "Sugar cane was a big crop and they sold it in stores for five cents a stalk," Lapsley said. "You could spend a lot of time cutting those things and peeling them and chewing them up. The stalks we got then were purple. We'd go to the store and pay a nickel, or people would come by with a horse pulling a little wagon, selling vegetables and milk and stalks of sugar cane. We all ate sugar cane. Shug ate sugar cane all the time."

Lapsley also recalled that shortly after he stuck Jordan with the nickname, Jordan appeared with a gray sweatshirt with the letters SUG on it, which to Jordan's thinking was the appropriate spelling of his nickname.

"What's that?" Lapsley asked Jordan.

"That's Shug," Jordan replied.

"No, that's SUG," Lapsley said, without the "sh" sound. "You don't want to be SUG."

In fact, the high school yearbooks during Jordan's prep years spell his nickname "Sug." Jordan's peers also called him "Sugar Cane."

Jordan lettered in football, basketball, baseball and track at Selma High School. Tepper remembered that he and Jordan were the first four-sport lettermen the school ever had. Jordan played varsity football and basketball in 1925, 1926 and 1927. He played for the varsity baseball team in 1926 and 1927.

His junior year the Selma High football team had a 4-2-3 record under coach Thomas Vaughan. During the summer prior to the season Vaughan participated in a coaching seminar conducted by Knute Rockne of Notre Dame. This would be the first of Jordan's many indirect links to Rockne.

Of Jordan the yearbook stated, "'Sug,' playing his first year at the pivot position (center), made a name for himself as a steady, dependable passer."

Jordan, playing forward, was captain of the basketball team his junior year. The team finished 6-4. Of one of those games the yearbook stated, "Then came Uniontown, a close neighbor. Jordan ran wild in this game and when the bewildered visitors recovered and the final whistle sounded, the count was 51 to 18 with Selma on top."

Jordan was also captain of the football team his senior year. He weighed about 155 pounds and almost reached six feet, which was as tall as he'd ever get. His hair was parted on the right side, combed left and wavy.

The gridiron team completed Jordan's final season with a 4-4-1 record. The yearbook read, "The team this year was captained by Ralph Sug Jordan, who played center and proved to be one of the best pivot men S.H.S. has ever had. He gave trouble to the opponents throughout the season."

His senior year was Jordan's best on the hard court. His ambidexterity enhanced his ball-handling and shooting. He was again captain of the team. Coached by T.H. McDonough, the Black Tornado, as Selma was called, finished 11-3 and advanced to the state tournament in Tuscaloosa. The *Times-Journal* picked up on the team's and Jordan's success, referring to the "floor play of Jordan" during a 34-17 win over Greensboro. The story of Selma's 27-12 win over Plantersville said, "A marked feature of the game was the brilliant scoring of Captain Jordan who accounted for 13 of the 27 points." After another victory the paper stated, "Captain Jordan played his best game of the season. He ran the floor unusually well, made most of the points for his team and seldom missed a close-in shot."

Jordan scored twenty-one points in the team's 31-17 win over Plantersville in the finals of the district tournament. The Selma yearbook said of the game, "Captain Jordan played the best game of his career and his teammates all were up to form." The yearbook also wrote, "Captain Ralph Jordan, forward, playing his last game for S.H.S., leaves a brilliant basketball career behind him and we expect much from him in college."

Teammate Tepper, who played guard, recalled that Captain Jordan didn't mind telling a teammate what he thought.

"In one game I was trying to do a little trick with the basketball and it slipped out of my hands and the opposing team stole the ball," Tepper said. "During the half, Shug said, 'Some of these people are trying to get kind of fancy with the ball instead of playing basketball.' Shug didn't like it one bit. I said, 'Shug, I know you're talking about me. It won't happen again.'"

Years later Jordan would credit himself and guard Lapsley with inventing the give-and-go play. Lapsley explained, "We would come down the court and the other team would go into a five-man defense, three across and two behind. Shug would come down, I would run forward and he would bounce pass the ball to me. He would run by me and I would hand him the ball and he would make the shot. I can see that in my mind now. It was as simple as could be."

Lapsley also said that the basketball coach, McDonough, probably was an early influence on Jordan in the way McDonough understood teamwork and knew how to get the best effort from his players. Lapsley related the story of a mother of one of the non-starters approaching McDonough and questioning why the coach started Lapsley over her son, who was obviously a better shot than Lapsley, jumped higher than Lapsley, ran faster and stood taller, since Lapsley was barely five-feet tall.

"I agree with everything you say," McDonough told the lady. "But the reason I play little Lapsley is that when he's playing, everybody else plays twice as good as they do when he's not playing."

Jordan's athletic endeavors continued into the baseball season. The yearbook stated that "'Sug' Jordan is showing his old hitting eye and probably will be useful on first and in the outfield."

Perhaps the first time Jordan's name appeared in a headline came on May 1, 1927 in the *Times-Journal*: "Ralph Jordan Wins Shot Put Event At State Track Meet." His toss, at Birmingham-Southern College, was thirty-nine feet, six inches.

That Jordan was captain of two sports says much for what his coaches and youthful peers thought of him. Some entertaining lines in his senior class yearbook provide additional insight. One section listed all eighty-five seniors with a short description of each. For Jordan, it read: "Favorite pasttime—sports; probable future—physical director; remarks—all round sport."

Another passage in the yearbook was "J is for Jordan, a captain athletic, a sport courageous, a scholar poetic." He was also named "Most Athletic Boy."

Roswell Falkenberry, four years younger than Jordan, remembered Shug as a town hero. Falkenberry and his mates would follow Shug and the bigger boys around.

In 1930, Falkenberry served as captain of the Selma football team. Selma traveled to Montgomery to play Sidney Lanier High School. Just before the game Falkenberry received a telegram from Jordan, then playing football for Auburn. The message wished Falkenberry and the team the best of luck.

"Shug was more of a gentle person than most of us were at that time," Tepper said. "He was conscientious. He was very quiet. He didn't go out of his way to be noisy."

Tepper remained deeply touched by a remark Jordan made at the fifty-year reunion of the senior class. Jordan commented during his speech that Tepper's brother, Milton, who had been killed during the war, had been the finest soldier in the war.

"I don't know why he said that," Tepper said. "It wasn't the subject we were discussing. It was a fine thing to do."

Lapsley recalled that he and Shug were both "elephants" when it came to girls. "I was the shiest person and he was probably about as shy," Lapsley said. "There were two girls, sisters, who taught dancing in their house. Shug and I took three or four lessons together over there. But we were more-or-less satisfied with each other's company."

Lapsley attended the U.S. Military Academy and became a Major General in the Army. He said when he and Jordan crossed paths in the ensuing years, including a couple of times during the war, they picked up right where they left off. "There wasn't any, 'What've you been doing?' It was, 'What are we going to do to-night?'"

Another person in Jordan's graduating class was Caroline Marshall, who became Caroline Draughon, wife of the late president of Auburn University, Ralph Brown Draughon, who was a key figure in hiring Jordan as head coach in 1951. Mrs. Draughon remembered Jordan in high school as very well liked, very intelligent, possessing many of the characteristics and qualities of Shug Jordan the man in later years.

"Those boys weren't too interested in the girls," she added of Jordan and his running mates.

Marjorie Moss Anderson, also a classmate, didn't recall Shug dating any girl in particular. "He was in a group. He was a good old boy that everybody admired, a regular fellow," she said. "He didn't seek popularity. He did not have anybody regular that he went with, I'm sure of that. It was all sports for him in those days."

Mrs. Anderson said Shug and his crowd would visit her family's country home during the summer. "They came in a little old car with no sides on it. They didn't have paved roads all the way in those days and sometimes they'd have to push it. We would just chat, play some tennis. Shug always had a good sense of humor."

Other images of Jordan in Selma are wonderfully normal: breaking piggy banks with the late Harmon Carter to buy a cherry smash at the drug store; hiking to Camp Fremont with Tepper and other pals and spending the night; meeting in the morning at an empty lot to play baseball — just knowing there was a game and everybody showing up; reporting late to class and being told to stay after school to memorize bits of the *Iliad* and the *Odyssey* — then skipping the punishment to play baseball; gathering with his friends around a radio to listen to Alabama in the 1926 Rose Bowl; taking black walnut ice cream to the girls at Camp McGee with Lapsley, Carter and Bill Floyd — then finding out the girls already had ice cream, forcing the boys to eat it themselves (Jordan got sick to the point that he never ate black walnut ice cream again); riding the trolley back and forth in Selma past J.C. Penny, Carter Drug Co., Cook Hardware, Swift Druggists, Stewart Dry Cleaning, Tissier's Sporting Goods and Lilienthal's clothing store; catching the train with his buddies and Judge Sam Hobbs, who always had tickets for them to see Alabama play in Birmingham; gathering with his senior-class pals around a newspaper and reading of boxer Gene Tunney taking the heavyweight title from Jack Dempsey and Charles Lindbergh landing his *Spirit of St. Louis* in Paris after a 33-hour flight across the Atlantic.

And, like many boys at that time, Jordan had a reputation for trying to sneak a cigarette or two. His senior yearbook imagined a whimsical moment between Jordan and his father.

Mr. Jordan: "Ralph, is that your cigarette stub?"
Sugar Cane: "Aw, go ahead, you saw it first."

Of his upbringing, Jordan said, "We accepted and did what we were told to do because we had respect for our elders. We always said 'yes sir, yes ma'am.' We practiced good table manners. With my family and Paul Grist and other people, I felt like I had been raised right and had an evaluation of the real things in life."

The immediate reality for Jordan was that he was not able to attend college in the fall after his high school graduation. His father's income had carried Jordan's athletic interests in high school, but there wasn't enough money to put the boy through college. Jordan sought an athletic scholarship and financial assistance from Alabama Polytechnic Institute (as Auburn was then called), the University of Alabama and the University of Florida. Judge Hobbs wanted Jordan to play at Alabama and recommended him to Wallace Wade, head coach at Alabama. Hobbs had lettered on Alabama's 1907 team and played in what was the last Auburn-Alabama game until 1948. (Auburn and Alabama had tied the 1907 game, 6-6, in Birmingham. Hobbs explained that the custom was for the winner of that game to walk off the field holding the football high in the air. Since the game ended in a tie, the two teams had a good-humored struggle for the ball, but the fans were more aggressive and rushed the field. A melee developed.)

Hobbs's recommendation didn't persuade Alabama, and neither Auburn nor Florida offered help. Jordan later commented on their lack of interest, "I had what is now known as the deadly combination: I was too little and too slow."

While money was a problem, a knee injury during his final football season may have encouraged Jordan to take his time about college, where he had definite plans to at least play basketball. Sol Tepper recalled the injury because he also sustained a knee injury his last year in high school.

Tepper said Jordan told him he had talked to his Catholic priest about the injury and the possibility of letting the knee heal for a year. It's very likely Jordan's conversation with the Father dealt with his whole situation regarding college, including the lack of funds. Tepper thought the injury may have been a cartilage problem. He said it continued to bother Jordan a year later when he entered Auburn.

As some of his classmates traveled to college in the fall of 1927, Jordan found employment with the state highway department. He worked out of the town of Orrville, driving stakes and handling the level rod and the red-and-white range pole for the transit. When he wasn't working, Jordan kept his ball-handling skills intact and his shooting eye sharp. He also refereed and served as the timekeeper for Paul Grist's games at the Y and for Selma High School games.

By fall of 1928, able to live at home during his year out of school, Jordan had saved five-hundred dollars. He felt his year of employment had been an excellent experience. His work had fueled an interest in transits, levels and the preciseness of building roads and bridges. Auburn, which offered an expansive farm management program and excellent vocational preparation, also had a reputation for its engineering studies. Jordan decided to specialize in civil engineering while playing basketball at Auburn.

About to turn eighteen, Jordan pooled his earnings with cash assistance from his father and made off for Auburn. He entered A.P.I. with a freshman class of 550, which represented one-third of the student body.

4

"Nothing but headlights"

In one way Auburn was like Selma High School: Shug Jordan became one of the most popular students on campus. Of course he participated in all of the major sports — during his freshman year he participated in football, basketball, baseball and track. His sophomore, junior and senior years he lettered in football, basketball and baseball. Jordan was especially gifted on the basketball court. For three seasons he was one of the top forwards in the Southern Conference, which was the league that preceded the SEC.

Jordan played sparingly his sophomore and junior seasons on the football team, but started at center as a senior. He was less of a factor on the baseball team, serving as a left-handed pitcher, utility first baseman and outfielder.

To get an idea of Jordan's reputation as a hoopster, a newspaper account of a baseball game in which Jordan pitched and won referred to him as "the basketball star." Something else happened to Jordan during his playing career at Auburn. He lost the nickname "Shug," at least in some mentions, and gained another nickname: "Lefty."

But his devotion to athletics wasn't the only reason for Jordan's popularity. He was visible in other campus activities, as well. He became a brother in Theta Chi fraternity. He served as treasurer of his senior class. He became a member of Spades, composed of "the most prominent and influential men of the senior class and the institution." Jeff Beard, who later became athletic director, was also a member of Spades. Jordan was also in Blue Key, which promoted "the spirit of fraternalism among the students."

Elmer Salter, who graduated when Jordan was a freshman, recalled Jordan as "an all-around fellow."

"He dated regular and went to the dances," Salter said. "He was popular with the girls."

Jordan's photographs in the annual *Glomerata* reveal that a handsome young man with a soft face, deep eyes and full lips had emerged from the gangly, bumpy-faced boy who had attended Selma High School. Jordan's untiring campus activities stood him tall in a student body that barely topped two thousand when he graduated in 1932.

Long before spacious Eaves Memorial Coliseum began housing the Tigers' basketball team, and even before the tiny, now-famous Sports Arena — better known as "The Barn" — caused opponents to shake in their shoes, Auburn played its home basketball games in an upstairs matchbox called Alumni Gym. Fans sat right up to the out-of-bounds lines and next to the benches.

"When you went up for a crip shot, you would probably land halfway up in the crowd," Jordan said. "The fans would literally throw you back on the court and you would take off again."

Fans also sat in a balcony that smothered the ends of the court. Hundreds of legs and feet dangled over the edge of the balcony within knocking distance of the backboards. Jordan liked to recall that as a player, and later as the head coach, he and his team took advantage of all the intimate delicacies of the home court. He told of a dead spot in the floor the size of a desktop. As opponents dribbled toward it, Auburn players anticipated and then pounced toward the ball as it hit the spot and went dead.

Jordan's performance on the basketball court as an Auburn freshman picked up where he left off as a Selma senior. The varsity squad, while Jordan competed on the freshman team, suffered through a 6-15 record and eagerly pointed to the following season when Jordan would make his appearance. Jordan lived up to his billing as a sharpshooting sophomore forward. He scored 112 points during the eleven-game season at a time when averaging in double figures was unheard of. He scored eleven points in the season finale to win the conference scoring title. Upon his snatching the scoring crown, a February 1930 newspaper article boasted of the sophomore: "His work this season on the hardwood stamps him as one of the leading cage performers ever to matriculate at the Cornerstone."

Jordan said in 1968, "In those days you had a wide-open game when the team scored forty points, and we won some in Alumni Gym by scores as low as 16-14, but they were as exciting as today's games. My points looked big then, but Maravich gets that many in two games now."

Unfortunately, Jordan was one of the few bright spots as Auburn won only one game against ten losses. Another strong performer was senior captain Louie James. As a sophomore in 1927-1928, James had played on an Auburn team which won twenty and lost only two. The two star performers of that team had been Louie's older twin brothers, Fob and Ebb.

Jordan was captain of the basketball team his junior season in 1930-1931. The new head coach was Sam McAllister. Jordan continued his brilliant play, finishing ninth in conference scoring, and the team came together around him. Auburn won eight and lost six. It won a first-round game in the Southern Conference Tournament in Atlanta, beating Virginia 33-26. The Tigers fell in the second round to Georgia, 31-27, as Jordan scored seven points. A newspaper reported that the flu bug had bitten the team going into the tourney.

Paced by Jordan and captain Jack Stewart, again with McAllister coaching, Auburn's roundball squad in 1931-1932 was rated the second best team in the school's history, behind the 1927-1928 team. Auburn won twelve and lost three, relying on a "quick-break and short passes." Other starters included Tom Lumpkin, Lindley Hatfield and Charles "Slick" Kaley. The team advanced to the semifinals of the Southern Conference Tournament in Atlanta by beating North Carolina State in the opener, 34-33, and knocking off LSU in the second round, 30-22, with Jordan scoring seven. North Carolina sent the Tigers packing in the third round.

Jordan's senior yearbook stated, "Lefty is truly one of the greatest forwards ever to don an Auburn uniform. His left-hand pass work has constantly proved a stumbling block for all Tiger opponents."

Jordan was a member of the varsity baseball team for three years, but played mainly in a utility role in the field. His best moment on the ball diamond came as a pitcher during his senior season. Prior to the season his only starting role on the mound was a four-hit 3-2 win over Dothan High School in an exhibition game in May 1931.

But Lefty pitched and won an important Dixie College Baseball League game his senior year. The league, composed of Auburn, Georgia, Florida, Georgia Tech, Oglethorpe and Mercer, had started up in 1931. Auburn, under coach Sam McAllister and with leading hitter Joe Burt, had won the title that year.

Auburn held a 3-3 record and Florida was 2-0 when the Gators visited Auburn for a two game series April 22-23, 1932. Auburn's ace pitchers, Clifford Smith and Ripper Williams, had taken ill, and the Tigers were just off a tough road trip that had taken its toll on a lot of pitching arms.

"The coach walked up and said, 'Let's see your stuff, Lefty,'" Jordan recalled. "I threw my fastball, which really looked like an annie-over (screwball), and my ole round-house out curveball, and coach said, 'You got it, Lefty. Get in there.' Porter Grant, my old friend from Dothan, claims every inning was two outs, three and two on the batter, and the bases loaded. He claims Florida had twenty-seven men left on base." Grant was barely exaggerating.

Jordan didn't fool the Gator batters, but he won the game 5-2. He surrendered eleven hits, walked five and struck out two. Florida left thirteen men on base. Jordan had a shutout going until the eighth inning. A newspaper article called Jordan "invincible with Floridians on the basepath."

Florida tallied once in the eighth and again in the ninth. The first three Gator hitters singled in the final frame, but a great catch by

Grant in center saved Jordan and Auburn.

Auburn scored first when Jordan homered to left in the third inning. Shortstop Jimmy Hitchcock, who would eventually take a shot a pro baseball and was Auburn's leading performer on the gridiron, also homered.

The clutch victory sparked the Tigers and they didn't lose again the remainder of the season, finishing with a 13-3 record and winning the Dixie League for the second straight year. Other seniors on that squad were Harry Lloyd, Duck Riley, Ike Lewis, Carl Creel and the right-handed hurler Cliff Smith, who posted a 17-5 record during his three years on the mound for the Tigers.

Jordan later admitted, "I was an atrocious pitcher. I didn't have a fast ball and didn't have very much of a curve and darn little control."

But for one day in April in 1932, with the season tilting on his left arm, Jordan had what it took to go the distance.

In today's lightning-paced, specialized game, it's hard to imagine what football was like when Jordan played at Auburn. It was the era of leather footballs and leather helmets, though headgear wouldn't become an NCAA requirement until 1939. Face masks were nowhere in sight. Not until 1932, the year after Jordan's final season as a football player, did the NCAA forbid defensive players from striking opponents on the head, neck or face. The latest substitution rule allowed players withdrawn during the first half to return to the game only in the second half, and a player taken out in the second half couldn't return at all. Some players wore numbers, some didn't. Passing was legal, but the ball was still a little too big to throw. A fairly new rule made it illegal for receivers to go out of bounds during a play and come back in and participate. (This rule burned Auburn and Thomas Gossom in 1974 against Alabama. Its reversal would help Auburn and Alexander Wright against Alabama in 1989.) A new rule moved the goal posts off the goal line and ten yards back into the end zone.

But it was still largely smash-mouth football. J.D. Bush was

Jordan's age and played tackle on the line with him. Bush was co-captain of his and Jordan's senior-year squad in 1931. During one game, Bush felt Jordan needed a rest from an ongoing dogfight he was in with a much larger lineman.

"Go on out," Bush told Jordan.

"No," Jordan replied.

"Go on," Bush repeated.

"Dammit, I'm not going to go out," Jordan snapped.

"You are going to get out or I'm going to go to the ref," Bush said.

"Let me just play another down or two," Jordan pleaded.

Bush finally consented with a nod of his head. At the end of the next play Bush turned and found Jordan flat on his back, knocked out cold. Bush had to smile as the players carried Jordan to the sidelines, the stubborn center having finally been forced to leave the game without even knowing it.

While Jordan attended Selma High School, Alabama had been a major power on the college football scene. Alabama had gone 10-0 in 1925 and 9-0-1 in 1926 under head coach Wallace Wade. The Tide played in the Rose Bowl on New Year's Day 1926 and 1927, beating Washington 20-19 and tying Stanford, 7-7. Major Bob Neyland's teams at Tennessee were also coming on strong, going 8-1 in 1926 and 8-0-1 in 1927.

But for years Knute Rockne's Notre Dame squads had been the primary power in the game. From 1919 to 1927, Rockne had coached Notre Dame to a spectacular 78-7-3 record, including undefeated seasons in 1919 and 1920, and again in 1924 — a team which featured the famous "Four Horsemen" backfield: Don Miller, Elmer Layden, Jim Crowley and Harry Stuhldreher.

Auburn, meanwhile, had been struggling, failing to win a game in 1927. The Tigers had not fared particularly well since Mike Donahue vacated his head coaching position at Auburn following the 1922 season to take a similar post at LSU. Donahue had coached Auburn into the national picture with undefeated teams in 1913 and 1914, winning the Southern Intercollegiate Athletic Association (SIAA) title both years, and winning the league title again in 1919 with an 8-1 record. He implemented the "line divide" formation which featured an unbalanced offensive line with gaping holes, and offensive backs lined up in the I formation before shifting.

Jordan had not intended to play football at Auburn, but was going to concentrate on basketball and his engineering studies. While in Auburn to register for his freshman classes in September 1928, Jordan decided to watch the varsity work out on Drake Field. While also observing the freshman team in action, and in particular the centers, he saw that no one could accurately snap the ball back to the punter.

"Now that I could do," Jordan said. "I was not big and I was not fast, but I could snap the ball with anybody."

Jordan went out for the team, which was coached by Red Brown. He made it as a center and linebacker. The freshmen "rats," as they were called, figured to see playing time on the varsity their sophomore years, since the varsity compiled a dismal 1-8 record in 1928, including a 54-0 loss to number-one-ranked Georgia Tech, coached by Bill Alexander. Tennessee, under Neyland, had contended for the national crown with a 9-0-1 record, and Vanderbilt under Dan McGugin and Charles Bachman's Florida team also had strong seasons.

Auburn improved little in 1929 with a 2-7 record, losing its final four games to Tennessee, Tulane, Georgia and Georgia Tech by the combined score of 122-0. Tulane, coached by Bernie Bierman, beat the Tigers 52-0 and finished number two in the nation behind another undefeated Rockne team. A tie to Kentucky was the only record blemish for Neyland's Tennessee, but it cost the Vols a share of the national title. Jordan, a sophomore, made only one appearance that year. He found himself entrenched as a second-stringer behind Dunham Harkins.

The gridiron situation could only improve for Auburn and Jordan. When Auburn named ex-Rockne player Chet Wynne head football coach and athletic director on May 1, 1930, the football program began moving forward. Notre Dame men would continue to shape Jordan's career and influence Auburn football for many of the following twenty years, culminating with Jordan's hiring as head football coach in 1951.

Wynne came to Auburn from a head coaching job at Creighton University in Omaha, Nebraska. Wynne brought with him as an assistant coach Chicago lawyer Roger Kiley. These men had played together on the undefeated, number-one-ranked Rockne teams of 1919 and 1920, which showcased halfback George ("Win One for the Gipper") Gipp. Wynne and Kiley's senior season in 1921 would have produced a third consecutive national title except for a close loss to undefeated Iowa. Wynne ran at fullback and Kiley played end. Kiley made All-American in 1921.

"When they came in it was the difference between day and night," said J.D. Bush. "We were just fumbling up until that time. It was a science after they got to handling it. They were terrific people."

During Wynne and Kiley's brief stay at Auburn, fans and writers seldom mentioned one's name without the other. The 1932 *Glomerata* was dedicated to "Wynne and Kiley" following a modest 5-3-1 record. The 1932 Auburn-Howard game at Cramton Bowl in Montgomery was designated "Wynne and Kiley Day."

Because of Wynne's late hiring, Auburn held a late spring practice. "Wynne began to develop pride and determination and many of those things with which we identify today," Jordan said. Auburn people felt it was the best spring practice in several years. Jordan acknowledged that it was a physically taxing one.

It probably taxed the players mentally, as well. Wynne, who coached the backs, and Kiley, who coached the line, implemented the Knute Rockne Notre Dame system. "It was deception, and half-spins and full-spins and quickness," Jordan said.

Smash-mouth football had taken on a little finesse.

It was called the Notre Dame Box. The offense lined up in the T formation with one back behind the center and three backs side-by-side in the backfield. Sometimes the offense ran a play from the T, but most of the time it shifted from the T to the Box. Six players executed the shift. When shifting to the right, for example, both ends moved out a yard away from the tackles, allowing the ends to move downfield easier or giving them a better blocking angle. The quarter-back moved over and lined up between the right offensive guard and tackle. The right halfback moved up and stationed himself as a wingback just outside the right offensive end. The fullback stepped right and lined up behind the right offensive tackle. The left halfback stepped right and lined up behind the center. The shift worked to the left or right. The defense had to be prepared to defend against a possible play out of the T and be ready to adjust its alignment to the left or right if the offense shifted into the Box.

When Wynne and Kiley played at Notre Dame, the rules didn't require the offense to remain set for a one-second count once it shifted into the Box. Notre Dame was so successful with it that a rule change in 1927 imposed a one-second pause after the shift. This allowed the defense time to move to a new alignment against the shift before the ball was snapped.

Wynne and Kiley built the system around sophomore halfback Jimmy Hitchcock. While Auburn won only three games in 1930, a season-ending 25-7 win over South Carolina provided a glimpse of the new offense's potential. Hitchcock scored on two long runs in Auburn's first Southern Conference win since 1926. Jordan again saw limited action during the season behind starting center Harkins. Following the 1930 season, Wynne added basketball and baseball coach Sam McAllister to his staff as a line coach.

Auburn fans hoped some of that Notre Dame stardust was about to rub off on the Tigers. Rockne's Notre Dame had again gone undefeated and again won the Rissman National Trophy, based on the Dickinson selection, which was considered the most authorita-tive. (The Associated Press didn't enter into the national champion-ship picture until 1936.) Alabama fans refused to endorse Notre Dame as the national champion. Wallace Wade's Tide had finished 10-0 and beaten Washington State 24-0 in the Rose Bowl.

With a year of the Notre Dame system under its belt, Auburn went into the following spring practice with a positive outlook, expecting to field a winning team. Jordan, at 5-11, 175 pounds, which was ten pounds less than the starting line averaged, and ten pounds more than the backfield, appeared to be winning the starting center position.

On March 31, 1931, not long after Auburn completed an excellent spring practice, the sports world went into shock. Rockne was dead. He had boarded a plane that morning in Kansas City, intending to fly to Los Angeles to look into some investment matters. The plane had crashed on a Kansas farm. Rockne, six other passengers and the two pilots were killed. He was only forty-three years old, but his dynamic personality, his inspirational messages, and his great football teams had gained worldwide fame. He had coached Notre Dame to a near-unbelievable 105-12-5 record in thirteen seasons. His teams won five national titles. He was coming off consecutive national titles and unbeaten seasons. His family received condolences from kings and queens. Flags flew at half mast. The funeral service played to more than fifty-million people on the radio. Two former Rockne players devastated by the tragedy were Auburn's Wynne and Kiley. They attended the funeral in South Bend, Indiana.

"They admired Rockne tremendously," recalled lineman Bush of the two coaches. "They spoke of Rockne like he was a high religious figure."

Jordan must have been disappointed when Wynne and Kiley didn't start him in the opening football game of his senior season. Buddy McCollum got the starting nod instead as Auburn beat Birmingham-Southern 24-6 in Montgomery. But Jordan was about to make his mark on the gridiron.

Auburn had two weeks to prepare for its second game, to be played in Madison, Wisconsin, against traditional slugger Wisconsin. The Badger program was still riding high after defeating a Rockne team a few years earlier. During the off-weekend Wynne announced he was moving McCollum to tackle and starting Jordan at center to give the line more muscle. A newspaper article referred to "snapper back" Jordan as "one of the most improved players on the team."

On October 10, Jordan and Auburn established the return of the Auburn football program by tying Wisconsin, 7-7. The game was played in sleet and snow, which many Auburn players were seeing for the first time. Only fourteen players saw action for Auburn. Jordan and the line played the entire game. Alongside Jordan were guards Boots Chambless and Sleepy Molpus; tackles McCollum and Bush; ends Porter Grant and Gump Ariail. Hitchcock played the entire contest at right halfback and Thomas Brown wasn't spelled at fullback. Firpo Phipps and Lindley Hatfield platooned at left halfback. M.V. Davidson, W.D. Parker and Ripper Williams platooned at quarterback.

Wisconsin, meanwhile, threw several dozen players at the Tigers. At halftime, Tiger guard Molpus remarked to Jordan and Bush, "You know that third guard I played against, he was pretty good."

Stuart X. Stephenson of the *Montgomery Advertiser* wrote that "the Auburn football team played the game as men play it....The starting line remained intact throughout the game and came out dragging and tired but game to the core and winners of as much glory as any line ever achieved in the face of such overwhelming odds....They were the heroes, the tackling fools who gave no quarter."

After a scoreless first half, Wisconsin returned the second-half kickoff for a touchdown. An offsides penalty on Auburn allowed Wisconsin a second chance at the point after, which the Badgers converted. But a Hitchcock touchdown and his point-after kick, with Jordan snapping, tied it. Jordan would later compare the pressure of that extra-point kick to the PAT by Gardner Jett that beat Alabama 17-16 in 1972.

Jordan would not relinquish his starting role at center the remainder of the season. A tremendous crowd turned out to greet the team as it returned by train to Opelika. "Usually we had to catch rides back to Auburn ... this time I remember looking out the back window of the car and seeing nothing but headlights all the way to Opelika," Jordan said.

The following week a special roundtrip train fare of four dollars transported a large Auburn contingency on the Atlanta & West Point Railroad line from Montgomery to Atlanta to see the Tigers battle

Georgia Tech. During the previous eleven seasons, Auburn had tied Tech twice and lost nine times. Seniors on the Auburn squad like Jordan still smarted from Auburn's 51-0 loss to Tech in 1928.

Jordan and the line's play excelled again as Auburn shut out Tech 13-0 and held the Yellow Jackets to 102 yards total offense. Brown and Phipps scored touchdowns for Auburn.

Auburn would lose, 13-12, to Florida in the next outing; rip Spring Hill 27-7; lose to the nation's number-two ranked team, Tulane, 27-0; shut out Sewanee 12-0; and fall to Georgia 12-6.

Prior to the season-ending clash in Montgomery against South Carolina, a newspaper article stated of Auburn's center: "Jordan has had to wait until his senior year to break into the starting lineup, but this has not kept him from being one of the leading players in Auburn's forward wall. He has performed superbly in every game that he has played."

By this time, Hitchcock, a junior, had received national attention for his running, passing and kicking. A fifty-yard touchdown pass from Hitchcock to Sterling Dupree, and running back Casey Kimbrell's eighty-yard touchdown dash gave Auburn a 13-6 win over South Carolina. One of the starters in the game for Auburn, right end Cary "Shot" Senn, would be a member of head coach Jordan's first staff at Auburn in 1951.

The 1932 school *Glomerata* stated of Jordan: "There wasn't a harder fighter or a more likeable man on the Tiger squad than Ralph Jordan. Although basketball is Lefty's first love, he is mighty hard to beat on the football field. Light but aggressive, he was a real pivot of strength in the line. He was as dependable a center as any team in the South could boast of. According to the records, not one bad pass to the backs is recorded against him in his last year of play."

The 1931 team finished with a 5-3-1 record. Jordan, Bush and their fellow seniors had laid the foundation for Wynne and Kiley's undefeated, once-tied powerhouse squad of 1932. Hitchcock would become Auburn's first All-American. Kimbrell, Phipps, Grant, Ariail, Williams and Chambless, all of whom played alongside Jordan in 1931, would contribute mightily to Auburn's number-five national ranking the following year.

Jordan was impressed at how Wynne and Kiley had reorganized Auburn's football program, instilled spirit into it, and guided the Tigers over the hump in two short years. Jordan must have also been intrigued at how they implemented a new offensive system. And Jordan, being the center and prepared to hike the ball to any number of backs, must have marveled at the mechanics of the Notre Dame shift. Certainly these observations strengthened any earlier considerations he had given to becoming a coach.

Teammate Bush recalled Jordan having ambitions to teach school and coach sports. "Athletics was his life," Bush said. "He wanted to teach so he could coach."

Elmer Salter, who covered Jordan's playing days as the sports publicity director, recalled that it was obvious Jordan the student-athlete was "impressive, level-headed and smart enough to be a good coach."

Jordan was one of 214 seniors in a student body of 2,007. In June 1932 he graduated with a degree in education, specializing in history and physical education. He had dropped engineering because it demanded too much of the time he preferred to spend playing sports, and because the idea of coaching had begun to appeal to him. He was a member of Company B of the ROTC Engineer Corps, and he graduated with a reserve commission.

Jordan never received financial assistance for playing sports at Auburn. To help pay his way through school he hopped tables at a boarding house. Still, it had been a good time to be in school, somewhat estranged from the country's economic quagmire. While the Great Depression knocked the wind out of the country, Jordan gained strength on Auburn's playing fields.

Ralph Jordan was not intent on making a lot of money. He didn't even imagine himself as the next Knute Rockne. He just wanted to teach history and coach high school ball. But first he had to learn a lesson about his own history, and it wasn't a pretty one.

5

"Auburn is just too damn tough"

Life was easy for Jordan in the decade between his college graduation and his military career. Things were good. But they didn't start out that way.

Before leaving Auburn Jordan had accepted a job to coach and teach history for one hundred dollars a month at a high school in north Alabama. But when the board of education received Jordan's formal resume it was noted that he was a Catholic. The board reneged on its offer. A strong Ku Klux Klan presence in the area and an accompanying anti-Catholic prejudice prompted the board's reaction.

This late-summer development hit Jordan like a ton of bricks. Depression still ravaged the country. It was tough enough to find a job, but to have one in his pocket — and then to lose it over his religious affiliation — was a crushing blow.

But again, the Notre Dame-Auburn connection came to Jordan's rescue in the persons of Auburn coaches Wynne and Kiley. The prejudice displayed toward Jordan incensed the Notre Dame grads, who were of course both Catholic. They hired Jordan on September 27, 1932, as assistant freshman football coach for one hundred dollars a month. When Wynne-Kiley Day was held at Cramton Bowl in Montgomery for the Auburn-Howard varsity game on November 5, Jordan surely led the applause.

As Jordan scratched his initial mark as a college football coach in 1932, Amos Alonzo Stagg was stepping down as head coach at the

University of Chicago and Pop Warner was still going strong at Stanford. Stagg and Warner would rank one-two in all-time wins with 314 and 313, respectively, until Paul "Bear" Bryant finished his phenomenal career with 323 wins. Bob Neyland had coached Tennessee to a 9-0-1 season in 1931, the nation's only unbeaten team, but the polls ranked the Vols behind once-beaten Southern Cal and Tulane. The Alabama football team, coached by Frank Thomas, had turned in another fine performance at 8-1-1. Notre Dame, without Rockne, had fallen to 6-2-1.

Though the Auburn freshmen had a four-game schedule in 1932, the Rats' primary function was to scrimmage the varsity. The new assistant coach's input made it unusually tough on the varsity because of his knowledge of his former teammates. Certainly the young and able Jordan itched to be on the field, as halfback and kicker Hitchcock led Auburn to a 9-0-1 season and a number-five national ranking. A season-ending 20-20 tie with South Carolina in Birmingham cost the Tigers a legitimate claim to the national championship, which undefeated and untied Michigan and Southern California shared. South Carolina had been the only team to score more than seven points against Auburn. The flu had racked the Tigers the week of the game and they got in little practice. The tie so disappointed Wynne that immediately after the game he turned down a bid to play in the Sugar Bowl. The tie also cost Auburn an outright Southern Conference championship. Three teams claimed a piece of it: LSU at 4-0 in conference play, Tennessee at 7-0-1, and Auburn at 6-0-1.

Jordan's buddy Hitchcock had a superb year. Two great games for Hitchcock under the national microscope — against Duke and Tulane—propelled him to first-team All-American. He was Auburn's first.

A footnote to the 1932 season was a new rule: any player could be replaced and returned to the game in any quarter except the quarter in which he came out.

A major development following the 1932 football season was the formation of the Southeastern Conference. The Southern Conference, which had been formed in 1920, had simply grown too large: it included twenty-three teams. This prevented any system for determining a true conference champion. The fiasco of 1932, when LSU, Auburn and Tennessee each played a different number of conference games and each claimed the title, demanded a resolution. At the annual Southern Conference meeting in Knoxville on December 8-9, the thirteen members west and south of the Appalachian Mountains reorganized as the Southeastern Conference. The ten coastal members remained in the Southern Conference. The charter SEC members were Alabama, Auburn, Florida, Georgia, Georgia Tech, Kentucky, Louisiana State, Mississippi, Mississippi State, Sewanee, Tennessee, Tulane and Vanderbilt. Some of the head coaches in addition to Wynne were Thomas at Alabama, Harry Mehre at Georgia, Dan McGugin at Vanderbilt, and Neyland at Tennessee. Dr. Frank McVey of Kentucky was elected president of the SEC and gathered the school presidents in Birmingham and Atlanta in February 1933 for the first SEC meetings.

A second major development following the 1932 season was that Shug Jordan became Auburn's head freshman football coach. He succeeded Earl "Bull" McFadden, who moved into the professional ranks with the Charlotte Bantams.

Jordan's first step as coach was to assemble a team. He already had one great player to build on.

During the 1932 season, a LaGrange, Georgia, sportswriter, Sam Adams, wrote Wynne about a local prospect. Wynne sent Jordan to scout the boy at the LaGrange-Darlington Prep game. The sportswriter's prospect didn't excite Jordan but the center on the Darlington team did. Charles Scott, Darlington's coach, introduced Jordan to the boy, a 6-3, 180-pounder named Walter Gilbert. Jordan asked Gilbert if he had thought about college.

"Yes sir, I've already made my mind up," Gilbert replied. "Auburn."

Jordan would always refer to Gilbert as the easiest player he ever recruited. Gilbert made All-American at Auburn in 1936 and was later inducted into the National Football Foundation Hall of Fame.

Gilbert and Jordan remained close friends until Gilbert's death in Auburn in 1979.

In the summer of 1933 Jordan was initiated into the recruiting arena. Porter Grant, a lineman from the 1932 team, traveled with Jordan throughout the South in a blue V-8 Ford with yellow spokes that cost the athletic department $350. Jordan, for the most part dealing with youngsters he had never seen play, offered a tryout and the "possibility" of aid if they made the team.

An Atlanta boy named Joel Eaves was one of the recruits Jordan and Grant brought to Auburn. The coaches had actually gone to Atlanta to offer a make-good scholarship to a high school quarterback named Sid Scarborough, who would letter three years at Auburn. As the coaches waited on Scarborough at the hotel, they read in the sports section that Eaves, a football teammate of Scarborough's who played end, had pitched a shutout in a summer baseball game. They asked Scarborough if he thought Eaves would be interested in attending Auburn. Scarborough called up Eaves and Eaves came to the hotel and took up Jordan and Grant on their offer. Eaves became a first team All-SEC end, and captain and guard of Jordan's basketball team. He would later coach ends under Jordan for fourteen years, and at the same time establish himself as one of the SEC's best basketball coaches, winning 214 games and coaching Auburn in 1959-1960 to its only SEC basketball title. Eaves became athletic director at the University of Georgia in 1963 where his first major act was to hire Vince Dooley — then the freshman football coach at Auburn — as Georgia's head football coach.

Jordan, Grant and the blue Ford rolled through Georgia, South Carolina, Mississippi and Alabama. No prospect was out of their reach. One stop was in Anniston, Alabama, at Fort McClellan. A Montgomery prospect out of Sidney Lanier High School named Herbert Bummie Roton, serving in the National Guard, was doing KP when Jordan and Grant walked in. Roton was an end in high school but would play tackle at Auburn.

Jordan and Grant's efforts resulted in a record-breaking first-practice turnout of ninety-five freshmen on September 7, 1933.

Assisting Jordan were Jimmy Hitchcock, Lee Johnson and Tom Shackelford.

In Jordan's first game as a head coach, his freshmen defeated Birmingham-Southern 39-6 in Birmingham on September 29. A newspaper article stated, "Coach Ralph Jordan, Hitchcock and the others are due considerable praise for the fine work they have accomplished in a short time."

The Auburn frosh then beat Lanier High School in Montgomery, 25-0, and the University of Tampa, 18-6. "Coach Ralph Jordan has one of the finest groups of frosh performing under his wing this year that has ever worn the orange and blue of Alabama Polytechnic Institute," another article reported.

Bummie Roton remembered the young freshman coach as "easygoing, no rough stuff, no profanity. He told you what he expected in the nicest way he could. As long as you did it, you were the number-one boy."

The success of the team began to draw interest and the final game against Georgia Tech received tremendous press. An article referred to the showdown at Drake Field in Auburn as "a football game that will rival many that have been played this season between varsity elevens."

Jordan's Rats beat Tech 21-13 to finish the season undefeated. Backs Wilton Kilgore, Rupert Scott and Floyd McElroy scored. Frank Gantt played well on the line, as did Hamp Williams, Eaves and Roton.

The report on the game called the offensive effort "an exacting attack between the tackles, surcharged by the black-headed Wesley Loftin and Wally Gilbert, and on the flying heels of Scott, McElroy and Kilgore."

When the freshman team wasn't winning games, it was scrimmaging the varsity three and four times a week. But the Wynne and Kiley magic wore off in 1933 and the varsity record fell to 5-5. Wynne left Auburn following the season to become head coach at Kentucky, but in four seasons there his teams played only .500 ball. Kiley returned to Chicago to continue his legal practice and later became a federal judge. Alabama had won the first Southeastern Conference championship in 1933 with a 5-0-1 record in conference play.

Wynne and Kiley's overall success made an impression on the Auburn faithful — the school immediately hired another Notre Dame man. Jack Meagher played end for the Irish teams of 1915-1917, which were coached by Jesse Harper, who was assisted by Rockne. Meagher came to Auburn from a coaching stint with Rice Institute in Houston.

Meagher coached at Auburn until 1942 when he entered military service. Three of Jordan's college teammates — Buddy McCollum, Boots Chambless and Jimmy Hitchcock — assisted Meagher the entire time. Del Morgan coached the line most of that period. Jordan remained head freshman coach and then joined the varsity staff in 1938 as centers coach.

Just as Jordan had learned about offensive football under Wynne and the Notre Dame shift, he now learned defensive football under Meagher. Meagher's defenses were very unpredictable, lining up in different formations and shifting men off and on the line. His three teams from 1936-1938 recorded fifteen shutouts.

Jordan's was a textbook case to become a head coach. He was in charge of a football team as freshman coach. He witnessed two new head coaches, Wynne and Meagher, come in cold, implement their systems and organize their football programs. He was the primary recruiter. He scouted opponents regularly for Meagher. He was tasting it all.

When scouting, Jordan often sat high in the corner of the end zone with his field glasses. "You just keep looking and looking, and finally it dawns on you that something is wrong with the situation," Jordan said. His most famous scouting report concerned Frank Sinkwich, Georgia's great back, who won the Heisman Trophy in 1942. In 1940, Jordan spotted a mannerism in the sophomore Sinkwich who guided Georgia's single wing offense. "On his half-spin, when he looked at the line he was going to run; when he looked back he was going to pass," Jordan said. Auburn lost low scoring games to Georgia in 1940 and 1941 and then gave Rose Bowl-bound Georgia its only loss of the 1942 season by the score of 27-13 in Columbus. The game is considered one of Auburn's greatest upsets. Jordan's tip proved valuable in holding Sinkwich in check. Jordan didn't see the game because he had entered the service, but Jeff Beard filmed the contest and shipped it to Jordan in North Africa. Jordan showed it to his Army buddies again and again as he moved through the European Theater and then took it with him when he went to the Pacific operation.

Jordan brought in another excellent group of freshmen for the 1934 season. As seniors in 1937 they would lead Auburn to an Orange Bowl win over Michigan State. As juniors in 1936 they played in the Rhumba Bowl in Cuba against Villanova. The bowl games were Auburn's first ever, and not until 1953, Jordan's third year as head varsity coach, would Auburn play in another bowl.

One of Jordan's freshmen, halfback Billy Hitchcock, was an easy recruit because Billy wanted to follow his brother Jimmy to Auburn. Billy would letter on the varsity team from 1935-1937. Jordan also coached Billy on the freshman baseball team. The younger Hitchcock went on to play nine years of major league baseball as an infielder, and managed the Baltimore Orioles and Atlanta Braves. Hitchcock recalled that Jordan "exhibited then the qualities that he exhibited later in his coaching career that made him a success."

"He didn't come on real strong and outwardly he was very soft-spoken," Hitchcock said. "But you could see that inward toughness that he had."

Hitchcock recalled that it was a "great day for the freshmen to go up on the hill to play the varsity."

A running mate in the freshman backfield with Hitchcock was Jimmy Fenton. That same year, 1934, Fenton's older brother Benny made first team All-SEC as a senior end. Another brother, Collins, had made the varsity's first team as a sophomore guard when he broke his leg in October 1933.

The Fentons came from Lakeland, Florida. As a senior in high school Jimmy met Jordan in the lobby of the Terrace Hotel in Tampa, when Jordan's freshman team played Tampa. Fenton was actually leaning toward going to the University of Florida, but Jordan so impressed the youngster that he stayed the family course and attended Auburn.

Fenton recalled that Jordan never raised his voice as freshman coach and seldom got angry. But one afternoon on the practice field Fenton's antics didn't sit well with the 24-year-old coach. Word had come down that the freshmen should try to keep out of the training room and allow head trainer Wilbur Hutsell to tend to the heavily-wounded varsity. Fenton had seriously bruised his ribs and on this day wore a pad during the scrimmage. But Fenton hurt the ribs again. He grimaced from the pain as he walked over to Coach Hutsell.

"Don't come to me now," Hutsell said. "You didn't come to me when you first hurt them, did you?"

As Hutsell walked away, Fenton's temper got the best of him. He slammed his blocking pad on the ground and hollered profanities. Jordan had seen and heard it all, and approached Fenton.

"You can go in," Jordan told Fenton, motioning toward the locker room.

"Thank you," Fenton replied, still burning.

"You can stay in," Jordan ordered.

"THANK YOU!" Fenton stormed.

Fenton left the field and met up with his brother Benny.

"I'm packing up and going to the University of Florida," Jimmy said.

"No you're not," Benny explained. "You're going to apologize to both Coach Jordan and Coach Hutsell. You were wrong."

Fenton finally cooled down and returned to the practice field. "Shug put his arm around me and took me down to the end of the field and we talked awhile. After that we got along fine," Fenton said.

Fenton remembered Jordan focusing on the basics of blocking, tackling and timing. "Jack Meagher taught him a lot," Fenton said. "Jack was a pure football man. He was always thinking. Jack's wife told me she hadn't seen their dining room table in ten years because it was covered in stacks of paper with Meagher's offenses and defenses."

Fenton starred as a back and kicker for the varsity team. Several years after he graduated, when much of Meagher's coaching staff, including Jordan, had entered the service, Fenton filled in and coached the backs for Meagher during the 1942 season.

One of Jordan's freshmen in 1934 would provide Auburn all of the offense it needed in the 6-0 win over Michigan State on New Year's Day 1938. Ralph O'Gwynn, also of Selma, scored the lone touchdown of the Orange Bowl on a two-yard run. A 24-yard pass from George Kenmore to O'Gwynn had set up the score. O'Gwynn holds the Auburn record for the longest rushing touchdown with a 92-yard romp against Loyola in 1936.

Jordan's 1934 freshman team tied the only two games it played, against Birmingham-Southern and Georgia Tech. Meagher's varsity squad recorded a 2-8 record, but the 1934 freshmen would be instrumental in pacing Auburn to 8-2, 7-2-2 and 6-2-3 records in 1935, 1936 and 1937, respectively.

Jordan's 1935 frosh squad won both of its games, beating Birmingham-Southern 21-0 and Georgia Tech 7-0. The largest crowd ever to view a freshman game at Auburn turned out for the Tech tilt. A fumble return for a touchdown by Malvern Morgan accounted for the game's only score.

Another of Jordan's 1935 freshmen, Torance "Bo" Russell, wasn't good enough to play high school football at Birmingham's Woodlawn High, but the 165-pounder walked on at Auburn and Jordan liked what he saw. Jordan found him a uniform and by the time Russell finished his playing career at Auburn he weighed two-hundred pounds and was bound for the Washington Redskins. Russell, playing left tackle, was a leader in Auburn's stellar defensive effort in 1937. Auburn finished with a 6-2-3 record and recorded seven shutouts, with all three ties being 0-0. One of Russell's greatest performances at Auburn came in the Tigers' 6-0 spanking of Michigan State in the Orange Bowl. Auburn held the Spartans to two first downs and just fifty-eight total yards. Russell made first team All-

SEC his senior season in 1938.

Russell would later figure in Jordan's good fortunes as a member of the screening committee involved in hiring Jordan as Auburn's head coach in 1951.

Jordan's fourth freshman team in 1936 beat Birmingham-Southern 12-7 and Georgia Tech 25-0. It was Jordan's fourth straight season as head frosh coach without a defeat. Prior to the season Jordan interviewed for the head coaching position at Sewanee, which at that time was still in the SEC, but the school and the man couldn't reach an agreement.

Jordan's 1937 freshmen finally broke his unbeaten string, losing twice and tying once. Jordan's first loss as a head football coach came against Birmingham-Southern, 13-12.

Of note during this period were several varsity clashes between Auburn and Tennessee, from 1935 to 1939. Auburn had only played Tennessee twice previously, in 1900 and 1929. Auburn and Tennessee split the 1935 and 1936 games, and Auburn's Orange Bowl team won in 1937. Meagher's coaching term peaked with the 1937 team and his squads played roughly .500 ball from 1938 to 1942. But the 1938 and 1939 teams gave Tennessee all it could handle.

After fielding several great teams in the early part of the decade, head coach Bob Neyland's Vols came back down to earth for a few years as Alabama and LSU dominated conference play from 1934-1937. But in 1938, Neyland, utilizing the single wing offense, fielded the first of three major bowl teams before he departed for the service. Despite an 11-0 record and a 17-0 Orange Bowl win over Oklahoma, Tennessee finished second in the Associated Press rankings in 1938 behind Texas Christian University. Tennessee struggled to a 7-0 win over Auburn early in the season.

The 1939 Tennessee team was equally great with a 10-0 mark in the regular season. The leading ball carrier was tailback George "Bad News" Cafego. Bob Suffridge was among Tennessee's greatest guards.

Auburn held a modest 5-4-1 record when it traveled to Knoxville and Watkins Field to close the season on December 9, 1939. The undefeated Vols were bound for the Rose Bowl and a match against Southern Cal. Jordan, now the centers coach under Meagher, remembered the 1939 battle and its impact on the Auburn-Tennessee rivalry.

"That was the height of the General Neyland regime up there. Course he was Major to us back in those days. The 'General' came along during World War II. In the mid-1930s Auburn and Tennessee got together for a series of games and it was even-steven: everyone was a blockbuster and a close game. In 1939 Tennessee had one obstacle in its way and that was Auburn. We went up to Knoxville and the Tennessee fans were singing 'California Here We Come.'

"In the middle of the fourth quarter Tennessee led 7-0. Auburn took over the ball on the twenty and began a steady march down the field. There was no passing. It was a rainy, drizzly day and the field was a quagmire by then. Tennessee had to have this ballgame, and we were making first downs all the way down to the Tennessee nineteen. I can remember looking at the General across the field. He was about to have a conniption fit. It didn't look like there was any way to stop Auburn. But for some unknown reason we decided to pass on first down. That sort of threw our continuity of downs off. We could make that two-and-a-half, three yards a down and consequently make a first down. So finally the ball went over to Tennessee and they punted out of danger. But this game created some anxiety on the part of Major Neyland, the Tennessee fans and also the Rose Bowl officials. I talked to Major Neyland many times about it during the basketball tournaments, which were held in Knoxville at that time. He always held court up there at the old Farragut Hotel. And he said to the press it just wasn't worth it to play Auburn. First of all, Auburn didn't draw many people and secondly Auburn was just 'too damn tough,' as he put it, to have an alley fight with before ten-thousand people. Of course his estimate of the situation was wrong because not only was Auburn drawing ten-thousand, but not many other people were drawing more than ten-thousand, including Tennessee."

Neyland and Tennessee stayed clear of the Tigers until the series resumed in 1956.

Another landmark event that occurred for Auburn during Jordan's years as an assistant was the construction of Cliff Hare Stadium. Hare had played on Auburn's first football team in 1892, served as president of the Southern Conference and served as chairman of Auburn's Faculty Athletic Committee. The new stadium comprised 7,500 seats, what is now the bottom part of the lower west stands in the 85,000-seat capacity Jordan-Hare Stadium. Jordan was an assistant coach when Auburn tied Florida 7-7 on November 30, 1939, in the first game ever played in the stadium. Thirty-four years later Jordan's name would be placed beside Hare's on the stadium brick.

There was a close-knit coaching staff under Meagher that included Jordan, McCollum, Chambless and Hitchcock. Trips such as the famous Rhumba Bowl in Havana, Cuba following the 1936 season tended to bring the coaches and players together. Practical jokes became commonplace and a good one was pulled on assistant coach McCollum during the return trip from Cuba. Citizens returning to the U.S. could bring in a gallon of rum without paying taxes and McCollum had stored away several straw-covered fifths. As the coaches and players enjoyed the voyage back home, someone would call McCollum out of his room and somebody else would replace one of McCollum's full bottles with an empty one. When the team reached customs, McCollum was out of rum.

In addition to his football duties, Jordan served as head coach of the basketball team and as the head mentor of the freshman baseball team. He once said of major league player and manager Billy Hitchcock, "I helped him become a .300 hitter: .100 his sophomore year, .100 his junior year and .100 his senior year."

The 1942 *Glomerata* said of Jordan: "As proficient a football scout as he is a center coach, and as fine a basketball mentor as a scout, he has that knack of getting the most from the least."

From 1933 to 1942, Jordan coached his hoopsters to an 88-66 record. After two subpar years, Jordan's teams recorded impressive marks of 10-5, 11-4, 14-5 and 16-6 from 1935 to 1939. Joel Eaves lettered on Jordan's 1935-1937 teams and served as captain. Jordan seldom got rough with the players unless they were performing below their capabilities. During half time of one game Jordan cleared the dressing room except for his starters and said, "You couldn't beat Loachapoka, Wetumpka or Wedowee the way you are playing tonight."

The 1936-1937 team finished third in the SEC. Along with captain and guard Eaves, other contributors included guard A.D. Curlee, forwards J.C. Holmes, Rex McKissick, and Malvern Morgan, and centers Thomas Edwards Jr. and Edron Childers. Regular opponents on the Tiger schedule during this period included Sewanee, Birmingham-Southern, Georgia, Georgia Tech and Florida.

Jordan's 1941-1942 team finished 11-6 and reached the semifinals of the SEC tournament. The Tigers beat Vanderbilt 36-34, and Tulane 45-36, before succumbing to one of Adolph Rupp's powerhouse Kentucky squads, 40-31. Shag Hawkins and Frank Manci made the All-SEC team for Auburn.

When he wasn't coaching, Jordan enjoyed the life of a bachelor. In fact, after he graduated and until he married in 1937, he was a member of the Tognby Club in Auburn. The group for bachelors had been formed by several professors and the club name was an acronym for the founders — Taylor, Odom, Guiton, Naftel, Barrett and Yotter. When a member married he lost membership status and another man would join the club to fill the vacancy. Jordan's playing and coaching mate, Jimmy Hitchcock, was also a member. The group maintained a clubhouse for socializing and frequently held parties for former members and their wives.

In 1934, while on a basketball trip, Jordan met his wife-to-be, Evelyn Walker, who was a student at the University of South Carolina in Columbia. They met at a school dance in the gymnasium. Evelyn received her undergraduate degree from South Carolina in social work. After graduating, she attended Tulane in New Orleans and gained a master's degree in the same field. They dated throughout this period and married on June 11, 1937 in St. Petersburg, Florida.

The Jordan's first child, Susan, was born in February 1939. A second daughter, Darby, was born in 1942.

In the ten years since graduating from Auburn, Jordan had built a family and was building a coaching career. But he would be forced to leave both behind. America was at war and Jordan would be in the thick of it.

6

"Where you from, son?"

Dear President Funderburk:

Some time ago I noticed in the paper the death of your football coach, who was known to the athletic world as Shug Jordan. My association with Coach Jordan was of a very short duration during the early part of 1944. We were in the same outfit in England, preparing for the invasion. He was a fine gentleman and an inspiring officer.

There was an incident during the D-Day operation which I am not sure that his many friends around Auburn University knew about, but I think it should be brought to the attention of the university and to you. Early on in that operation, Coach Jordan caught a piece of shrapnel in his shoulder. I am sure it was very painful as you could see the feverish look in his face and the suffering he was going through, but he refused to turn himself in to have it removed since he probably would have had to be sent back to England as all surgical effort was being applied to the very seriously wounded, of which there were many. It was this quiet type of heroism that is so seldom recognized. Several days later when things quieted down he was hospitalized and the shrapnel removed. I am not aware of any further problems with his arm but he returned to duty shortly thereafter. I do not remember how long the medical procedure took but he never complained. Best personal regards.

Sincerely,
Henry K. McHarg III
March 10, 1982

Captain Ralph "Shug" Jordan received the Purple Heart for the shrapnel wounds to his left arm and shoulder sustained during the June 6 invasion of Normandy, known as Operation Overlord. Jordan's unit had been part of the landing at Utah Beach. Perhaps the odds had run out on Jordan since the clash marked his fourth major invasion since entering the service.

Jordan had activated his military commission and was appointed a Lieutenant in the Army Corps of Engineers early in 1942. He reported to Camp Edwards in Massachusetts and in August sailed to Scotland to await orders for the American-British invasion of North Africa. He was assigned to the 1st Engineer Special Brigade, an amphibious assault force.

Jordan told how he and his men were issued white overcoats, long underwear and heavy boots, hinting of a trip to Norway. But after boarding ship the soldiers discovered they were sailing south to North Africa. The cold weather clothes had been meant to mislead them in order to maintain the secrecy of the mission. Jordan stated he was apprehensive about the assault at Oran in French North Africa because it was unknown whether the French defenders would fight with the Germans or support the Free French effort. There were problems with craft and communications during the November 7-8, 1942 invasion, referred to as Operation Torch, but weak resistance was overcome. Jordan's work included the design of docks, roads and bridges.

In February 1943, Jordan wrote home from North Africa: "I have been made to feel very much at home by the sight of basketball courts in the small towns of the region."

He told of celebrating New Year's Day with six other Auburn men and of their letting go with a lusty "War Eagle!" that they hoped would echo across the Mediterranean to the ears of Hitler and Mussolini.

Also during this period after the North African landing, Jordan met up with his Selma High School pal Billy Lapsley, who later achieved the rank of Major-General in the Army. The two enjoyed a couple of beer-drinking nights. Jordan commented to Lapsley that he had played in one bowl game, referring to the North Africa invasion, and now he had to keep going until he played in the Rose Bowl, referring to the much anticipated, though still to be agreed upon, cross-channel invasion.

In January 1943 the powers-that-be had met at the Casablanca Conference and decided on the invasion of Sicily. Jordan was assigned responsibilities planning and was with the first American soldiers under General George Patton's command to land on the island in July 1943. The Allied forces completed the conquest on August 8.

Years later Jordan recalled, "God, I loved that Patton's style. I still remember him coming over with a radio message to the effect that he was taking command of the newly-born 7th Army, which would have its baptism of blood on the beaches of Sicily the next morning."

Even before the Sicily landing, the Trident Conference in May pointed to Italy as the next target after Sicily. Jordan participated in the landing on the European mainland at Salerno, Italy in September 1943. The allies experienced fierce fighting with the Germans.

Jordan recalled while waiting aboard ship for orders to move, he stood watching the eruption of a volcano with fire and ash spitting into the dark sky. Alongside Jordan stood a soldier from Texas who had gained a reputation for boring his mates with tall tales stemming from the many giant wonders of his home state.

Jordan, gesturing toward the volcano, said, "I'll bet you don't have anything like *that* in Texas."

The young soldier thought a moment and then replied in his Texas drawl, "No, but we sure have a fire department in Dallas that could put it out!"

By the end of May in 1944, more than a million-and-a-half U.S. troops, including Jordan, had gathered in the United Kingdom to prepare for the massive ship and troop movement across the English Channel and the invasion of Normandy. This was Jordan's Rose Bowl.

Full-scale rehearsals were held in late April and early May.

Troops and equipment embarked in the same ships and for the most part in the same ports from whence they would leave for the real invasion. During landings and convoy maneuvering in late April, German E-boats torpedoed several allied Landing Ships Tanks (LSTs), killing 441 soldiers and 197 sailors.

Jordan was again placed in charge of a landing boat outfit and participated with his troops in numerous practice runs, usually moving out into the channel past the Isle of Wight and sweeping left back toward the England shore. Jordan knew the real invasion was finally at hand when his superiors told him and his troops to "pack all your personal possessions in your footlockers and put the name and address of your next of kin on the top."

By June 3 almost every vessel was in her assembly port and loading was nearly completed. They began to move early in the morning of June 4 as D-Day was scheduled for June 5. General Eisenhower was at Southwick House, Admiral Ramsay's headquarters, to hear the latest weather forecasts. Early in the morning of June 4 Eisenhower was informed that a low ceiling would prevail the next day which would prevent the air forces from carrying out their part of the assault, and heavy seas would swamp landing craft. Eisenhower postponed the operation for twenty-four hours. All ships and craft already at sea were recalled to their emergency postponement ports. Jordan's unit and thousands more remained uncomfortably on ship. Seasick men, the odor of gasoline and the stench of backed-up toilets stayed in his memory.

In the darkness of the morning of June 5, General Eisenhower turned out for the final weather conference. A fair interval of two days was predicted beginning the morning of June 6, with moderating winds, an overcast sky, and two-foot waves off the far shore. Eisenhower made the decision: "O.K. We'll go."

This time Jordan's ship sailed into the channel and swept right toward France. During the night his thoughts turned to his wife, Evelyn, and their seventh wedding anniversary upcoming in five days, to his two daughters, to his Selma upbringing, to those wonderfully timeless days when he competed on the athletic fields for

Auburn and to his ten most satisfying years as an assistant coach.

As the morning came the number of sea vessels astounded Jordan. Their crowded movement had run very close to schedule. The Germans remained completely unaware of what was going on. German E-boats had failed to make their routine patrol on the night of June 5 because of foul weather.

The airborne landing began in the early hours of June 6. Approximately thirteen-thousand paratroops in the 101st and 82nd Airborne divisions began to dominate several miles of the French inland from the beaches.

Jordan was bound for the nine-mile stretch of the Cotentin east coast named Utah Beach. Its appearance was not unlike the beaches that ran along the east coast of the U.S. from the Carolinas to Maine. The German defenders had planted lines of anti-boat obstacles at shallow water. The beach proper was a gentle slope of yellow sand. Low sand dunes partly covered with grass formed a 100-yard belt behind the beach. On the seaward side the Germans had constructed a low concrete wall. Behind the dunes, flooded pasture lands ran one to two miles inland. U.S. ships bombarded German fortifications. The Germans were estimated to have more than 110 guns — ranging from 75 mm to 170 mm — defending the Utah sector. Twenty landing craft of the first wave touched down at H-Hour, 0630 (6:30 a.m.). The men waded through one-hundred yards of water to reach dry land. With them was Brigadier General Theodore Roosevelt, a cane in one hand and a map in the other.

Jordan and his troops departed the cross-channel ship and boarded the landing craft. Jordan later recalled many times that although "there had been a lot of carrying on the night before, it was silent in those landing craft. I never saw an atheist or an agnostic when it came time to hit the beach."

Just over two hours after the first troops hit Utah Beach, Jordan too sprinted ashore and scrambled for cover. The landing had mistakenly occurred south of the designated point. Smoke from the Naval bombardment had obscured landmarks, and the landing control boat encountered a strong current as it guided the first wave of troops. As a result, enemy gunfire was not as thick as that experienced by U.S. troops storming nearby Omaha Beach, but shells flew consistently enough. Shrapnel from a German 88 pierced Jordan's left shoulder and upper arm. He considered the wounds minor and with the 1st Engineer Special Brigade organized the beaches and directed the mammoth movement of troops and supplies inland. The engineers made contact with the airborne divisions; tapped the French telephone system for communication purposes; blew gaps in the concrete seawall so that troops could cross the flooded pastures; repaired and constructed roads and cleared the area of mines.

By the early evening of D-Day, more than 21,000 troops, seventeen-hundred vehicles and seventeen-hundred tons of supplies had landed on Utah Beach. By June 10, more than 62,000 troops, 4,100 vehicles and ten-thousand tons of supplies had come in; and by June 17 some 110,000 troops, fifteen-thousand vehicles and 42,000 tons of supplies had moved inland thanks to the efforts of Jordan and his fellow engineers.

Captain Henry McHarg, who wrote Auburn University President Hanly Funderburk about Jordan's performance, was also in the engineer brigade and had crossed the channel in the same vessel as Jordan. He worked alongside Jordan out of the hastily-established beach headquarters.

"It hurt him like hell, but he knew he wasn't going to die," McHarg recalled of Jordan's injury. "After awhile he couldn't use his arm and he broke out in a tremendous fever. It was a fine thing to have done to stay on the beach."

Four days later, the weary Jordan looked forward to taking a whiff of ether and sleeping as doctors removed the shrapnel and stitched up the wounds. But the field surgeon heard Jordan's dialect and asked, "Where you from, son? You're from Alabama, I know by hearing you talk." Jordan acknowledged the doctor's observation. By an amazing coincidence the doctor, Leslie Taylor, was a cousin of J.D. Bush, Jordan's football teammate and fellow member of the prestigious Spades student organization at Auburn. Dr. Taylor, from Mobile, wanted to carry on a conversation. His assistant gave Jordan a local anesthetic. Jordan later told J.D. Bush that his cousin the doctor nearly killed him digging for the shrapnel as they talked about their home state and football on Utah Beach. After two days of rest, Jordan returned to duty.

"I don't think it affected my personality at all," Jordan said about his experience in the European Theater Operation many years after the war. "It made me appreciate being here. I saw 'em stacked up like cord wood. I could have easily been one of them. I felt like I had been raised right and had an evaluation of the real things in life. The things I saw in the Army just enhanced my feelings and made them more profound. So no, I don't think it changed me personally at all. I had been scared before I went over there and I was damn sure scared over there. If you ever meet anybody that's been in combat with bombs and mortars and that German 88, and they say they weren't afraid, you say well that son of a bitch is crazy."

Jordan worked the beaches into November. "We did go to Paris. That's as far inland as we got," he said. "I never got to Germany because they brought us back. I thought we were going to be school troops and teach everybody how to do it. We had made the North African invasion, Sicily invasion, invasion of Italy, and D-Day in Normandy, but they didn't bring us back to teach anybody, they brought us back to go to the Pacific for the Okinawa invasion. So we made that one on a very unusual day, April Fool's Day, 1945."

Before heading to the Pacific, Jordan received a month of stateside leave at the beginning of the year. His wife had left Auburn with the two girls to stay with her mother and sister on the Walker's family estate in east Georgia. Evelyn's father, M.E. Walker, and her mother, Rose, had built a home on four-hundred acres between Keysville and Matthews, just southwest of Augusta. It was called Rose Acre Farm. Jordan also worked in a visit to Auburn during his leave.

On January 27 Jordan departed for the West Coast, where he was scheduled to fly out of Fort Lewis, Washington on February 1. But when he reported there he received orders to fly out near San

Francisco. He didn't depart for the Philippines until February 10. En route he stopped at Tarawa, Guadalcanal, Hollandia and Spaipan.

"In no time at all I found myself ten-thousand miles from Alabama, crossed the equator twice and also the international date line," Jordan wrote a friend on March 15: "You can see that I've been rushed. The trip home was wonderful and I do believe the five weeks were about the happiest I've ever known."

The Okinawa campaign, the last great amphibious campaign of the war, was hotly contested against a backed-up Japanese army. During it, President Roosevelt died on April 12 at the Little White House in Warm Springs, Georgia. Roosevelt of course frequently retreated to Warm Springs for polio rehabilitation. One of Jordan's daughters, Darby, also received treatment for polio there during the war. Just eighteen days after Roosevelt's death, Adolf Hitler shot himself in Berlin. On June 21, the Japanese garrison, having lost 103,000 of its 120,000 men, ended resistance on Okinawa. U.S. casualties reached 48,000, a quarter of them killed.

Following V-E Day on May 8 and Japan's official surrender aboard the *Missouri* in Tokyo Bay on September 2, Jordan was honorably discharged and promoted to the rank of Major upon the resignation of his commission.

Jordan would often refer to World War II when speaking to his football teams before games, though he seldom spoke in detail about his experiences, even to his family.

"It was hard to get much out of him about the war," said his son, Ralph, Jr. "Most of what you got had some message, whether it was a life-lesson, a commitment, a responsibility or something humorous. He didn't talk about the Normandy invasion or the circumstances surrounding his wound and rehabilitation. I remember the scars of course."

Upon his return, Jordan prepared to move his family back to Auburn and resume his coaching career in time for basketball season. But he was in for a shock and a heartache. A hero at war, Jordan received something less than a hero's welcome from Auburn.

7

"Close the joint down"
•••••••••••••••••••••••

The world — and Auburn — had changed when Shug Jordan returned in time to coach Auburn's 1945 basketball team. Jack Meagher had relinquished his position as head coach of the football team following the 1942 season to enter the service. Meagher's last hurrah had been Auburn's 27-13 upset of top-ranked Georgia in Columbus. The Tigers finished the 1942 season with a 6-4-1 record.

Auburn didn't field a football team in 1943. Only Georgia Tech, Tulane, LSU, Georgia and Vanderbilt did among the SEC schools. Notre Dame won the 1943 national championship. All of the SEC schools played full schedules in 1944, and at Auburn's helm, as head football coach and athletic director, was Carl Voyles.

Voyles had been head coach at William & Mary where his team won the Southern Conference championship in 1942. He began his career as an assistant at Illinois from 1925-1931, moved to Duke as an assistant until 1938, then started at William & Mary. Voyles's Auburn squads finished 4-4 in 1944 and 5-5 in 1945, winning only two conference games.

The Jordans returned to their old home in Auburn and Jordan's cagers fought to a 7-9 record his first year back. Voyles looked on Jordan and several other returning coaches as excess baggage. Even Elmer Salter, who had served in the Army air corps, was demoted to a secondary public relations position answering "to somebody who didn't know football from baseball," Salter said. (Jordan and Salter had kept in touch during the war, with Salter sending Jordan a carton of cigarettes each week.)

"Voyles didn't want any of us to return to his staff," Salter said. "But he was obligated by law to take us back for a year. He did everything he could to make us want to leave. I wouldn't say he advertised the fact, but people knew the situation."

The man Shug Jordan confided in during these difficult days was Cliff "Fesser" Hare. Living out his remaining years quietly, Hare frequently invited Jordan to sit on his front porch and converse.

"I guess we were just two lonely men talking about old times," Jordan said. "He was old, lonely, and in declining health. I was a lonely young assistant coach. Those afternoons we spent together — there must have been fifteen or twenty of them in the course of a year — have meant a great deal to me."

"Never lose faith," Hare told Jordan. "Never lose faith and keep working."

Hare also told Jordan how he and Dr. Steadman Sanford — for whom the stadium in Athens, Georgia is named — used to go to Hare's Auburn home every year after the Auburn-Georgia game in Columbus to divide the gate money. They would sit down in the kitchen, take the money out of a cigar box and divide it dollar-by-dollar. Little did Jordan realize he would soon be coaching in Sanford Stadium, or that his name would one day shine alongside Hare's on the stadium in Auburn.

On June 1, 1946 Jordan resigned from the Auburn staff. He was practical enough to understand that a head coach wanted his own people around him and proud enough not to endure the humiliation.

Jordan joined the staff of his former mentor, Jack Meagher, who had become head coach of the Miami Seahawks in a new professional league, the All-America Football Conference. Another assistant coach for the Seahawks was Hank Crisp, who had served as an assistant coach for Frank Thomas at Alabama in the 1930s. But the Miami team didn't put fans in the stands and the franchise was doomed from the start. On October 11, only weeks into the season and the day Miami won its first game over the Buffalo Bisons, Jordan announced that he had accepted a job offer from the University of Georgia as an assistant football coach and head basketball coach. Georgia head football coach Wally Butts had telephoned Jordan and offered the position.

"I was in a hotel on the cheap end of Miami Beach when Coach Butts called," Jordan said. "My roommate was Hank Crisp of Alabama. I guess you could say we were both in exile."

Jordan's decision to leave the pro team proved to be a good decision. Two weeks later head coach Meagher resigned, turning the team over to Crisp. At the end of the season, with Miami sporting a 2-10 record and equally-poor attendance figures, the league gave the franchise to Baltimore.

The Georgia job elated the Jordans. It seemed tremendously secure following the post-war occurrences at Auburn and Miami. Mrs. Jordan, who had remained in Auburn with the children when her husband went to Miami, would be moving back within one-hundred miles of her childhood home in Georgia.

Once again Jordan's coaching career was on track. He was joining a nationally-acclaimed football program that was rich with tradition. In fact, Georgia had played its first football game ever on February 20, 1892 at Piedmont Park in Atlanta. It had lost, 10-0, to another school also competing on the gridiron for the first time — Auburn.

Georgia had accumulated an impressive lineup of head coaches through the years. Pop Warner, who would become famous for coaching the legendary Jim Thorpe at Carlisle and who produced great teams at Stanford, began his head coaching career at Georgia after graduating from Cornell. He coached the Bulldogs in 1896 to an undefeated season. W.A. Cunningham, who learned his football under Dan McGugin at Vanderbilt, came to Georgia as head coach in 1910 and his teams produced winning seasons seven times in eight years. H.J. Stegeman, a great athlete under Amos Alonzo Stagg at the University of Chicago, coached Georgia to an undefeated season and the Southern Conference championship in 1920. George "Kid"

Woodruff, a captain and star quarterback at Georgia, coached the Bulldogs from 1923-1927 and implemented the Notre Dame system, bringing in two Rockne disciples, line coach Harry Mehre and backfield coach Frank Thomas. Mehre, who played on the line for Rockne during the era of the Four Horsemen, coached Georgia from 1928 to 1937.

Wally Butts was into his eighth season as head coach in 1946. Born in Milledgeville, Georgia, Butts had come to Athens in 1938 as an assistant following coaching stints at Madison A&M, Georgia Military College and Male High. His first staff as head coach at Georgia included J.B. "Ears" Whitworth, J.V. Sikes, Bill Hartman, Howell Hollis, Spec Towns and Quinton Lumpkin.

Butts immediately established himself as a master of the passing game. His teams in 1939 and 1940 played .500 ball, but the 1941 team went 9-1-1 and beat TCU in the Orange Bowl. The star performer of the bowl game had been junior back Frank Sinkwich, who threw for 243 yards and three touchdowns and rushed for 139 yards. In 1942 Sinkwich was joined by sophomore sensation Charley Trippi in the backfield and Georgia went 10-1, losing only to Auburn while winning the SEC title and beating UCLA 9-0 in the Rose Bowl. Sinkwich won the Heisman Trophy that year and set an SEC total offense record with 2,187 yards (1,392 of them through the air). Georgia lost Trippi temporarily to the service but still produced 6-4 and 7-3 seasons in 1943 and 1944. Trippi returned for most of the 1945 season and Georgia finished 9-2. Trippi set a conference record in the Georgia Tech game, passing for 323 yards.

Much was expected of Georgia's 1946 season with Trippi returning for his senior season along with highly-touted sophomore Johnny Rauch, whom Butts had taught the mechanics of passing. Four other players on that Georgia team were sophomore back Buck Bradberry, freshman end Gene Lorendo, sophomore guard Homer Hobbs and sophomore guard Joe Connally. Jordan would hire all four of them as assistants when he took the reins at Auburn in 1951.

The team was 3-0 when Jordan joined the staff in 1946 as an assistant to head line coach Whitworth. Jordan recalled his first day on the practice field in Athens when Butts took him aside and moaned that Georgia didn't have any material. Butts questioned whether Trippi really wanted to play football, said Rauch couldn't throw and that even if he could the squad didn't have any ends who could catch the ball. Jordan would find such pessimism fairly common for Butts.

Jordan recalled that Butts loved the passing game, developed it first and then built a running game to go with it. Jordan may not have acquired Butts's thirst for the aerial attack, but he learned a great deal from Georgia's "Little Round Man."

"Under him I saw for the first time a head coach give assistant coaches great responsibility," Jordan said. "The only time Wally entered the picture, as far as constructive criticism to his coaches, was the next day in private. I tried to bring a lot of that philosophy with me to Auburn. He was probably the most generous coach I ever knew. He would literally give you the shirt off of his back."

While Jordan may have borrowed from Butts's approach to his assistants and showed similar off-the-field generosity, he didn't take with him Butts's style of motivating his players. Joe Connally remembered playing for Butts "out of fear." Bradberry called Butts "a tyrant on the field" who confronted and chewed out his players during practice. Bradberry said Butts became theatrical at a moment's notice in efforts to charge up his team.

"Coach Butts could pull some of the damnedest things you've ever seen," Bradberry said. "We lost a game probably because of that. We were playing Tech in 1947. Trippi had graduated. We still had Rauch. We were behind 7-0 at half. As usual we all went in the dressing room with the trainers and managers, while the coaches were outside getting their heads together. Then the coaches came in and then Coach Butts came in. We were sitting on the benches against the locker. He paced back and forth and didn't say anything. That was the way he usually did it and then he'd start cussing out this guy and that guy, jumping up and down, ranting and raving. But this day he came in and paced back and forth, then he walked over to the door to leave, then looked back and just scanned the room and looked into each person's eyes. One rule was if he looked at you and you weren't looking at him you were in trouble. He hit somebody in the face over at Furman in Greenville once because he was looking at the floor. He lifted him up with an uppercut. But this time he stopped at the door, scanned the room and said 'Shit' and walked out.

"Coach Whitworth was sitting over there on the training table and everything was just quiet as a mouse. Coach Whit started whimpering and then he started crying and then he looked around and tears were coming down his face and he said, 'Godammit, you're killing the little man.' We all started crying and we were so damn down, they beat us 7-0. That one didn't work."

Years later as head coach at Auburn, Jordan took a page out of Butts's book, but smoothed out the rough edges. Jordan walked into the dressing room at halftime, told his squad he was ashamed to be the head coach of Auburn and ashamed to be a part of this football team and walked out. Unlike Butts's Georgia team, the Auburn players came out and destroyed the competition in the second half.

End Lorendo remembered Jordan at Georgia as "always well prepared, ready for an opportunity." Lorendo also played on Jordan's basketball team. Bradberry recalled Jordan at Georgia as "a very kind person, easy to talk with, very studious, very methodical in his coaching, not in the mode of a Whitworth who was ranting and raving at his linemen. Coach Jordan was the same all of the time."

In addition to assisting Whitworth with the line, particularly the centers and defense, Jordan became the main scout as he had been for Auburn prior to the war. Until the 1950 season, when Whitworth left to become head coach at Oklahoma A&M, and Jordan became head line coach, Jordan was seldom on the Georgia sidelines on game day, except for the season closer against Georgia Tech, because he was scouting an upcoming opponent. Coaches Thomas and Lumpkin assisted Jordan with scouting.

Jordan participated in one of Georgia's greatest seasons ever in 1946. Georgia finished the regular season with a 10-0 record, winning the SEC, and beat North Carolina in the Sugar Bowl, 20-10, to close a perfect season. The offense scored a whopping 392 points. Halfback Trippi was a unanimous All-American and won the Maxwell Award as the nation's outstanding player. He finished second in the Heisman Trophy voting to running back Glenn Davis of Army. He led the SEC in scoring with eighty-four points, rushed for 744 yards and passed for 622 yards. He was also an outstanding defensive back and an excellent punter. Many years later Jordan said of the Georgia star, "Trippi was the greatest football player I have ever seen. He could do everything: great runner, passer, blocker, tackler, punter, great return man. He is, without question, the greatest football player I have ever been associated with."

Also starring for Georgia in 1946 were Rauch at quarterback, guard Herb St. John, end Joe Tereshinski and tackle Jack Bush. Despite being the only unbeaten, untied team in the country, Georgia finished third in the nation behind Notre Dame and Army, who had played each other to a 0-0 tie in Yankee Stadium in New York City.

In the second game of the 1947 season North Carolina snapped Georgia's seventeen-game winning streak. Georgia finished the season 7-4-1, including the season-ending loss to Georgia Tech when Butts's halftime ploy backfired. Georgia tied Maryland in the Gator Bowl, 20-20.

Meanwhile at Auburn, head coach Carl Voyles's Tigers continued to slide. His 1946 and 1947 teams had posted a combined record of 6-13 and won only two conference games, both against Florida. One of the few bright spots for the Tigers was quarterback Travis Tidwell. As a freshman in 1946 he led the nation in total offense with 1,715 yards.

In December of 1947 Auburn bought out the remaining two years of Voyles's contract, named long-time track coach and trainer Wilbur Hutsell as athletic director and began looking for a head coach. Voyles became head coach of the Brooklyn Football Dodgers, owned by baseball legend Branch Rickey, of the professional All-America Conference.

A newspaper article reported a lineup of coaches rumored to be under consideration by Auburn: Nurmi Nelson, Ears Whitworth, Scabs Scarborough, Slick Morton, Ralph Jordan, Ed McKeever, Red Sanders and the former Auburn head coach, Jack Meagher. Indeed Jordan felt the position was ripe for picking and interviewed for the job. He was thirty-seven years old and had thirteen years of coaching experience in the SEC. But Auburn snubbed its favorite son again.

Jordan appeared before the athletic committee but said the members gave him no encouragement. "They said something about there being too many factions among the alumni for them to hire an Auburn man," the bitter Jordan said. "I told them if they had no confidence in Auburn men, they ought to close the joint down."

Once again Auburn looked north to Notre Dame. Athletic Director Hutsell named thirty-two-year-old Earl Brown as head coach on January 21, 1948. Brown had starred as an end under Elmer Layden at Notre Dame from 1936-1938. Prior to getting the Auburn job, Brown was head coach at Canisius College in Buffalo; before that he was head coach at Dartmouth. Auburn's choice of Brown prompted Jordan to return to Georgia and dig in as an assistant coach. The Jordan family, now including James Ralph Jordan Jr., born in August 1947, was ready to call Athens home.

"When Brown was hired, I thought — and had every reason to think — that I'd never return to Auburn," Jordan said. It appeared Jordan or Ears Whitworth would replace Butts whenever Butts stepped down, though that didn't seem likely anytime soon.

Butts put together another scoring machine in 1948 led by senior quarterback Rauch. Georgia won its third SEC title under Butts with a 9-2 record and then lost to Texas in the Orange Bowl, 41-28. But the next year, in 1949, Butts's squad dropped to 4-6-1. Following the season head line coach Whitworth accepted the head coaching position at Oklahoma A&M, and Butts put Jordan in charge of the line. Georgia fared better in 1950, going 6-3-3 while losing to Texas A&M in the post-season Presidential Cup in College Park, Maryland, 40-20. Two of Jordan's top linemen were tackle Marion Campbell and guard Rocco Principe.

While the Georgia football program had begun a descent into an eight-year trance of mediocrity, Auburn's gridiron program had hit rock bottom. Earl Brown's 1950 Auburn team lost all ten of its games, failed to score in seven games, and accumulated only thirty-one points the entire season while opponents devoured the Tigers with 255 points. Cliff Hare Stadium, as Auburn's home field was now called, had increased capacity to 21,500 in 1949, but fans seldom filled up more than half of it.

Brown's first year at the helm in 1949 saw the Tigers go 2-4-3, relying almost exclusively on senior quarterback Travis Tidwell, who made All-American and led Auburn to a victory over Alabama, 14-13, in the final game of the season. Believing the win over Alabama signaled brighter football days ahead, Auburn alumni promptly gave Brown a new car. Then Auburn lost its 1950 opener in Montgomery to Wofford, 19-14. The season went downhill from there.

After the season Auburn followers again bickered over whether to buy out the remaining year of their head football coach's contract. From Athens, Jordan sympathized with young Brown's position. He also shook his head in disbelief at what had become of his alma mater's once-proud football tradition.

8

"A graveyard for coaches"
••••••••••••••••••••••••••

On January 17, 1951, only two days after his inauguration, newly-elected Alabama Governor Gordon Persons, an Auburn supporter, announced publicly that Alabama Polytechnic Institute needed a new head football coach and new staff. A circle of the governor's supporters in the capital city who also supported Auburn, including lumberman and confidant Billy Thames, had encouraged Persons to place the "Fire Brown" campaign into high gear.

Auburn President Ralph Draughon wasn't impressed that the governor had made the status of Auburn's head football coach his number-one priority upon taking office. But Persons maintained that he had this authority "by virtue of being governor and because I am the president of the (Auburn) board of trustees."

On the night of January 19 Persons met with Draughon, Auburn alumni and faculty — twenty-one people in all — at the governor's mansion in Montgomery. About the only person who wasn't there was head coach Brown. Persons indicated he had received three-hundred telegrams, telephone calls and letters since his announcement two days earlier and all but a handful had sided with him.

According to a report by the *Montgomery Advertiser*, an unexpected development occurred during the meeting. Two Auburn football players showed up at the door with a petition in support of Brown signed by sixty-two players from the 1950 squad. Persons left it up to Draughon whether to invite the two players into the meeting. Draughon ruled they could come in. Their petition, aimed at the governor, stated: "We, the Auburn football players, disagree with your action taken with our head football coach, Earl Brown. We want you to know we have full confidence in Coach Brown and know that you have made a grave mistake."

Governor Persons went around the room and asked for the opinion of each person in attendance. Draughon presented the recommendation of the faculty athletic committee that Brown be retained, but that the coaching staff be strengthened. Draughon said he approved the committee's recommendation and told the governor that a change at this time would not be helpful to the football program. All others in attendance also suggested that the remaining year on Brown's contract be honored. At meeting's end, Governor Persons conceded he had "lost his point" and that Brown would remain. If the situation didn't improve, Persons said, another meeting would be held in one year.

The next day Persons issued a public statement for Auburn people "to get behind Brown." Of his new lease on life, Brown stated, "It is heartwarming and it is with every hope I have that all Auburn men work together with us for a greater Auburn."

As agreed, Brown went about boosting his coaching staff. He dismissed two line coaches and the freshman coach and began interviewing to fill the positions. Another assistant coach soon resigned. Brown also continued to sign recruit after recruit. From December 1, 1950 to January 31, 1951, Brown signed the unheard-of total of 115 prep players, twice as many as he had signed during the same period the previous year.

But Brown's position wasn't secure yet. On February 3, a group of Auburn alumni in north Alabama publicly pressed for Brown's dismissal. The group's letter to Governor Persons stated: "The record of Coach Brown is marked with a sense of dismal failures on the football field. We believe that the degree of alumni loyalty which has been unparalleled throughout the nation heretofore will be seriously strained if Coach Earl Brown is retained during the present year."

More than seventy Auburn supporters signed it. Meanwhile, the governor's office, sensing renewed momentum to oust Brown, turned the pressure back on.

Jeff Beard, Auburn's business manager since 1944, later said he went before the athletic committee and suggested firing Brown. The department was $100,000 in debt. "We were wallowing in misery," Beard said. "We put in a ticket office but we weren't selling any tickets." Auburn had just constructed fourteen-thousand seats on the east side of Cliff Hare Stadium in 1949, enlarging capacity to 21,500.

In the February 6 edition of the *Montgomery Advertiser*, sports editor Max Moseley broke the story that the remaining year of Brown's contract would be bought out and that either Georgia's Jordan or LSU line coach Norm "Shorty" Cooper would get the head coaching position. Brown, meanwhile, continued to interview assistant coaches.

On Friday, February 9, two Auburn football players visited influential Auburn alumnus and Mobile banker Ken Lott, who had played freshman football at Auburn in the late 1930s. According to Lott, the players told him Auburn was not going to have a football team if Brown stayed. "Why not?" Lott asked. The boys answered that half the squad was going to quit. Apparently the players' petition presented at the meeting with the Governor was losing names quickly. Lott phoned Roger Allen of the faculty athletic committee and passed on the story.

If something wasn't done the situation was going to tear the program apart and create a crevice that would run all the way to the Governor's office.

Two days later, on Sunday, February 11, Auburn's faculty athletic committee voted unanimously to pay Brown for the final year of his contract, approximately nine-thousand dollars, and begin the search for a new head coach. President Draughon approved the action. Governor Persons refused to comment. Brown didn't hold back his feelings.

"I've always felt that I was working with men of honor, but this is the first time I have ever had reason to doubt that," he said. "I have never been called in on any of these meetings that have been taking place behind my back. And today, when the committee met, they were supposed to be taking action on assistant coaches. As far as I can see, the faculty athletic committee wanted to get back in the good graces of the governor. I hope they have succeeded. Auburn is a graveyard for coaches. God have pity on the man who comes here."

Not everyone felt as badly as Brown. "The atmosphere in Auburn was 'thank goodness Brown is gone,'" recalled trainer Kenny Howard.

President Draughon and the faculty athletic committee asked athletic director Hutsell to name an alumni screening committee that would narrow down the list of applicants. On February 13, Hutsell, with input from President Draughon and Jeff Beard, announced the five participants on the screening committee. They were Jimmy Hitchcock, the great All-American back who played from 1930-1932; Bo Russell, the first-team All-SEC lineman from the 1936-1938 teams; Marion Talley from the 1931-1933 teams; Bobby Blake from the 1934-1936 teams; and Ken Lott.

Lott, because he showed up late for the first meeting, was appointed chairman of the committee by the other members. He suggested three criteria: that a credit report be received on every applicant due to some bad experiences with previous coaches; that Auburn hire a coach with SEC experience; that they give the head coach they hired an opportunity to take on the athletic director post. At that moment President Draughon knocked on the door. He informed the committee that Hutsell, who had reluctantly become athletic director when Voyles departed in 1947, had just passed the position to Jeff Beard. Hutsell stated that the ongoing search for a new head football coach provided an appropriate situation in which to bring in a new athletic director. The date was February 15, 1951.

Beard knew whom he wanted as head football coach — his old friend Jordan. He relayed that message to Draughon. Certainly the wheels appeared greased for Jordan. Jordan and Hitchcock were longtime best friends. Russell and Blake had played on Jordan's freshman team and Blake later helped Jordan coach the freshman team. Talley had played on the same team as Jordan in 1931. Lott played on Jordan's freshman team in 1937. Over in Montgomery, influential businessman Billy Thames had also recommended Jordan to Governor Persons. Thames would remain one of Jordan's biggest boosters during his career.

"I knew who it was going to be," Russell said of his preference for Jordan going in. "Jim Hitchcock, myself and some others were going to get Coach Jordan in there."

First Beard had to get Jordan to apply for the job. Jordan, remembering the snub when he had previously applied for the position, played hard-to-get. Russell recalled that Beard had a difficult time even getting Jordan to write a letter of application. When Beard asked Jordan about the delay, Jordan said he had received no encouragement in 1948, he and his family were happy in Athens, plus he was working for a fine coach in Butts. At that point Beard became impatient with his old friend's stubbornness.

"Write the letter!" Beard demanded. Jordan promptly penned the now-famous condensed letter of application: "I hereby apply for the head coaching job at Auburn. Sincerely, Ralph Jordan." Jordan was playing fickle, but he had heard the call of his struggling alma mater.

It still wasn't set in stone. The screening committee began reviewing an onslaught of applications that eventually numbered 225. The committee didn't have much time. SEC teams were gearing up for spring practice. Beard attempted to sit in on one of the committee's sessions and Hitchcock invited him to leave. Auburn banker Monk Wright asked the committee to allow former Auburn great Walter Gilbert to participate. The committee wouldn't do it. It plowed through the applications and reduced the list to four coaches: Jordan; Cooper, line coach at LSU; Bowden Wyatt, head coach at Wyoming and an All-SEC end on Neyland's great Tennessee team in 1938; and Ray Graves, line coach at Georgia Tech. The committee decided to invite Jordan, Cooper and Wyatt to Auburn to talk with Draughon, Beard and the faculty athletic committee. Hitchcock called and invited his buddy Jordan. Lott contacted Wyatt, who said he'd be there. But two days before the scheduled interview, Wyatt called back and said he had earlier signed a multi-year contract with Wyoming and was going to honor it. Beard later said that Wyatt had talked with Dudly Noble, the athletic director at Mississippi State, about the Auburn coaching situation. Noble told Wyatt: "Don't fool with it. Auburn is a hot spot."

"I'm out," Wyatt told Beard.

"Thanks for your interest," Beard said.

Another story was that Wyatt had talked with his mentor, General Neyland of Tennessee, and Neyland advised him to be patient, that the Tennessee position could open up in the near future. Tennessee would hire Wyatt as head coach in 1955, and he would direct the Vols to an SEC title with a 10-0 record in 1956, before losing to Baylor in the Sugar Bowl.

Shortly after midnight, on the morning of February 26, 1951, after a vibrant day of interviewing and negotiation, President Draughon and Athletic Director Beard named Jordan as the new head football coach. Jordan signed a five-year contract for $12,500 annually, nearly five-thousand dollars more than athletic director Beard was making. Draughon was leery about a five-year deal, but Jordan had insisted, given the low ebb of the program.

The faculty athletic committee had interviewed Jordan and Cooper during the day. Assistant coach Dick McGowen chaperoned Cooper and said Cooper offered him a position on his new staff at Auburn. McGowen appreciated the offer but thought to himself that Cooper wasn't head coach material and doubted Cooper was going to get the call.

The committee reported a 3-2 vote in favor of recommending Jordan to Draughon. Beard said one of the points working against Jordan was again the peculiar mindset that Auburn should hire a non-Auburn man who would be free of previous Auburn associations and thus not tied to any school politics.

Jordan, who had been using Beard's house as a base, received word to come to the president's mansion. After hashing out the contract, Beard and Jordan walked out on the front porch and Beard introduced Jordan to the press in the darkness of the new day.

"Auburn is my home," said Jordan, the first ex-Auburn player to be named head coach at the school. "I played football here and I helped Jack Meagher coach here. I know Auburn people and Auburn troubles and Auburn hopes. Auburn met my terms and promised cooperation so I decided to take the charge.

"I have a lot of faith in Auburn and am optimistic about the future. I want no sympathy but do need the support and help of all Auburn men and women in the tremendous task ahead."

The lone sad note about the situation was that Jordan's father, Harry Jordan, didn't get to see his son become a head coach. Harry Jordan had died in 1950 at the age of sixty-eight. He was buried in Selma.

Jordan returned to Athens to wind up his affairs, and reported back to Auburn in early March. "It was a great day when Shug came in," Beard said. "Talk about two people facing insurmountable obstacles. We didn't have any money. I had to go to the bank and borrow money to keep the doors open for Shug when he got here."

Writer Max Moseley wrote in the *Montgomery Advertiser* on March 1: "The Auburn University situation appears to be solved. Ralph (Shug) Jordan has been chosen to bring the Tiger gridiron sport out of the wilderness, and he'll do just that unless we miss our guess."

The *Birmingham News* wrote on March 13: Jordan takes over "in the Tigers' darkest hour." He is "charged with the toughest job in the SEC. He is expected to restore the Tigers to their old gridiron glory."

First Jordan had to assemble a coaching staff. "Football talent, personality and character will rule in their selections," he said. He wanted assistants who would abide by his discipline, instill it in the players, and endorse his conservative approach to the game. He intended to give his coaches a fair amount of leeway.

Jordan pulled three veteran assistants from Brown's staff. Shot Senn became the line coach. Joel Eaves focused on the defensive ends. Dick McGowen became the head freshman coach. The three were hardly strangers to Jordan. Senn had played beside Jordan on the Auburn line in 1930 and 1931. Jordan recruited Eaves as an end in 1933, coached him on the freshman football team and coached him on the varsity football and basketball teams. Jordan coached McGowen on the frosh team in 1937 and McGowen played halfback and punted from 1938-1940 when Jordan assisted Meagher on the varsity. Eaves and McGowen had made All-SEC in 1936 and 1940, respectively. Jordan knew them both as solid Auburn men. Jordan also added Charlie Waller to the staff as offensive backfield coach. Waller came from a very successful coaching stint at Decatur High School in Georgia. Former coach Brown had considered Waller as a possible addition to his staff.

Now Jordan turned to younger men to fill out his staff, men who could bring the more conservative side of the successful Georgia system to Auburn. Jordan knew these men because he had coached them in Athens. Buck Bradberry became Auburn's defensive backfield coach and also assistant to Waller on offense. Gene Lorendo became the offensive ends coach, and covered for Eaves on defense when basketball season consumed Eaves's time. Homer Hobbs became assistant line coach.

Bradberry, from Athens, lettered four years for Georgia — 1944, 1946, 1947 and 1948 (he spent the 1945 season in military service). Bradberry played regularly as a defensive back as rules of the day permitted substitutions for the quarterback on defense. Bradberry ran at third string as a running back. In 1949 he became a student-assistant backfield coach on the Georgia freshman team under Quinton Lumpkin.

"When I got to be a student assistant, Coach Jordan and I conversed a lot," Bradberry recalled. "I don't know whether he thought he was going to be a head coach some day or what, but I can remember when I was in his office he would get me on the black-board and ask me questions about certain things. I was kind of surprised that he would be asking a guy like me questions. 'What do you think about this, Buck? Tell me now if this, this, this and this. Show me some of the stuff that you feel strongly about.' Sometimes it would be techniques in relationship to fundamentals, which are basically on-the-field things, but you could demonstrate it."

Jordan had also called on Bradberry to assist him with scouting Auburn and Georgia Tech during the 1949 season. In the four games Auburn played before playing Georgia, Bradberry sat in on the first two and Jordan observed the next two.

In 1950 Georgia assistant line coach Whitworth accepted the head coaching position at Oklahoma A&M and took along Bradberry as head freshman coach. After Auburn named Jordan head coach in late February 1951, Jordan called Whitworth who gave the okay for Jordan to talk with Bradberry.

"He gave me a ring in my office," Bradberry said of Jordan. "He said he wanted me to coach the defensive secondary. I said, 'Goodness, Coach, tell me about it.'"

"You know Auburn didn't win a game last year," Jordan said.

"They didn't?" Bradberry replied. "No games, Coach?"

"That's right," Jordan said. "I just want you to know now, when you're considering this, that we don't have but one way to go and that's up."

Bradberry asked for a couple of days to think about it. Jordan agreed but indicated time was short. "I was surprised by the offer, but then as I thought about it we had had a good freshman team when I was coaching the freshmen at Georgia," Bradberry said. "We beat Alabama and Georgia Tech, and consequently those were the ones that were our main competitors. It could have impressed him possibly. Another thing was at that time there were no defensive specialists around. But with the wild card substitution I happened to be a defensive secondary player, so in that sense I was a natural for Coach to take."

Lorendo, from northern Minnesota, began attending Georgia in 1942, following the recommendation of a Minnesota acquaintance who coached on the football and basketball staffs at Georgia. But because of military service Lorendo didn't play as a freshman until 1946. He lettered at end for the varsity in 1947, 1948 and 1949. He also played on Jordan's basketball team. In 1950 Lorendo coached football and basketball at Presbyterian College in Clinton, South Carolina.

In March, Jordan called Lorendo and offered him the position of ends coach.

"Golly, Coach, they lost all ten games last year," Lorendo responded.

"Well, the only way we can do worse is to schedule eleven and lose them all," Jordan replied.

Lorendo remembered Jordan's coaching budget was limited. "We all started out at about five-thousand dollars," he said. "I lived out of my suitcase."

Hobbs lettered in 1946, 1947 and 1948 as a lineman at Georgia. He made third-team All-SEC guard in 1948. He had played two years for the San Francisco 49ers in the National Football League when Jordan called.

Bradberry, Lorendo and Hobbs had played on great Georgia teams. "Georgia had such success while Coach Jordan was there, that naturally he would be impressed with players off of that team," Bradberry said. "He knew we had good backgrounds. He knew we had good training. He knew us inside-out, even if we were somewhat young."

Jordan had assembled a unique and talented mixture of veteran Auburn football men and young Georgia football men. As Jordan had told them, they could only improve upon the situation on the Plains.

George Atkins, who became a star guard at Auburn and played pro football for a season before joining Jordan's staff in 1956, was a freshman in 1950 when Auburn went 0-10 under Brown.

"When I was a freshman we had Vince Dooley and a bunch of good people who were freshmen," Atkins said. "We would go up on the hill and scrimmage the varsity. We were supposed to be their dummies so to speak. But we would beat them so bad, we thought we were good. Then we found out how bad the varsity really was when they went 0-10."

Late in his career, Jordan recalled his first spring practice as Auburn head coach. "I don't think we've had another spring as demanding as the first one," Jordan said. "It was grim. We didn't know anything about our squad except that Auburn had won only three games in the last three years. It was a volatile situation. The hiring of me and the new coaching staff hadn't solved anything because some people weren't sure it was a step in the right direction. Our assistant coaches were mostly young and unproven. We didn't know the players, just a few names and that there was enough material to win more games than they had been winning. It was mysterious, even eerie, what we were getting into.

"The first thing we had to do was make some estimate of our personnel. The only way to do that was find out who could play football. We wanted to find out who was here for a free ride and who was here to make a contribution to Auburn.

"Our practices that spring were rough. We scrimmaged every day after we got into the swing of things, six days a week for six weeks. It was nothing fancy, just hammer-and-tong, dog-eat-dog football. We worked every day until we just had to quit. We lost a lot of people. In a way, that was the idea. We wanted to see who would submit to discipline and we didn't try to deter anyone from leaving.

"We ended up with maybe not as much talent as we thought we had, but we had some real fine football players. We taught our players to play when they were tired. We developed a kind of Spartan spirit. We shamed all the guys who hollered when they got kicked in the shin and tried to teach them to laugh."

Spring training began on March 26. "It was Marine boot camp football," Bradberry recalled. "It was survival of the fittest. We had some people hear how tough it was going to be who didn't even show up for the first practice."

The younger assistants — Bradberry, Lorendo and Hobbs — were in tremendous physical shape. Bradberry and Lorendo were only a year or two out of Georgia. Hobbs was fresh from a two-year stint in the pros. The first day of organized, group-work practice found Waller and Bradberry with the backs and Lorendo and Eaves with the ends up on the main field, while Senn and Hobbs worked the linemen down on the lower part of the practice field. Standing near the backs and ends, Jordan blew his whistle, which meant all players and coaches were to sprint to him and rest on one knee while he talked to them before beginning other drills. After Jordan blew the whistle the linemen sprinted up. Their coach, Hobbs, aggressively set the pace. When they reached Jordan and the remainder of the squad, Lorendo and Bradberry glanced at each other and broke into laughter. Jordan smiled. Blood ran from the attentive Hobbs's ear and down the side of his face. While demonstrating a technique without a helmet on to a lineman, the contact had split the top of his ear.

Bradberry, just twenty-four years old, showed the players a lot of leadership and personality on the practice field. Big Lorendo cussed-out the players and stayed on their backs. The gritty Senn also put them through "holy hell," as some players recalled it. Eaves was quiet, but drilled his players relentlessly until they reached perfection. Jordan observed and, if necessary, made a point, which was totally opposite Butts's style at Georgia.

Jordan could get mad, but he didn't scream and bounce around. His tone of voice, a grimace on his face, a tug on his left ear indicated his displeasure. Jordan allowed his assistants to be the bad guys during practice. To the players, Jordan — the man standing in the background, the man responsible for putting the best food in the county, and lots of it, on the chow line, the man responsible for bringing in top-notch equipment, the man most definitely in charge — was the good guy.

"I don't think anybody got abused, but we put them to the test," Lorendo said of that first spring. "We were sort of like the Marines — we were looking for a few good men. Those that survived were good men."

Vince Dooley survived. The sophomore from Mobile was vying for the quarterback and safety positions. Dooley had never heard of Shug Jordan, but he figured a coaching change couldn't be any worse than an 0-10 season.

"We thought it couldn't be any worse until we got into spring practice," Dooley said. "It did get worse. A lot of guys left. But it was needed. Discipline was needed. Real tough hard work was needed."

Dooley even considered leaving, but not because of the tough practices. The coaches had moved him to halfback on offense. "I was very discouraged," he said. "They didn't think I could play quarterback. But I ended up having a pretty good spring game and my morale got back up."

George Atkins also survived. "It was the toughest thing I have ever been through in my life," said Atkins, who was redshirted for the 1951 season. "We used to live in those little cabins, six to eight people inside, didn't have air conditioning, windows open, screen doors. At night you could hear a click and hear the screen door creak — one or two more were gone. You wouldn't believe how they quit and left. The coaches wanted to find out who would hit and who wouldn't—who would go when they were tired and who wouldn't."

Trainer Howard and coaches Lorendo and Hobbs lived with the players in a series of cottages around the amphitheater at Graves Center.

"We were keeping up with players on and off the field and if they didn't live by our rules, we'd fire them," Jordan said. "All that caused some unpleasantness, of course."

Fundamentals, drills, scrimmages — the early going was as slow as Jordan had anticipated. "We're not kidding ourselves," he said a week into practice. "The men aren't there and we are starting work on our T from scratch just as if none of the men had ever played the system."

On May 5, following six weeks of separating the men from the boys, the Orange and Blue game ended in a 20-20 tie. Allan Parks served as Blue captain, and Ed Bauer led the Orange. The Blue, with Parks, freshman Bobby Freeman and Bill Alford scoring touchdowns, pulled out to a 20-0 lead. But the Orange fought back behind quarterback Bill Tucker and young halfback Charlie Hataway.

A sports column the following day stated, "We saw more blocking and tackling by those Auburn gridders out there yesterday than we have seen in some time."

In his first spring practice as head coach, Jordan had built up confidence and morale for a team that was accustomed to losing. He had established discipline and hard work as part of his football program. He had planted the seeds for growing a winning tradition at Auburn.

9

"Find who wanted to play"
● ●

"He was the greatest public relations person we ever had," said athletic director Beard of Jordan.

The summer of 1951 was a time for putting into action the plan to rebuild Auburn's athletic program. Auburn needed someone to be in charge of rallying the alumni. Joe Sarver, an Auburn insurance executive, remembered that he and President Draughon kept trying to think of such a person, until one day Draughon said to Sarver, "How about you?"

"Me?" Sarver replied. "Well, okay."

Sarver became Alumni Secretary and remained so for twenty-five years. He, Draughon, Beard and Jordan attacked the athletic department's desperate situation. The plan was simple: make as many trips to as many towns to talk to as many alumnus and supporters as possible. Sometimes Draughon accompanied them, but usually Beard, Jordan and Sarver jumped in the car and traveled throughout the South and even beyond for nearly a week at a time. Jordan felt it was absolutely necessary to meet the people face-to-face. His charm and humor delighted them. His memory fascinated them. It was said of Jordan that he could meet a man, his wife and their three children for the first time, and a year later encounter only the man, remember his name, and ask how his wife and three children were doing, by their names.

Vernon Wells, a Selma High classmate of Ned Jordan, Shug's younger brother, said he ran into Jordan about every ten years or so.

"Every time he'd see me he'd call me by name as if we had spoken yesterday," Wells said.

Sarver recalled that they usually set up the meetings for the evening at one of the local restaurants or at a civic club room. "At first all three of us would make a speech," Sarver said. "After awhile I just let Shug and Jeff do the talking while I tried to collect the money."

They made three, four and five meetings a week. They didn't always draw a crowd. Jordan said the low point came in Macon, Georgia, when only six people turned out. Auburn was, after all, coming off an 0-10 football season and had not had real success on the gridiron since Meagher's 1937 Orange Bowl team. But Jordan, Beard and Sarver believed it was only a matter of getting the juices of the alumni flowing again.

Dollars began to tumble in as Beard sold tickets and Jordan sold the folks on his plan for rebuilding the football team. But Jordan and Beard didn't only talk about football and sports. They spoke of their undying love for their alma mater. They recalled hopping tables and washing dishes to put themselves through Auburn during the Depression, and how the faculty, students and citizens of the community weathered the economic storm. "Adversity drew us together," Jordan said. "It drew the early Christians together."

Jordan spoke of his encounters with Auburn people overseas during the war and of the affection and sense of strength that immediately developed. "I like to say that the Auburn spirit is Auburn people," Jordan said. "This I believe very much."

In three years the athletic department moved from $100,000 in the red to $250,000 in the black. Beard quickly gained a reputation as a hands-on penny-pincher and maintained that tradition until he resigned in 1972.

For example, a younger brother of an assistant coach hitchhiked to Kentucky to see Auburn play. The coach had the hotel put a cot in his room for his brother to sleep on Saturday night following the game. Monday morning, Beard phoned the coach and told him he owed the athletic department three dollars for the rented cot. The coach wrote a check.

Near the end of his career, Jordan would look back on the early years. "It's been about 2,500 speeches since then for me. Today our stadium seats over sixty-one thousand, our Auburn Alumni Association is sixty-thousand strong. We are not in debt. We are very, very much in the black because of a successful football program. It has not been a job done by me, but a job done by many, many people."

What made it work was a mutual love of Auburn, and winning football games.

Enthusiasm ran high as eleven seniors, nineteen juniors, twenty-nine sophomores and ninety freshmen reported for fall practice in 1951. During the summer Jordan had added Joe Connally to his coaching staff to assist freshman head coach McGowen. Connally was yet another player Jordan had coached at Georgia. Connally had played guard in 1943, 1946 and 1947 and defensive end in 1948. He then joined Charlie Waller's staff at Decatur High School. When Waller came to Auburn as part of Jordan's first staff, Connally stepped in as head coach at Decatur, but he didn't make it to fall practice. During the summer Jordan had felt his staff was too thin and that McGowen, whose strength was the backfield, needed a line coach. Connally remained an assistant for all of Jordan's twenty-five years.

Fall practice picked up where spring practice had left off. Many of the 115 recruits Brown had signed had made it to the Plains.

"Some of them had been second and third team in high school," Lorendo said. "They (Brown's staff) took anything that was warm and walked. We started with fundamentals. Half of them didn't know how to line up. We had to find out who wanted to play."

Lorendo said the practice sessions on Drake Field drew hundreds of fans each day. "It was a homey and folksy affair," he said.

Going into the 1951 season, along with Jordan, the SEC head football coaches included: General Neyland at Tennessee, Wally Butts at Georgia, Johnny Vaught at Ole Miss, Bobby Dodd at Georgia Tech, Red Drew at Alabama, Bear Bryant at Kentucky, Bob Woodruff at Florida, Gaynell Tinsley at LSU, Slick Morton at Mississippi State, Bill Edwards at Vanderbilt, and Henry Frnka at Tulane. Bryant's Kentucky had won the SEC in 1950, edging out Tennessee because Kentucky had played one more conference game. Tennessee, which beat Kentucky during the season, finished 11-1, including a Cotton Bowl win over Texas. The Vols wound up fourth in the nation. Kentucky finished seventh nationally. The Wildcats completed an 11-1 season with a major victory in the Orange Bowl over undefeated Oklahoma, but Oklahoma held on to its number-one ranking.

Jordan's thoughts weren't on national rankings as the 1951 season started. He was thinking more along the lines of playing competitive football. He knew he needed to pick up a few early wins to avoid a season resembling the 1950 disaster. The 1951 schedule would close with several heavyweights. In later years, remembering his most special victories, Jordan always mentioned the season-opening win over Vanderbilt in 1951. It was Jordan's first of 176 wins. It soothed the bite of the previous season's 0-10 performance and immediately restored a spirited following for Auburn football.

Vanderbilt had won seven and lost four in 1950. Bucky Curtis made first-team All-SEC at end, and quarterback Bill Wade made second team at quarterback. Both returned for the 1951 season and hoped to open it with a repeat of the 41-0 pasting Vandy had given Auburn in 1950 in Nashville.

Montgomery Advertiser sports editor Max Moseley went out on a limb and picked Auburn to win, 26-13.

Jordan believed Auburn had to dominate possession of the football to win the game, which Auburn did in winning 24-14. Auburn, wearing orange pants and blue jerseys, ran the ball a staggering eighty-six times, which is second in SEC history for team rushes in a single game.

The game was tied at 14-14 with less than five minutes to go when Auburn's Bob Burns, a defensive back, recovered a fumble at the Vanderbilt thirty-yard-line. Homer Williams, a senior who was converted from center to fullback during the spring, carried four times and made two first downs to the one, and plunged in from there for the score.

On the second play from scrimmage following the kickoff, Auburn safety Vince Dooley batted one of Wade's passes and intercepted the ball just before it hit the ground at the Vanderbilt thirty-three. Auburn placekicker Joe Davis kicked a 45-yard field goal to ice the game at 24-14. Williams had rushed for 122 yards and sophomore halfback Hataway ran for 120 yards. Allan Parks had started at quarterback. Billy Tucker, who had played a lot of quarterback during the spring, had contracted polio. Dooley was back in the quarterback picture as a second-stringer in addition to his starting role at safety.

"We looked in the stands and Auburn people were shocked," Lorendo said of the victory. "They didn't know what had happened." The game drew 17,500 fans.

The victory guaranteed Auburn a better season than it experienced in 1950. As Jordan had told many of his assistants when hiring them, there would be no place to go but up. Auburn was already up after one game, and after six games the Tigers stood at 5-1. A 14-13 win over Florida, which gave Auburn a 3-0 start, also gave Jordan his first honor as a head football coach. The *Atlanta Journal* voted Jordan Coach of the Week in its weekly sportswriter poll. But Florida was not strong and two of the wins had come over Wofford and Louisiana College, while the loss was a 27-7 affair to Georgia Tech. The Tech game provided a more accurate picture of how Auburn would fare down the stretch, and bore out Jordan's preseason concerns. Auburn proceeded to lose to Ole Miss, 39-14; Georgia, 46-14; Clemson, 34-0; and Alabama, 25-7. The lopsided losses to Ole Miss, Georgia and Alabama, none of which had outstanding teams, indicated, as Jordan said, that the spirit brought on by a new regime had finally succumbed to the reality of a lack of talent and depth.

Dooley made second team All-SEC at defensive back. Offensive guard Ed Bauer also made second team. Bill Turnbeaugh at defensive tackle, Ed Duncan at offensive guard and future Auburn athletic director Lee Hayley at offensive end all made third team.

Neyland's Tennessee gave the SEC its first national title, while

Georgia Tech finished fifth in the nation and Kentucky dropped to seventeenth.

Jordan's reason for wanting a five-year contract instead of Auburn's customary three-year contract had been this: "I thought we'd do well the first year, enthusiasm would die down some the second year, and with one year left they might buy me off."

He was on target regarding the second-year blues. Auburn won two and lost eight in 1952, beating only Wofford and Clemson. It wasn't expected to be quite that bad. Dooley had earned the starting quarterback job in the spring. Hataway returned in the backfield and sophomore back Bobby Freeman had made his presence felt. The spring game drew eight-thousand fans on March 8 with the Blues winning, 32-14.

Fall practice began on September 1 with fifty-seven players reporting. Auburn worked four hours that day, split between shorts and full uniform. Meanwhile Kentucky's Bryant was padding his reputation as a preseason pessimist. "This was the worst opening day practice I've seen in fifteen years of coaching football," Bryant groaned about his squad. "They have no conditioning, no leadership, no spirit and no talent."

Auburn opened its season in Birmingham against Maryland, which had finished the 1951 season ranked third in the nation. Maryland came into the first game of the 1952 season ranked number one. Maryland was heavily favored, but barely escaped with a 13-7 win before 37,000 fans at Legion Field on September 27.

Maryland scored first to go ahead 6-0, but Auburn, running out of the T, drove sixty-five yards for a touchdown in the second quarter. The best play of the drive came at the Maryland twenty-five. Dooley drifted back to pass and was almost trapped, but got the ball away to Hayley who made a circus catch for a first down at the ten-yard-line. Dooley, Hataway and Freeman each ran once as Auburn moved to the two. Then Dooley faked a pitchout to the left side and slid between the guard and tackle for the touchdown. Davis kicked the point after to put Auburn ahead, 7-6.

The lead held until mid-way through the fourth quarter. Maryland quarterback Jack Scarbath completed passes of forty-two and thirty-two yards to Lloyd Colteryahn, the second one for a touchdown. Maryland held on to win.

A newspaper account of the game said Auburn's performance ranked with that of the 1942 team that beat number-one-ranked Georgia in Columbus. Following the game, Jordan said of his team, "They reflected honor to Auburn and to themselves by never giving up." Down through the years, when remembering games past, Jordan always recalled Auburn's heroic loss to powerful Maryland in 1952.

Building on the Maryland game, Auburn might have launched a successful season but a bad break befell the Tigers the next weekend in Memphis against Ole Miss. Dooley, seemingly on his way to making his mark as an SEC quarterback, went down with a seriously twisted knee in the third quarter. Auburn lost the game, 20-7, and lost Dooley for much of the season.

"We were going to be an option team, but after I got hurt we went pass crazy," Dooley said. Auburn never recovered and finished last in the conference with an 0-7 mark. Auburn was probably not as bad as its record. Only Georgia Tech and Alabama shellacked the Tigers. Tech finished the season ranked second in the nation. Alabama finished ninth. Opponents Ole Miss, Maryland and Florida finished seven, thirteen and fifteen, respectively.

"In 1951 I think we showed that if we had the players we could win," Bradberry said. "The players who were reasonably good athletes were very young. Later on some of those players really developed, but there weren't that many of them. We didn't expect to go two and eight in 1952. We didn't beat Clemson but 3-0. I was the placekicking coach and I do remember that Dooley had to shag the ball and put it down. Joe Davis kicked the field goal and we beat them. We were zero and seven against SEC opponents in 1952, but five years later we were seven and zero and they only scored seven points. That's a helluva damn thing."

Jordan had expected a poor season in 1952. But during dozens of alumni dinners on the road the following summer he assured supporters the future was bright; that recruiting had been going well. He also recognized that his third year at the helm had to produce something Auburn fans could sink their teeth into.

Following the successful start of the 1951 season, Jordan's teams had won two and lost twelve. Jordan had the support of President Draughon and friend and athletic director Beard, but such support couldn't hide poor numbers on the field. Jordan tried not to think of failure, but the tension ate at him. His hair began to fall out of the back of his head in patches the size of silver dollars.

10

"Tough? Yessir."
• • • • • • • • • • • • • • • • • •

Nineteen fifty-three to 1958. On the field it was the best of times. Off the field it was the worst of times. Away from the gridiron, the NCAA slapped Auburn with two penalties, in early 1956 and again in early 1958, for separate recruiting violations. The penalties made Auburn ineligible for bowl games from 1956-1960. Auburn would have gone to bowl games in at least four of those years.

On the field, Shug Jordan enjoyed his greatest years as Auburn's head coach. Auburn played in three Gator Bowls — 1953, 1954 and 1955 — and finished seventeenth, thirteenth and eighth in the nation, respectively. Auburn won, while on NCAA probation, the Associated Press national championship and the SEC championship with a perfect 10-0 record in 1957; and, while still on probation, went 9-0-1 in 1958 and finished fourth in the nation. Beginning with its seventh game of the 1956 season, Auburn won seventeen games in a row. From the beginning of the streak in 1956 through the entire 1958 season, considering a tie in 1958, Auburn played twenty-four straight games without a loss.

It began to come together for Jordan in 1953. New and rigid substitution rules suited Jordan's conservatism. The talent of younger players kicked in. Jordan and backfield coach Charlie Waller's offensive schemes jelled. And Jordan hired a defensive coordinator whose innovation meshed with Jordan's passion for defense and belief that you had to keep from getting beat before you could win.

The new defensive coach was also an Auburn man. Hal Herring, after playing high school ball at nearby Lanett, had lettered in football at Auburn from 1946-1948 and made second team All-SEC at center/linebacker in 1948. From 1949 to 1952 he played linebacker for the Cleveland Browns. Herring worked closely with the Browns' defensive chief, Blanton Collier, and called the defensive sets and coverages on the field. Collier would later become head coach at Kentucky. During Herring's years at Cleveland, head coach Paul Brown led his team to the National Football League championship game three times and won the title once, beating Los Angeles 30-28 in 1950.

Herring had just signed a new contract with the Browns when Jordan contacted him prior to the 1953 season. Herring's pro-oriented and somewhat radical defensive mind impressed Jordan. Auburn's defense, Jordan believed, required major surgery, having allowed more than twenty-five points in seven of its fourteen conference games since Jordan took over. Jordan offered the position to Herring, who figured his pro career had reached a pinnacle after winning the NFL championship. Coaching at his alma mater excited him, and the freedom Jordan offered challenged him. That two sons had just begun elementary school ultimately convinced Herring that he needed to embark on a career.

Herring's defense began in the film room when he viewed the upcoming opponent's previous games. He charted each of the offensive sets and the multiple combinations of downs, yards to go for a first down, position on the field and particular plays run. This of course told Herring the tendencies of the offense, and from this he drew up his defensive plan. Having played linebacker himself, a position that required instinct, skill and intelligence, Herring built his defense around bright players.

"We had very smart, gifted young men at Auburn who enjoyed the heat of battle," Herring said. "With smart players you could tailor a defense. You could tell them that if the back cheated out and up a foot he was going to do this or that. Sometimes we put three on the line, sometimes four, sometimes six. Sometimes we'd take the best defender and put him on the best receiver man-to-man and we'd play zone otherwise. We had four or five different sets on the line and six or seven different coverages."

Herring remembered that he was one of the first coaches to call the defensive plays from the sidelines. "That was Coach Jordan's idea," he said.

Scouts went home befuddled because Herring's defense never seemed to do the same thing in the same situation.

"Sometimes I didn't know what the defense was doing," Herring said modestly. "The players would ask me, 'What do we do coach?' I said, 'Hell, tackle the guy with the ball.' They said 'Who do we cover on them passes?' I said, 'Cover the ones they're throwing to; don't cover them decoys.'"

Herring, who specifically coached the defensive line and linebackers, brought his own style to the practice field. He preferred method instead of madness. "I always taught safety," Herring said. "I told them to keep their head up and tackle 'em in the chest. All I did was try to refine their skills and put them in the best position they could be."

Jordan had found his man to direct the defense. He also felt that the offense was on the verge of clicking. Jordan and offensive coach Charlie Waller had studied Maryland and head coach Jim Tatum's Split-T formation. The Terps had finished third nationally with it in 1951. Bud Wilkinson's Oklahoma Sooners won the national title with a Split-T offense in 1950. Compared to the T formation, the Split-T spread out the offensive guards, tackles and ends in order to spread out the defense. This potentially gave an alert ballcarrier more room to run, with or without perfect blocking. It also accented the skills of versatile option quarterback Vince Dooley, who would be a senior on the 1953 team.

It was probably no coincidence that Jordan collided with great success at the same time the NCAA altered its substitution rules. The NCAA had liberalized its substitution rule in 1941 and again in 1948 to allow substitutions on each play and unlimited substitution on the change of team possession. For the first time, in 1951 and 1952, the Associated Press named separate offensive and defensive All-SEC teams. But for the 1953 season the NCAA basically abolished offensive and defensive specialization by permitting players to enter the game only once in each quarter. As when Jordan played, players for the most part would have to go both ways. They would have to be "complete" football players.

Jordan liked this survival-of-the-fittest style of football. It required, however, extremely talented and durable athletes. During the 1952 season Auburn supporters had strained their eyes in search of such talent. But in 1953 Jordan discovered he had enough athletes to field two teams.

He called them the X and Y teams. Dooley quarterbacked the X team, which was the more conservative offense, and junior Bobby Freeman ran the Y team, which tended to open up and pass the football. "We'd start one team and they'd play ten minutes and we'd put the other one in and they'd play the last five minutes of the first quarter and the first five minutes of the second quarter," Jordan said. "But when they went in there they were in there. They played offense. They played defense. They went down on kickoffs, they returned kickoffs."

Bradberry recalled, "They started out as kind of a first and second string, but then as you got into the season they were both good football teams and Coach Jordan decided he had some people on the second team who were coming along real fast and could have moved up and been a first-teamer. As we got into the season he decided to play the X and Y teams. Coach Jordan thought up the X and Y because he was some kind of lay psychologist. He knew if one was the A team and one was the B team then it would make a difference psychologically if you were on the B team. But if you were on the Y team, so what? X is as good as Y, and Y is as good as X, but B is not as good as A."

Sophomore Fob James ran in the X backfield behind his roommate and quarterback, Dooley. But James almost wasn't around for the 1953 season.

"Life at Auburn in the 1950s was like you thought you had died and gone to heaven," James said. "Auburn was home to me. I knew the area. Had a lot of relatives. Some of them were farmers. The hunting and fishing areas that were available were very inviting and they certainly took precedence over way too many classes.

"One day Coach Jordan called me into his office. Over in the corner he had my shotgun, my shells, my fishing tackle. My father was there, too. Coach Jordan said I wasn't here to fish or hunt or to play football, and that I was grounded from the football team until my grades were back on track. He knew how to mean business when he wanted you to know he meant business. It became very very plain."

In 1955, James's senior year, he would make All-American at halfback and be named Academic All-SEC in his curriculum of Aerospace Engineering.

"Coach Jordan was an extraordinary fellow," James said. "He was thorough enough in his observation of his kids that he knew when they were getting off the beaten path. He was a great teacher. He was interested in kids being exposed to their respective religions. I remember a bunch of us boys were having a conversation about who believed in God and if you should or shouldn't, like kids will talk about. He had heard us and he came up and said, 'You know, I never saw a man in a fox hole who didn't believe in God; think about that.' What he was saying was when death looks you in the eye, you get honest with yourself."

Along with Dooley and left halfback James, the X backfield included senior right halfback Bobby Duke and senior fullback Charlie Hataway. Running behind Freeman on the Y team were senior right halfback Joe Davis, senior left halfback Johnny Adams and sophomore fullback Joe Childress. Also starting for Auburn in 1953 were Frank D'Agostino, a sophomore tackle, and sophomore end Jim Pyburn, who, according to Fob James, "had the best pair of hands I've ever seen."

An impressive cast of football talent had suddenly emerged on the Plains. They paced Auburn to a 7-2-1 regular season record in 1953. Waller's offense averaged 25.7 points per game, compared to fourteen points per game the previous year, and led the SEC in scoring per game. Auburn also led the conference in total offense with 339.8 yards per game, and was first in rushing yardage per game with 222.5. The defense, in Herring's first season, allowed 13.8 points per game compared to nearly twenty-one points per game the previous season.

"I think we wore down a lot of people because we had two teams working on one team," Dooley said.

D'Agostino and Pyburn made first team All-SEC. Junior guard George Atkins made second team.

Bobby Duke's 100-yard kickoff return sparked a come-from-behind 21-21 tie at Mississippi State. Duke scored three times in a 29-20 win over Miami. The Tigers whipped Georgia, 39-18. Going into the season-ending Alabama game, Auburn held a 7-1-1 record, its only loss a 36-6 licking by Sugar Bowl-bound Georgia Tech, which would finish eighth in the nation. Auburn needed to beat Alabama to win the SEC and go to the Cotton Bowl. But Red Drew's Tide prevailed 10-7, and snatched the conference title and the bowl bid away from Auburn. Auburn accepted a bid to play in the Gator Bowl in Jacksonville, Florida.

The Gator Bowl had begun in 1946 and was the youngest of the major bowls, following the Rose, Orange, Sugar and Cotton. The Sun Bowl in El Paso, Texas had been around since 1936 and the Tangerine Bowl in Orlando had begun in 1947, but neither had big-name drawing power. The Gator Bowl on the other hand had featured the likes of Oklahoma, Maryland, Georgia and Missouri in its brief history. But this didn't impress the Auburn players.

"We were going to the Gator Bowl and we were not happy about it," Dooley said of the players. "We were all down. The coaches kind of talked us into going. They said, 'Well, they're going to give you watches and jackets.' So we said 'we'll go.'"

The bowl bid forced the Tigers to practice during the Christmas holidays. Dooley recalled it was a grim, lonely bunch of players going through typical rigorous practices on the vacated campus. During warmups prior to one practice, trying to psych themselves up for the bowl appearance, they began talking about the Gator

Bowl gifts the coaches had mentioned. An assistant coach promptly hollered, "You damn guys, you ain't going to get anything. You're going to play the game and that's it."

"It took morale which was not too good and sunk it to the bottom," Dooley said. "That night all the players got together and said they were going to strike, they were going to leave, that the coaches had promised (the gifts) and the coaches had lied to them. I was the captain of the team. I said, 'Let me go talk to Coach Jordan.' They said 'He'll talk you out of it.' I said 'I'll represent the football team, that's my job. Let me talk to him before we do anything.'"

Dooley scheduled a morning appointment with Jordan. When he entered Jordan's office he sat down and explained the players' feelings.

"I just don't think that's fair to tell us you're going to do something and then have a coach out there saying you're not going to do it," Dooley said to Jordan.

When Dooley finished, Jordan began talking. "Down through the years..."

"Coach Jordan starts giving the history of things," Dooley recalled. "He started going back to when he first came to Auburn."

Dooley cut in: "Coach, what does all that have to do with the Gator Bowl?"

Jordan looked sternly at Dooley. "Did I interrupt you when you were talking?"

"No sir," Dooley replied.

"You don't interrupt me when I'm talking," Jordan said.

"Yes sir," Dooley said.

Jordan eventually explained that what was told to the players about the gifts was in good faith, but that the coaches had apparently been misled by the Gator Bowl. Dooley said he understood but that Jordan needed to explain it to the team because morale was terribly low and the players were serious about striking. Jordan agreed. Dooley went back to his teammates and told them Jordan would explain the situation that afternoon at practice; if the players wanted to ask questions, that was the time.

"They said, 'Yeah, we're going to do it, we're going to tell him exactly how we feel,'" Dooley said.

At practice Jordan called the players together and explained the mix up.

"Are there any questions?" Jordan asked.

The players remained silent.

Two days later while speaking to the team, Jordan said, "Incidentally, I just got word we're all getting watches and jackets."

The good news didn't carry on to the field, however. Texas Tech clubbed Auburn 35-13.

Still, it had been a remarkable third season for Jordan, and a total turnaround from the 1952 season. His team had fallen a field goal short of winning the SEC. He had experienced his first bowl game as a head coach and given Auburn its first bowl appearance in fifteen years.

Auburn finished number seventeen in the nation. To cap it off, the Associated Press named Jordan SEC Coach of the Year. The *Nashville Banner* did likewise in what it called a two-coach race between Jordan and Bryant of Kentucky. The Wildcats had also finished with a 7-2-1 record, though they didn't go bowling and wouldn't again until 1976. Bryant departed Kentucky following the season for the head coaching position at Texas A&M.

With so much talent from the X and Y teams returning, Auburn supporters dared to think that in 1954 the Tigers might finish in the top ten.

Though Dooley had graduated, along with several other starters, Jordan stayed with the X and Y formula as the 1954 season kicked off. But following an opening season win over Chattanooga, Auburn dropped close ones to Florida (19-13), Kentucky (21-14) and Georgia Tech (14-7). One of the keys to the 1953 X and Y had been its natural development from a first team and second team situation. "In '54 they kind of split the people up as opposed to letting it develop," Dooley said.

After the 1-3 start, "it was clearly evident that some of the very best players were on the Y team," Bradberry said.

"Neither the X or Y version in '54 quite had the overall ability to score like they did the year before," said James. "After we lost the three ballgames it was pretty obvious that it was time to make a change. Everybody knew it."

Jordan admitted he had made a mistake in sticking with the formula. He didn't have the number of front line players he had fielded in 1953, but it quickly became obvious he had a larger number of outstanding players. He decided to put his best eleven on the field at the same time.

All eleven of them would be offered professional sports contracts when they graduated. Senior quarterback Freeman would play six years in the NFL at Cleveland, Green Bay, Philadelphia and Washington; senior halfback Hoppy Middleton played seven years in the NFL at Detroit and Minnesota; junior fullback Joe Childress played ten years in the NFL for the Chicago Cardinals and then the St. Louis Cardinals; James played a year of Canadian pro ball in Montreal; junior end Jim Pyburn could have played in the NFL but chose major league baseball, skipping his senior season at Auburn to do so, and played three years for the Baltimore Orioles; senior end Jimmy Long chose to enter the service; junior tackle Frank D'Agostino played two years in the NFL; junior tackle M.L. Brackett played three years in the NFL; senior guard George Atkins played one season in the NFL; junior guard Bob Scarbrough was drafted by San Francisco but went into the Army; senior center Jack Locklear played for the Cleveland Browns.

"For the next seven games that was one of the best teams we ever had," Jordan said.

"You had a passing combination (Freeman and Pyburn) that would have been on par with Sullivan and Beasley," James said. "Jimmy Long and I were the only two non-super athletes on the team. That was a very explosive ballclub. After Coach Jordan made the change, it was easy. It was the best college football team I've ever seen."

"I still think the 1954 team was the best ever," trainer Kenny Howard said.

"The 1954 team was the best team we ever had, if you look at it from the standpoint of eleven men," Bradberry agreed.

The "new" team routed five of its remaining six opponents, including Florida State, 33-0; Tulane, 27-0; Georgia, 35-0; Clemson, 27-6; and Alabama, 28-0. Only Miami, which was ranked sixth in the nation, gave the Tigers a battle. Miami led 13-0 in the fourth period. Auburn's Freeman had blocked the extra point attempt following the second touchdown. Auburn rallied, driving sixty-three yards with Freeman scoring and Childress converting the extra point. Then following a fumble recovery by D'Agostino at the Miami twenty-seven, Auburn drove and Childress scored from three yards out. Childress kicked the point after to win the game, 14-13. Childress had rushed for 164 yards in twenty-nine carries. It was Miami's only loss of the season.

Auburn's convincing season-ending win over Alabama gave Jordan his first win over the Tide and gave Auburn another Gator Bowl berth. Auburn beat a strong Baylor team, 33-13, and finished thirteenth in the nation. Ohio State won the national title. Ole Miss won the SEC title.

Jordan and Herring's defense came of age. It shut out five opponents and gave up only 7.3 points per game.

Once again Auburn led the conference in rushing yardage per game with 249.6. The offense averaged 6.3 yards per play. Pyburn caught twenty-eight passes for 460 yards and was named All-American. Childress led the SEC in rushing with 836 yards and was named the conference's most valuable player by the Birmingham Quarterback Club. The Atlanta Touchdown Club named Freeman, who threw for 865 yards, the SEC Back of the Year. Tackle D'Agostino made second team All-SEC.

Something else happened in 1954. Tim Baker played freshman football for Auburn. He would serve as captain of the 1957 national championship team.

"The thing that made the 1957 team was the 1954 team," said Baker, who as a freshman competed regularly against the pro-bound stalwarts of the varsity. "We were their whipping boys. They beat on us pretty hard. They really toughened us up."

Baker recalled that seventy-five freshmen turned out in 1954. By 1957 the seniors that were left could be counted on two hands. But those few seniors formed the nucleus of the national title team. Among them were Baker, a 170-pound guard, running backs Billy Atkins and Bobby Hoppe, end Jimmy Phillips, tackle Dan Presley and tackle Ben Preston. What happened to the rest of the class?

"They left," Baker said. "It was tough out there under Coach Jordan. The assistant coaches were tough people. Coach Shot Senn was tough. During practice I saw Coach Senn lay down, put his head on the ground, look up in their face and call them everything in the world. He'd make the boys who weren't in shape go one-on-one. Then he'd say, 'give me another one on 'em.' It was pitiful to watch. Coach Gene Lorendo was tough. There was a game in Florida. The seats came right down to the field. Somebody was hackling him up there and he got up off the bench and went up in the stands and got the guy. Tough? Yessir.

"Coach Jordan was a quiet, nice type person. Very seldom would he ever raise his voice and get too riled up. He had things under control. He had good assistants. The great coaches do."

Jordan's Tigers ran up their best record so far in 1955. Auburn finished 8-1-1 in the regular season, came in second in the SEC, appeared in the Gator Bowl for a third straight year and ended the season the eighth-ranked team in the country.

Prior to the season, offensive backfield coach Waller accepted an assistant coaching position at the University of Texas, and Bradberry moved to offense. With Freeman graduated, junior Howell Tubbs played quarterback. For the third straight year the offense led the conference in rushing yardage per game with 241.3 yards. Herring's defense led the SEC in total defense by allowing only 183.2 yards per game.

Senior backs Fob James and Joe Childress provided a powerful one-two punch in the backfield. James rushed for 879 yards and a phenomenal 7.2 yards per carry. He finished his career with 1,913 yards rushing, which at the time was the best in Auburn history.

Childress settled in right behind him on the all-time Auburn rushing list with 1,667 yards. James and Childress accounted for 239 career points between them. They both made All-American teams in 1955. The Atlanta Touchdown Club named James the SEC Back of the Year. Senior tackle D'Agostino, known for his powerful blocking, also made All-American.

Two future national championship head coaches also made first team All-SEC in 1955. Howard Schnellenberger starred at end for Kentucky, and Johnny Majors shone for Tennessee in the backfield. Schnellenberger guided Miami to the national title in 1983, and Majors coached Pittsburgh to the crown in 1976.

The high point of Auburn's season came in the fourth game when Auburn broke its thirteen-year losing streak to Georgia Tech. Auburn won, 14-12, in Atlanta. Tubbs scored the winning touchdown from inside the one. Alton Shell had run seven yards for the first score. Childress kicked both extra points.

Again Auburn romped over Alabama, 26-0. The Tide finished the season 0-10 under first-year head coach Ears Whitworth. Auburn's only loss came to Tulane, 27-13, in New Orleans.

Closing strong with four consecutive wins encouraged Jordan and Auburn that a Sugar Bowl bid might be forthcoming. Instead it went to Georgia Tech, who had the same overall record as Auburn, but whom Auburn had beaten. The snub greatly disappointed the players and they found it difficult to rise to the occasion in the Gator Bowl, won by Vanderbilt 25-13.

Perhaps the strongest testament to the turnaround of the Auburn football program and the athletic department was that in 1955 Cliff Hare Stadium increased seating capacity another thirteen-thousand seats to 34,500. Indeed Jordan had shaped the Tigers into a national power in only four years. General Bob Neyland, who had ended his great career as head football coach at Tennessee after the 1952 season, called Jordan the best young football coach in America.

11

"Innuendo from some quarters"

Jordan recognized that 1956 would be a year for rebuilding. Auburn returned talented players, but the departure of three All-Americans left some gaping holes. Of the seventy-man spring squad, fifty were sophomores. Running back positions were up for grabs. Though the previous season's starting quarterback, Tubbs, returned, he had to battle Jimmy Cook for the job. Jordan worked his players harder in the spring of 1956 than any spring since 1951. It appeared to be paying off when the Orange and Blue squads dazzled a crowd of seven thousand with some offensive fireworks on March 10.

The Blues won 33-13 as the teams combined for 654 yards, seven touchdowns and twenty-six first downs, running out of the tight-T and split-T formations. Cook was voted the outstanding back. Jordan said he was more pleased over this A-Day game than any he had seen since becoming head coach. An article in the *Birmingham News* prophetically stated "The Tigers look good in '56, they might be great in '57."

The same newspaper, in an article that briefly described each of the current head coaches in the conference, said of Jordan, "Intelligent looking and talking, a man who weighs his conversations and views carefully for exact impressions... Perfectionist type, he can be quickly bitter toward player putting out only 99.4 percent."

Jordan showed such bitterness that September. As the team prepared for the opener two weeks away against Tennessee, he abruptly called off practice and told his players they were awful and he had seen all he could take of their "slouchy and unenthusiastic" drills. "We have had players who wanted to play for years now," Jordan told them. "You don't look like any squad we have had lately. Maybe you don't want to pay the price."

If Jordan's talk was meant to revitalize his squad, it didn't work. Tennessee, coached by Bowden Wyatt, blasted Auburn, 35-7. The game, played before a sellout crowd of 44,000 in Legion Field, was the first encounter between the teams since 1939. Senior tailback Johnny Majors paced the Vols' attack, which Auburn aided with four fumbles deep in its own territory. Jimmy Phillips, a starting junior end in the game for Auburn, commented, "The game in 1956 was the first time I had played against the single wing in a long time. That year, the defensive ends had the duty to step across the line and wait. Tennessee's pulling guards were running over us." A halfback named Lloyd Nix scored Auburn's lone touchdown.

Majors would finish second to Notre Dame's Paul Hornung in the Heisman Trophy vote, make All-American and be named the most valuable player in the conference. Four years earlier, Jordan may have let the small but agile Majors get away. Travis Tidwell, Auburn's All-American quarterback of the late 1940s, had returned to Auburn as a recruiting coach in 1952 following a brief career in the pros. He recruited Majors and thought he had him in the bag.

"I had Johnny and his dad, Shirley Majors, down for a homecoming game in 1952," Tidwell said. "Johnny committed to me verbally that he was going to enter Auburn. I had him down at the field house where the athletic department was and he and his daddy were in the open reception area. Coach Jordan was sitting in his office with Coach Lorendo with the door cracked open and you could see into the outer area. I told Shug about this boy I had who was head and shoulders above everybody in that league he played in and he was all-this and all-that. And Shug looked out of that crack in the door, and Johnny was standing beside his daddy, and Shug said, 'Travis, we can't give him a scholarship. He's too small.' Majors was only 5-8 or 5-9, 160 pounds. So Shug turned him down. The hardest job I ever had as a recruiting coach under Shug was to go out and unsell the sell I had made on him to go to Auburn."

Auburn's loss to Tennessee wasn't too shameful, considering that Tennessee proceeded to win all its games during the regular season before falling to Baylor in the Sugar Bowl. Tennessee finished second in the nation behind Oklahoma.

Auburn sputtered for the first two-thirds of the season and was 3-3, having also lost to Georgia Tech in Atlanta, 28-7, and to Florida in Gainesville, 20-0.

"At the time things needed to get tough under Coach Jordan, they did," said Lloyd Nix of Jordan's practices. "After Florida killed us, the rest of the year was very tough." Nix would never play in another losing effort. Auburn would win its next seventeen games in a row, tie a game, and win another six in a row before losing the opening game of the 1959 season.

Auburn began the streak with a 27-20 win over Mississippi State in Auburn. An incident during the following week's 20-0 win over Georgia in Columbus accented a closeness between the players that would carry over into the 1957 season and prove crucial when so many games went down to the wire. Auburn had scored on its first offensive play on a Tubbs-to-Phillips seventy-yard touchdown pass, and scored again in the first period to lead 14-0. Georgia then mounted a drive to the Auburn 31-yard line. On the next play Auburn guard Baker and end Jerry Wilson tackled Georgia quarterback Bill Hearn near the out-of-bounds line. Hearn was shaken-up and forced to leave the game. On the next play the new Georgia quarterback, Ken Schulte, set up to pass and fired toward the Auburn goal line, where a Tiger defensive back intercepted. Back upfield, Auburn's Baker brawled with several Georgia players.

"Georgia had a lineman named (Harold) Cook," Baker said. "I got by him as the quarterback dropped back to pass, but the halfback blocked me and the quarterback threw the pass. Cook got up, came back there and started a fight with me. Everybody else had gone downfield with the pass, but there we were, Cook, me, the quarterback, the halfback, fighting like cats and dogs. Everybody came running back up the field to us. I can still see Coach Jordan and all the boys coming out. Coach Lorendo grabbed me."

Fights broke out all over the field. Policemen and coaches struggled to pull apart players. Only when the band began playing the national anthem did the melee cool down.

Some post-game reports indicated that Baker's tackle on the quarterback the previous play had encouraged the fight. The day after the game Jordan came to Baker's defense. "There has been innuendo from some quarters that the tackle Tim Baker made on Georgia's Hearn is what started the thing," Jordan said. "In deference and fairness to Baker, the pictures clearly show that Baker made his tackle at least two or three yards in bounds, that Hearn kept moving and Jerry Wilson came in to finish the tackle. Hearn was well in-bounds until he was hit. If anybody thinks that sparked the trouble, it's certainly dead wrong thinking. Nothing happened on that play to make folks start fighting."

Newspapers continued to report on the fight two days after the game. Alf Van Hoose of the *Birmingham News* called it the "Battle of Chattahoochee." Van Hoose said accusing Baker of being the aggressor was "decidedly unfair."

Van Hoose added, "No denying this, however. Once the fighting flared, light-heavy Baker did not shirk any front-line trench duty. He went to the midst of the action, and...well, if he used a little subtle persuasion against the enemy, who could blame him?"

Jordan's final comment on the matter praised Baker. "He's a football player, not a fighter," Jordan said, "and we have high appreciation of his talents. He's got one of the quickest charges of any lineman I've ever seen...and he's quite a man."

Baker would always remember the incident for the support his teammates showed him in rallying to his side on the field. He said it proved to the players they were indeed a team.

Prior to the Georgia game, Jordan had instructed his assistants to work the second- and third-stringers more into the scheme of things. Non-starters such as Baker, Wilson, tackle Presley and several others played nearly half of the game against Georgia. The 1956 team only had nine seniors, including quarterback Tubbs, guard Ernie Danjean, end Jerry Elliott, guard Chuck Maxime and center Frank Reeves.

With the backups continuing to see a lot of playing time, Auburn closed the season with wins over Florida State, 13-7, and Alabama, 34-7. The Tigers finished 7-3 but unranked nationally. Still, the offense, for a remarkable fourth year in a row, led the conference in rushing yardage per game with 276 and led in total offense for the second time in four years with 374.9. Two running backs emerged in sophomore Tommy Lorino, who rushed for 692 yards with an unheard-of, nation-leading average of 8.4 yards per carry; and junior Bobby Hoppe, who gained 542 yards on 6.5 yards per carry. Lorino and junior end Phillips made second team All-SEC. Phillips caught twenty-three passes for 383 yards and four touchdowns.

So began the march toward the 1957 national title. Jordan had taken a major step toward the crown when a few years earlier he signed a prep fullback named Zeke Smith out of Uniontown, Alabama. Uniontown resident Carl Morgan Sr., a graduate of the University of Alabama, wanted Alabama to recruit Smith, but Alabama wasn't interested in the slow-footed fullback. Morgan, who knew Jordan well, mailed Jordan a photograph of Smith and encouraged him to talk to the youngster. Jordan grinned at the photograph and handed it to freshman coach McGowen. The photo showed Smith, in street clothes, squatting in a baseball catcher's position and wearing a mitt, while a young girl posed in a batting stance with bat in hand. "We gave Zeke a one-year scholarship based on Carl Morgan's say-so," McGowen recalled. "We normally never did anything like that." Jordan wasn't impressed with Smith as a fullback, but he saw the lineman in him and switched him to guard his freshman year. After a redshirt season, Smith, 6-2, 215, started at left guard his sophomore year in 1957, making third team All-SEC. He would win the Outland Trophy as the best interior lineman in the country in 1958 and make All-American in both 1958 and 1959. For many years Jordan gave Carl Morgan Sr. complimentary season tickets to Auburn home games because of his tip on Smith.

Going into the 1957 season most of Jordan's original staff was still intact. Offensive backfield coach Bradberry, offensive line coach

Senn, defensive ends coach Eaves, offensive ends coach Lorendo, line coach Connally and freshman coach McGowen were approaching their seventh season. Two members of the original staff had left — Hobbs, following Jordan's initial season in 1951 for an assistant coaching post at Navy, and Waller, after the 1954 season for an assistant's position at Texas. Herring, since coming to Auburn in 1953, had fast established himself as the premier defensive coach in the league, and his best was yet to come. Jordan had added two more to his staff before the 1956 season. George Atkins returned to Auburn as assistant line coach following a one-year playing stint in the NFL with the Detroit Lions. Vince Dooley, who had played quarterback and safety on Jordan's first three Auburn teams, came in as an assistant backfield coach and quarterback coach following two years in the Marine Corps.

Jordan went into the spring of 1957 knowing the potential was there to field a solid team, though he said, "we did not feel we were overly blessed with talent. We had too many sophomores and untried people we were counting on." Seven starters had graduated. Jordan's concerns focused on sophomore left guard Smith, and sophomore center Jackie Burkett, 6-4, 215, because of their inexperience. He knew they had talent. Also he was going with a sophomore backup at halfback, Lamar Rawson. Quarterback Tubbs had graduated and the quarterback position leaned to senior Jimmy Cook, with junior Frank Riley backing him up, and behind them sophomores John Kern and Bryant Harvard. A battle also brewed at fullback, between junior Donnie May and senior Billy Atkins. But Jordan had veteran talent at the ends, in the line and at halfback. Senior end Phillips, 5-11, 205, who had made second team All-SEC in 1956, was a preseason All-American. Junior end Jerry Wilson had played well the previous season and was expected to become all-conference material. Senior tackles Ben Preston and Dan Presley, and juniors Cleve Wester, James Warren and Jim Jeffery provided great depth. Senior guard Baker, with his scrappy demeanor, had come to symbolize the character of the team. He moved into the starting role and was named captain. Behind him at guard was a capable junior, Frank LaRussa. Junior halfback Lorino, 5-7, 165, who made second team All-SEC in 1956, and senior halfback Hoppe were respected throughout the conference.

During the spring Jordan and his staff worked the players hard, particularly on fundamentals and technique. The Blue team beat the Orange 12-9 before 7,500 in the March 9 A-Day game. The contest provided an accurate glimpse of the upcoming season: conservative, low scoring, aggressive blocking and tackling, a lot of punting. Jimmy Cook emerged as the number-one quarterback. Atkins appeared to have the edge on May at fullback.

Also during the spring of 1957, Jordan sent most of his staff to Oklahoma for a week to observe the Sooners in their spring workouts. Oklahoma, coached by Bud Wilkinson, and led by halfback Tommy McDonald, had won national titles in both 1955 and 1956. They had won forty games in a row. Many experts rated them with Army's 1944-1945 teams, which featured backs Glenn Davis and Doc Blanchard, as the best ever.

The Auburn staff specifically wanted to observe the Oklahoma quarterback option and the plays run off it. But Jordan's main intention was for his assistants to soak in a national championship program.

"We were trying to find out how you get to that point," Coach Atkins said. "What was the mystery? We came back all enthused."

On April 25 Jordan made a decision that, as unpleasant as it was, helped Auburn win the national championship: he dismissed quarterback Cook and fullback May from the team for "scholastic and disciplinary" reasons.

Atkins remembered, "They didn't handle themselves right. They went into a girls' dorm and had a few beers. Coach Jordan was embarrassed by the incident. It was a clear-cut decision for him. There was no agonizing. They were a little wild before that. He would give a man the first chance, a second chance and maybe a third chance. They had been there before, and he had warned them and this happened. He called them in and told them they were gone."

Bradberry remembered the incident, as well. "They had been on the fringes to some degree. These guys were good people, but we had strict rules in those days. When push came to shove these guys had been forewarned and they broke the rule again. Coach Jordan called Lorendo and I into his office and we talked about it. Coach went on and made the gut decision to let them go. Quite frankly there were three or four kids in that group, just cut-ups. This brought them into the fold."

In the book *National Champions*, Jordan wrote a short piece on the 1957 season entitled "By Reason Of Spirit."

"There are countless intangibles and unusual circumstances that lead to success or failure in almost every endeavor...I'm convinced that the underlying reason why Auburn attained the National Football Championship in 1957 was a spiritual one.

"Right after spring practice we had to make a move as a coaching staff that could make or break any season...it had a tremendous psychological effect on the team. They knew that the coaching staff was serious about team discipline and morale...They also realized that we would take any other disciplinary steps necessary to insure this team morale. As a result we did not have to push this team to get it out of them.

"From this type of co-operative attitude came the leadership that is so essential to a successful football team. The players sold themselves on dedication and realized that to have any kind of football team at all they would have to play better than many of them were capable of playing to make up for those losses."

Atkins stated it a bit more succinctly: "That put the fear of God in that team."

Jordan called the players together when they reported in the fall. "Adversity draws men closer together," he said. He told them that as good Auburn men they would get over the dismissals, they would work hard and work together and they would be proud of their accomplishments during the 1957 season. The players had only one question. Who was going to play quarterback?

Not only was the number-one quarterback in the spring out of the picture, the number-two quarterback, Riley, had left school. This left Jordan with two sophomores, Harvard and Kern, and a junior named Lloyd Nix. A 5-11, 175-pound southpaw, Nix had been an all-star split-T quarterback at Carbon Hill High School in Alabama. He was also a prep basketball star. Auburn freshman coach McGowen moved Nix to halfback in 1955. Nix saw limited playing time at halfback his sophomore year, carrying the ball thirty times and throwing one halfback pass. He finished the season as the third-string right halfback. At the time of the disciplinary action in the spring, Jordan and Bradberry decided to move Nix into the fall quarterback competition.

"We didn't know if he would win the job," Bradberry said. "But we had an idea that Nix, with his maturity, might be able to handle it."

Ten days into fall practice, Nix had the edge on the position and started the first game-like scrimmage. He completed ten of eleven passes for 125 yards and ran for a 69-yard touchdown. The job was his. "Nix was not a picture quarterback," Jordan said. "But he seemed to get the most done."

"With the type team we had he was a perfect fit," said quarterback coach Dooley. "He was really the missing piece of the puzzle that enabled that team to do so well. He could handle it because he was smart. He was a winner."

Nix's level-headed demeanor and consistency complemented the task of Jordan and Bradberry. "We had to really work hard at being very conservative in the handling of our offense," Bradberry said.

Two weeks into practice Jordan called for a "reckless fullback" to step forward. The senior fullback, Billy "Ace" Atkins, his main competition in the spring no longer with the team, answered Jordan. Atkins became the focal point of the T formation. Jordan and Bradberry implemented the H Belly Series, and the belly belonged to Atkins. It was a fullback off tackle option in which the quarterback put the ball in the fullback's belly and either let the fullback keep it or pulled the ball back and, depending on the position of the defensive end, kept the ball or pitched out to the halfback. At the snap of the ball the offensive guard had pulled to block the end; the other halfback had plunged straight ahead and filled the pulling guard's hole in order to block the defensive guard, or had followed the pulling guard and veered out and blocked the linebacker.

"That was our main stuff," Bradberry said.

Fall practice for the sixty-four players who turned out was rough, as usual. "You don't get fat playing for Shug," commented an observer at practice. Jordan not only intended to find eleven men to start the football game, he wanted eleven more to fill a second team that could replace the first unit at any point in the game, and continue gaining ground. "We worked the hell out of them," George Atkins said.

Baker remembered, "We didn't get any water or ice at practice. We'd go out in pads in that afternoon heat, then we'd run 100-yard sprints. But no water. I've seen other football players, plus myself, take sweaty towels and squeeze 'em to try and get moisture in our mouth and all we could spit out was cotton."

Practice always drew several pre-teen boys from the area and the players would pay them a nickel or a dime to sneak in a piece of ice or a cup of water. Coach Lorendo caught the youngsters in the act one day and made them run a lap.

"The games on weekends were fun," Baker said. "They were nothing like practices were."

Very little was mentioned during fall practice about the NCAA's no-bowl penalty that ran through the 1957 season. But when it came up the staff turned the situation into a challenge. "It's us against everybody else," Lorendo told the players. "We can't go anywhere, but we can win 'em all."

Preseason forecasts dribbled out and many of the experts liked Auburn's depth. A poll of twelve sportswriters who covered the conference placed Tennessee at the top, followed by Auburn, Georgia Tech and Ole Miss. They picked Alabama to finish last. Three of the twelve writers, Furman Bisher and Jesse Outlar of Atlanta and Tom Siler from Knoxville, picked Auburn to win the SEC. Head coaches going into the 1957 season included Jordan at Auburn, Bowden Wyatt at Tennessee, Bobby Dodd at Georgia Tech, Johnny Vaught at Ole Miss, Wally Butts at Georgia, Bob Woodruff at Florida, Paul Dietzel at LSU, Andy Pilney at Tulane, Blanton Collier at Kentucky, J.B. Whitworth at Alabama, Wade Walker at Mississippi State and Art Guepe at Vanderbilt.

Look Magazine picked Auburn number eighteen in the nation. *Saturday Evening Post* picked Auburn number nine. But the Associated Press didn't rank Auburn. And neither did *Sports Illustrated* in its annual college football preview. *SI* ranked Baylor at the top of its best eleven. It picked Georgia Tech number two and Tennessee number ten. Bryant's Texas A&M team, led by halfback John David Crow, and coming off a two-year NCAA probation for recruiting violations, was picked number eleven.

Auburn, *SI* wrote, had the best material in the conference; had the toughest and heaviest line in the conference; and in Lorino and Hoppe had two of the best running backs in the country. "The Tigers are the conference giant, but unless Coach Ralph (Shug) Jordan can come up with a smart quarterback his giant may be slow-moving and dim-witted...This team has championship material at every position except quarterback, and herein may lie Tennessee's claim to the SEC crown."

Two weeks prior to the opening game against Tennessee in Knoxville, Jordan stated: "I don't believe a team in the nation with as tough a schedule as ours will go through the year undefeated."

Jordan announced he would take forty players to Tennessee — eight seniors, fourteen juniors and eighteen sophomores. "We're ready," he said four days before the game. "It's the waiting that will be the toughest."

Jimmy Phillips recalled leaving the hotel in Knoxville the morning of the game to head for the stadium. Filling the air was the replay of the radio broadcast from the previous year's game, won by Tennessee, 35-7. "That got us fired up," Phillips said.

Approximately 42,000 fans sat in Shields-Watkins Field on September 28. Rain fell and the field grew sloppy. Auburn dominated the game statistically, 217 yards to 84, and had numerous opportunities to score but did so only in the second quarter. Jerry Wilson partially blocked a Tennessee punt and Auburn took over on its own forty-three. Nix showed nifty ball handing as he directed the touchdown drive. With Hoppe, Atkins, Lorino and Rawson carrying the ball and a Nix-to-Wilson pass for ten yards mixed in, Auburn drove to the five-yard line. Rawson gained two yards to the three. Then Atkins carried three straight times, finally scoring from the one on fourth down. Atkins kicked the extra point to put Auburn up, 7-0. That's how it ended. Nix completed one of three passes. Auburn didn't turn the ball over.

"From the beginning I could sense a determined attitude on the part of the players," Jordan said.

Tennessee's biggest scoring threat came in the first quarter when it blocked an Auburn quick kick and recovered at the Auburn eighteen. Zeke Smith dropped the ball carrier for a three-yard loss, then Phillips forced a fumble with a jarring tackle and recovered it himself. Tennessee moved the ball inside the Auburn thirty twice late in the game, but Auburn's defense stiffened.

Phillips and Wilson, as they would all season, played great defense at the ends. Phillips recalled that the defensive plan allowed the ends to play free, unlike the previous year when they stepped across the line and planted themselves. Tennessee's pulling guards in the single wing had run over them. But this time the Auburn ends wreaked havoc in the Tennessee backfield.

Herring said of the ends' play that year, "They came up field every time. There wasn't no pitty-patty or jumping around. Ole Joel Eaves did a great job as the defensive ends coach."

Jordan substituted eleven players at a time during the game. He would do this throughout the season. Starters and second-stringers in Knoxville included: left ends—Jerry Wilson and Leo Sexton; left tackles—James Warren and Jim Jeffery; left guards—Zeke Smith and Jeff Weekley; centers—Jackie Burkett and Jimmie Ricketts; right guards—Tim Baker and Frank LaRussa; right tackles—Dan Presley and Cleve Wester; right ends—Jimmy Phillips and Mike Simmons; quarterbacks—Lloyd Nix and John Kern; left halfbacks—Tommy Lorino and Pat Meagher; right halfbacks—Bobby Hoppe and Lamar Rawson; and fullbacks—Billy Atkins and Ronnie Robbs. Several other players saw action as well. An injury hindered the services of tackle Ben Preston.

The big question mark going into the game had been quarterback Nix, but he had proved his capabilities in a hostile environment and on a slippery playing surface.

"Coach Jordan being the way he was, I figured if I didn't mess up he wouldn't change anything," Nix said. "If we'd lost to Tennessee, then I wouldn't have been the quarterback of that team. He really was one of those people who felt, 'if it ain't broke, don't fix it.'"

"He had the best hands of anybody I've ever seen," McGowen recalled of Nix. "He went about his business. He knew what he was going to do."

The win over Tennessee served as a model for the remainder of the season: outstanding defense, excellent kicking, no mistakes. The Associated Press jumped Auburn from nowhere to number seven following the game. The next week Auburn defeated Chattanooga, 40-7, but dropped two places in the poll to number nine. Auburn then beat Kentucky 6-0 in Auburn. Atkins made the play of the game in the third quarter when he slapped down a Kentucky pitchout and recovered it at the Kentucky thirty-six. Auburn drove to the six, aided by a Lorino run and a personal foul on Kentucky's All-American tackle Lou Michaels. Atkins ran it in from the six for the touchdown. Atkins and Robbs averaged forty-five yards a punt during the game to keep Kentucky backed up. Kentucky never penetrated inside the Auburn seventeen and made it that far only because Auburn fumbled.

Auburn led the nation in total defense when it tangled with Georgia Tech in Atlanta on October 19. The defense gave up only 150 yards as Auburn won 3-0. The lone Tiger score came early in the second quarter on a drive that began late in the opening period at the

Auburn thirty-three. Jordan sent in the second unit with Harvard at quarterback, Meagher and Rawson at the halfbacks and Robbs at fullback. They drove forty-eight yards and Atkins kicked a 31-yard field goal, the first one he'd ever made.

"I felt confident the ball was going straight through those uprights," Atkins said. "I never saw a more beautiful sight."

"It was all I could do to watch him try it," Jordan said.

Georgia Tech drove to the Auburn four-yard line in the third quarter, but end Wilson's hit on Tech quarterback Fred Brasleton forced a fumble and Phillips recovered. "If we live for 100 years, I doubt if we will ever see finer end play than was put on by Jimmy Phillips and Jerry Wilson," Jordan said after the game. More strong punting by Atkins kept Tech at bay.

The AP ranked Auburn number five. "We just played one at a time," Baker said. "Then all of the sudden we had won a bunch of games and our name came up in the polls. Somebody said Auburn is getting on up there close to number one. We really didn't realize it."

"Suddenly the players realized that an unbeaten season and a conference championship were within their grasp," Jordan said. "These were no longer things to just talk and think about. Here they were for the taking. Paying the price for victory took on added meaning. They could not wait for the next practice or game."

Auburn blitzed Houston in Texas the following week, 48-7, and dominated Florida, 13-0, a week later. Auburn mounted 381 yards to Florida's eighty-three. The Tigers completed only two passes, but one of them was a 63-yard touchdown connection from Nix to Phillips with Phillips making a dazzling run.

The Associated Press ranked Auburn third as it put its 6-0 record and ten-game winning streak on the line against Mississippi State in Birmingham before 42,000. State brought in impressive offensive numbers, averaging 24.5 points per game. The Bulldogs scored first and led 7-0 at half, but Auburn drove seventy-six yards in eleven plays to tie it in the third quarter, the big play a 24-yard run by Lorino. Atkins scored from the three-yard line and kicked the extra point. Auburn then dropped State for a safety when Jackie Burkett broke through the line and forced the State punter to run. Auburn's John Whatley, playing for the injured Phillips, tackled the punter before he could get out of the end zone to put Auburn ahead, 9-7. Auburn's final score came after Zeke Smith recovered a dropped punt at the State ten. Auburn drove it in with Atkins scoring from the two. Auburn won, 15-7.

The Tigers maintained the number three position in the rankings — behind top-ranked Texas A&M and number two Oklahoma — as it prepared for the final three games. Jordan started the same lineup against Georgia, Florida State and Alabama: left end Wilson (220 pounds), left tackle Preston (215) left guard Smith (210), center Burkett (215), right guard Baker (195), right tackle Wester (220), right end Phillips (205), quarterback Nix (170), halfbacks Lorino (168) and Hoppe (175), and fullback Atkins (190).

Captain Tim Baker remembered seeing for the first time the saying, "When the going gets tough, the tough get going." An Auburn fan had written it on a piece of paper and mailed it to the team. Jordan posted it on the dressing room bulletin board in the field house.

The Georgia game in Columbus kindled memories of the previous season's bench-clearing brawl. Baker, who had not started the fight, but who had been at the center of it, again left his mark on the Columbus field in front of 27,000.

Head coach Butts and Georgia brought a dismal 2-6 record into the game but played Auburn to the hilt. Tackle Nat Dye, older brother of future Auburn head coach Pat Dye, made third team All-SEC for Georgia following the season.

Auburn scored in the second quarter on a four-yard pass from Nix to Phillips. The drive covered fifty-two yards in twelve plays. Jordan had again displayed his squad's depth. The second unit, with Harvard at quarterback, began the drive at the Auburn forty-three. Harvard mixed in two pass completions, to Whatley and Rawson, as Auburn drove to the Georgia thirty-one. Jordan rushed his first team back into the game. Following an offside penalty on Auburn, Nix passed to Atkins for eight yards, Hoppe ran for three yards and a

Georgia roughness penalty on the play moved the ball to the Georgia five. Atkins carried for a yard and then Nix leaped and hit Phillips with the pass for the score. Auburn missed the extra point.

Following Auburn fumbles, Georgia twice penetrated the Auburn ten-yard line, but Auburn held. Georgia had first and goal on the three when quarterback Charles Britt took the snap. Baker's quickness saved the day, and perhaps the national title for Auburn.

"I slipped through the gap between the center and the guard and got the quarterback as he was going down the line to hand the ball off," Baker said.

Baker's hit forced Britt to fumble. Zeke Smith recovered.

Auburn gained 227 yards on offense. The Tigers threw the ball more than usual as Nix completed nine of ten for seventy-two yards. Phillips caught five passes for thirty-four yards. Auburn's defense held Georgia to ninety-seven yards and three first downs.

While Auburn was whipping the Bulldogs, top-ranked Texas A&M lost to Rice and number-two-ranked Oklahoma lost to Notre Dame. But the Associated Press jumped once-beaten Michigan State ahead of Auburn. The Spartans had 1,851 points to Auburn's 1,842, but Auburn had one more first place vote, 88-87.

The poll corrected itself the following week after Auburn racked Florida State 29-7 to move to 9-0 on the season. The Seminoles attempted to beat Auburn through the air, throwing twenty-six passes, but Auburn picked off five. Auburn's offense gained 311 yards, a third of them by passing. Following the game, Florida State head coach Tom Nugent said, "Playing Auburn is like entering battle without any guns."

The win pushed Auburn into the number-one position, with Ohio State number two and Michigan State number three. Ohio State had lost its opening game of the season to Texas Christian University, 18-14. The polls looked like this: Auburn — 1,850 (85 first place votes); Ohio State — 1,769 (65); and Michigan State 1,713. Ohio State head coach Woody Hayes publicly questioned the strength of Auburn's schedule. But Auburn victims Tennessee, Mississippi State and Florida would finish the season ranked thirteenth, fourteenth and seventeenth, respectively.

The season-ending Iron Bowl would be Auburn's only bowl appearance because of the NCAA penalty. Alabama came into the game battered and bruised with a 2-6-1 record. The Tide wasn't hiding the fact that it wanted to hire a new head coach, preferably Bryant, to replace the outgoing Whitworth.

Before 45,000 at Legion Field, Auburn clinched the national title with a 40-0 annihilation of the Tide. Auburn led 34-0 at intermission and Jordan played everybody in the second half. Atkins scored the first two touchdowns. Nix scored the third. Lorino picked off a deflected pass and ran seventy-nine yards to put Auburn up 27-0. Burkett intercepted a pass and ran sixty-six yards for a touchdown to make it 34-0. Early in the second half Nix passed to Phillips for the final score. As the game ended the players carried the coaches to midfield and later tossed them in the locker room showers. Jordan stated of his team's effort, "They were sharp as razors."

On December 2 the Associated Press named Auburn its national champion. Auburn picked up 3,123 points and 210 first place votes to Ohio State's 2,645 points and seventy-one first place votes. Michigan State finished number three, followed by Oklahoma, Navy, Iowa and Ole Miss. Jordan, having caught a cold from the post-game antics in the showers, said, "As far as I'm concerned Auburn has been number one all the year. Team morale was the finest I've been around."

On December 10, twelve-thousand fans (school enrollment was 8,500) turned out at Cliff Hare Stadium to see AP General Sports Editor Ted Smits present the national championship trophy to Jordan and the Tigers. The city of Auburn hosted a parade for the players and coaches. Local schools let out for the day. Flags and banners decorated the Plains.

On the same day the Associated Press named senior Jimmy Phillips as a first-team All-American. During his three varsity seasons, Phillips caught fifty-two passes for 1,012 yards and nine touchdowns. He averaged 19.5 yards per catch. He dominated as a defensive end. "Red Phillips never went to practice that he was not dedicated to leaving the field a better player," Jordan said. The Birmingham Quarterback Club named Phillips the SEC's most valuable lineman.

Jordan and Herring's defense produced some mind-boggling statistics. It gave up only twenty-eight points the entire season. None of the opponents' four touchdowns came on the ground; one score came on a long interception return. The defense shut out six conference teams — Tennessee, Kentucky, Georgia Tech, Florida, Georgia and Alabama. The only conference opponent to score a touchdown was Mississippi State. The defense led the nation in total defense for fewest yards allowed per game at 133; and led the nation in fewest rushing yards per game at 67.4. The defense led the conference in fumble recoveries with twenty-two, and in interceptions with twenty.

Defensive coordinator Herring said, "We didn't give them anything up the middle. We made them run east and west and we could catch them when they did that."

Jordan's act of discipline in the spring had put the weight on quarterback Nix and fullback Atkins. They responded superbly and in effect enabled Auburn to win the national title. Nix, playing nearly mistake-free, completed thirty-three of sixty passes for 542 yards and four touchdowns. "He never missed anybody that was open," McGowen said. Atkins set a school record for points scored with eighty-two. He rushed for eleven touchdowns. Atkins was best with the game on the line. He scored the touchdown and kicked the point after in the 7-0 win over Tennessee. He scored the touchdown in the 6-0 win over Kentucky. He kicked the field goal in the 3-0 victory over Georgia Tech. He accounted for thirteen points — two touchdowns and a point after — in Auburn's 15-7 over Mississippi State. And in the Iron Bowl he scored twice and kicked four extra points. Also, Atkins's effective punting established field position for Auburn time and time again.

The offense finished second in the conference, behind Ole Miss, in yards per game with 288.4. Phillips caught fifteen passes for 357 yards and four touchdowns. Lorino led the team in rushing with 450 yards on seventy-eight carries.

Phillips and Wilson made first team All-SEC at the ends. Burkett at center, Preston at tackle and Atkins at fullback made second team. Smith at guard and Lorino at halfback made third team.

Jordan received the greatest honor of his coaching career when the Washington Touchdown Club named him National Coach of the Year. The Associated Press named him SEC Coach of the Year for the second time in five years. Auburn President Draughon rewarded Jordan with an annual extension clause in his contract.

Years later Jordan reflected on the 1957 team. "As individuals off the field they were gentlemen and scholars. As individuals on the field they were uncommonly rugged and aggressive."

At forty-seven years old, Shug Jordan was at the top of his game.

12

"In the interests of another institution"

··

As Jordan drove the Tigers to glory in 1957, something kept tugging at him. With his energies channeled into the tremendous task at hand, he usually pushed the discomfort aside. But it was there. The NCAA was again investigating Auburn for recruiting violations, looking specifically into Auburn's recruitment of Guntersville High School quarterback Don Fuell. What frustrated Jordan was that this was Auburn's second such involvement with the NCAA. Auburn was already playing under probation. The NCAA had handed down a punishment in spring 1956, charging Auburn with improper recruiting. The penalty prohibited Auburn from playing in bowl games following the 1956 and 1957 seasons. The penalty may have cost Auburn's 7-3 team a bowl bid in 1956. It undoubtedly cost Auburn's undefeated squad of 1957 a bowl invitation.

On December 15, 1955, the *Birmingham News* broke the story that SEC Commissioner Bernie Moore was looking into a report that an Auburn recruiter paid one-thousand dollars to Gadsden-area running backs Robert and Harry Beaube in an effort to coerce them to accept scholarships from Auburn. The twin brothers had just completed their prep careers at Emma Sansom High School. Harry Beaube had made Class AAA All-State. The father of the twins, the Reverend Albert Beaube, said he wished his sons "would just forget football."

A week later, the SEC fined Auburn two-thousand dollars for the incident. Auburn said it would not appeal the fine. Commissioner Moore revealed that Auburn defensive coach Hal Herring gave the twins five-hundred dollars each on November 28. Apparently, Herring acted on behalf of an alumnus.

President Draughon commented, "After full inquiry we accept as fact the statement that one of our coaches has made offers in cash in excess of normal grant-in-aid allowable." The existing grant-in-aid setup allowed players tuition, books, room and board, plus fifteen dollars per month for laundry.

But Draughon offered some additional information. He said, "Persons acting in the interests of another institution" had led the twins to believe they would be given a furnished apartment. When Herring discovered this, he "unwisely, in the heat of competition, was led to make a cash payment."

Draughon didn't mention any names, but he was referring to the University of Alabama. The twins said Auburn and Alabama had been the only two SEC schools to offer them scholarships. Auburn also believed that Alabama's recruiting coordinator had called the SEC Commissioner and reported Auburn's misdeed.

"We cannot excuse the fact that the excess upon Auburn's part occurred because persons acting in the interests of another institution made the original offer," Draughon said. But he added, "To penalize one institution and not the other can only result in sharpening the rivalry."

Jeff Beard, then the athletic director, said he and Jordan immediately drove to the home of Hueytown High School quarterback Richard Rush, who had just signed with Auburn. They gathered goods which, according to Beard, had been given to the player by Alabama during the recruiting season, and transported the goods to the SEC commissioner's office in Birmingham.

"We told him that if he wanted evidence, there it was," Beard later said.

On December 31, 1955 the *Birmingham News* reported that the SEC had fined Alabama one-thousand dollars because four alumni or supporters of the university gave Hueytown's Rush a television set, clothes, an overcoat and $28.47 in cash.

But Auburn, not Alabama, was in the hot seat with the NCAA, which had launched an enforcement program in 1952. Early in 1956, NCAA Executive Director Walter Byers reported that twenty-five schools were under investigation. The NCAA had recently slapped the University of Miami with a major penalty.

On May 1, 1956, an eighteen-man NCAA Council, meeting in New Orleans, put on probation Texas A&M, Mississippi College and the University of Kansas. The NCAA found Bear Bryant's Texas A&M program guilty of offering at least two prospective student athletes financial aid during April 1955. The penalty knocked Texas A&M out of two bowl games.

The next day, May 2, the NCAA put the boom on Auburn, Florida and Louisville. The council agreed with the SEC's finding on Herring and the cash payments to the twins. Executive Director Byers said the twins reported the incident to their father the same day they received the money, and their father returned the money the following day. President Draughon called the probation "rough stuff."

"We're going to do everything we can to restore the good standing of Auburn," Draughon said.

The NCAA also reprimanded and censured Jordan for failing to "take corrective action or punitive action upon learning of the incident."

In four years the NCAA had placed seventeen colleges on probation.

Years later Herring said, "I took the blame and we went on. It's amazing how all the agricultural colleges get zapped and the state universities don't."

The incident didn't seriously impact recruiting as scholarships weren't part of the penalty. Also, Auburn had already signed those players who were to be freshmen in 1956. The players Auburn would sign the following season, who would play freshman ball in 1957, wouldn't be affected by the lack of bowl participation anyway, since freshmen couldn't play on the varsity. Auburn signed lineman Ken Rice and fullback and kicker Ed Dyas, both future All-Americans, that year. Needless to say the penalty didn't affect the varsity team's play, as the 1957 team won the national title.

But the incident did, in Draughon's words, sharpen the rivalry between Auburn and Alabama. It created some bitterness in Beard, Jordan and the assistant coaches toward Alabama. However, Auburn's 34-7 and 40-0 whippings of Alabama in the no-bowl years of 1956 and 1957 helped mollify their anxiety.

And then it happened again, only this time it was worse. In April 1958, just as Auburn was coming off the initial penalty, the NCAA smacked Auburn with a three-year probation. No bowl games in 1958, 1959 and 1960; no sharing in the conference's bowl receipts; no television; no participation by the school's other sports including basketball, baseball, track, golf and wrestling in post-season regional or national tournaments or playoffs with NCAA championship ramifications. The NCAA said Auburn violated recruiting rules when an alumnus, who was an active recruiter, and whose actions were known by members of the coaching staff, offered substantial financial assistance and materials to Guntersville High School quarterback Don Fuell.

Once again Auburn insinuated that Alabama had a hand in Auburn's misfortunes. This time Auburn aggressively contested the charges.

Jordan had signed Fuell, a highly-recruited 6-2, 205-pound quarterback, on December 7, 1956. Fourteen schools had offered scholarships to Fuell. Almost immediately, allegations regarding recruiting improprieties — and in particular an automobile — surfaced. Auburn maintained that an Alabama coach contacted the SEC office and initiated the rumor about the automobile. Rumors of other gifts continued to abound into 1957 and the NCAA began its investigation in late August, shortly before the beginning of the 1957 football season. Fuell, meanwhile, played freshman football for Auburn in 1957, as well as baseball and basketball. The NCAA investigation continued throughout Auburn's national championship season and into the spring of 1958.

Fuell participated in varsity spring practice. He established himself as a hard-hitting ballplayer. "Everybody wanted to know where he was lining up before they snapped the ball," McGowen said.

Athletic director Beard argued Auburn's case a first time before the NCAA infractions committee in Kansas City. Then Beard, along with Opelika attorney Bob Brown, and accompanied by coaches Lorendo and Bradberry and young Fuell, argued it again before a seventeen-member NCAA Council during an April 19-21 meeting in New Orleans.

But on April 21, the NCAA Council announced the three-year penalty. The council said "Auburn offered a prospective student athlete illicit financial aid for himself and his family." Fuell was married and had a son when he entered Auburn. The NCAA said Auburn offered Fuell a motorboat and an air-conditioned apartment among other items. The NCAA stated..."the alumnus who primarily was responsible for arranging the various benefits has been identified as a rep of the institution in that staff members of API knew that he was actively recruiting the prospect...and at least one member of the staff conferred with the alumnus concerning living accommodations."

NCAA Executive Director Byers called it the third-most severe penalty in NCAA history. On October 16, 1952, the NCAA had placed the Kentucky sports program on probation for the academic year of 1952-1953 and denied Kentucky the right to play other NCAA member basketball teams. On November 13, 1956, the NCAA whacked North Carolina State with a four-year probation.

Beard immediately called a press conference in Auburn. He said the NCAA decision was based on unsupported statements that were disproven by signed affidavits. Beard produced a letter, which had been shown to the NCAA Council, from SEC Commissioner Bernie Moore to Byers dated March 26. "There is not sufficient evidence to substantiate the allegations against the boy or Auburn," Moore wrote. "At no time is it proved that Donald Fuell actually received any cash awards or gifts." Moore, however, following the NCAA decision, toned down his stance and said he wrote his letter based on information Auburn gave him and that he reserved the right to scrutinize all of the facts of the case.

Beard told the press that the NCAA Council had relied on a statement by its investigator who said two witnesses told him that they had seen a piece of paper reportedly containing Auburn offers of extra inducement. Beard said the NCAA believed that Carl Lay, Fuell's father-in-law in Guntersville, in late July 1957 showed the paper to an assistant line coach at Alabama. Beard also said the NCAA believed that a booster of Oklahoma State had also seen the paper.

But Beard produced a statement from the Alabama coach that he had seen or heard nothing about such inducement, and Beard produced a statement from the Oklahoma State supporter that he had been misinterpreted. Fuell's father-in-law, in a sworn statement, said, "Such a piece of paper never was in my house...I know that Auburn has not made any such inducement except a scholarship." The Alabama assistant coach had previously coached at Oklahoma State and Beard implied that in the summer of 1957, perhaps acting in Alabama's interest as well as Oklahoma State's, the assistant coach attempted to sway Fuell out of the SEC and toward Oklahoma State. At the time of the NCAA's decision on Auburn, the assistant coach was no longer with Alabama.

As for the NCAA's focus on the Auburn alumnus, Beard said the NCAA had merely made a connection between a Birmingham goods distributorship run by an Auburn alumnus who was courting Fuell for Auburn, and the fact that this alumnus guided Fuell and/or his father to the involved purchases. But Beard said documents showed that the alumnus made no purchases for the Fuells; he cut the Fuells no special deals; and that Fuell's father purchased the motorboat, and that the son, with his father's permission, bought the air conditioner.

Beard also implied that Alabama's involvement ran even deeper: he suggested that Alabama wanted so desperately to turn Fuell away from Auburn that an Alabama recruiter hired a Pinkerton detective to accomplish that task and possibly to work with the

NCAA investigation. Beard presented a statement from Fuell that said a Pinkerton detective asked Fuell in late August 1957 if he would consider a bonus to get him to enroll at Mississippi Southern or Tennessee. Beard said the detective visited Fuell twice and after one visit went to Tuscaloosa to confer with the Alabama recruiter.

"I knew he was some kind of agent or whatever," Fuell said of the Pinkerton detective. "We just played a game with him."

Beard also said that the Pinkerton agent received a call from an NCAA official who inquired about Fuell's material possessions. University of Alabama President Frank Rose denied that his university was involved in Auburn's predicament.

The NCAA's Byers stated, "The fact that Auburn failed to establish its innocence in two formal hearings when all the evidence was available, instead of just one side of the evidence, is more eloquent testimony to Auburn's guilt."

Auburn President Draughon continued to search the NCAA findings for the kind of hard evidence that would seemingly be required to hand out a three-year penalty. "Two years ago we were reprimanded and had no excuses," said Draughon. "If the committee on infractions based its findings on the charges submitted to us, I cannot see how they arrived at the conclusions they arrived at."

Birmingham News sportswriter Benny Marshall wrote, "There can be little doubt that NCAA conviction of Auburn guilt came...largely on circumstantial evidence...It looks from here like the councilmen determined their verdict for more on what they thought appeared to be than what actually was shown to be."

Draughon requested that the SEC Executive Committee meet on the NCAA decision, which the committee did on May 23 at the Georgia Terrace Hotel in Atlanta. The committee, along with Commissioner Moore, included university presidents Dr. Troy Middleton, LSU; Dr. Frank Dickey, Kentucky; Dr. T.A. Bickerstaff, Mississippi; Dr. A.R. Scott, Georgia; and Dr. S.M. Sarratt, Vanderbilt. Auburn was represented by Beard, Draughon, Jordan, attorney Brown, Atlanta attorney William Bentley, coaches Lorendo and Bradberry and quarterback Fuell. Auburn argued its case during the morning. The

NCAA's Byers presented his group's findings to the committee during the afternoon.

Once again the decision fell against Auburn. The committee endorsed the NCAA penalty and provided additional detail of the charges. The committee said that between May 18 and August 14 in 1957, Fuell came into possession of a forty-horsepower motor, boat trailer and boat at a total cost of fifteen-hundred dollars, of which five-hundred dollars was paid as a down payment; an air conditioning unit that cost $182; an electric range and refrigerator that cost three-hundred dollars; and a two-bedroom unfurnished apartment renting for seventy-five dollars a month, plus utilities.

The committee said, "Each of these items were connected in varying ways with the Auburn alumni who had been actively interested in Fuell. Staff members of Auburn knew of the alumni active recruitment and consulted with them."

The committee also said that possession of these items was not in keeping with the financial status of Fuell and/or his family; that cash outlay amounted to more than one-thousand dollars in a period of less than ninety days and at a time when his father did not have a bank account. The committee said there was no evidence that Fuell's parents ever provided him with these items.

"The evidence shows the boy was promised these benefits and as an enrolled student received them. Representatives of Auburn have failed to satisfactorily clarify or explain the financing of these items."

In addition to endorsing the NCAA three-year penalty, the committee kicked Fuell out of SEC athletics. Crying in the lobby of the hotel after hearing the decision, Fuell uttered, "It was a raw deal."

Jordan, quiet throughout the long investigation, made the most dramatic statement of all:

"The Southeastern Conference missed a great opportunity to grow up and become a real conference today. The commissioner missed a great opportunity to grow up and be a real commissioner. The Southeastern Conference has (in the past) backed up its stand that no school ever will be convicted on hearsay, suspicion and supposition. The commissioner has repeatedly made the statement. But that's what we were convicted on today. I am still fully convinced that Auburn is innocent of any wrongdoing or illegal recruiting in Donald Fuell's case."

Defense coach Hal Herring, who had been in the middle of the first probation in 1956, said years later, "If you're doing too well somebody is always trying to trump up something to knock you down. Instead of doing it on the field, they want to do it on the sly."

Auburn assistant coach Bradberry said that Auburn's investigation showed that a summer job could have provided Fuell with the funds to buy many of these items. As for the stove and refrigerator, Bradberry said the Birmingham distributor had told Fuell where to get a good deal at an appliance merchant in Tuskegee, which was having trouble because of a black boycott. Fuell subsequently bought the appliances in Tuskegee.

Bradberry said he had naturally associated with the Birmingham distributor because the distributor had helped Auburn recruit for several years "which was legitimate then." Bradberry said the alumnus asked him to help the Fuells find a place to live in Auburn, and Bradberry accompanied the Fuells to the apartment. "It wasn't a violation," Bradberry said. "It was just the connection. That's one of the problems when somebody starts coming at you. You have to prove you're innocent with the NCAA. There's no such thing as due process with the NCAA."

Thirty-five years later, Fuell recalled his ordeal with heartfelt sadness and more than a little bitterness.

"The thing that really smacks still about the situation is the way the verdict came about, without ever hearing my side, without ever getting any of the supposedly-conflicting depositions resolved. Auburn was on top of the SEC at that time in football, basketball, baseball, had great wrestling, swimming, just an all-around good program, and for kids to be punished for that was a tough thing to handle.

"I sat out my sophomore year in 1958. We tried to get in a court of law. We took it to court but they would not hear the case. There was no legal precedent at that time. But since then there have been a number of lawsuits against the NCAA, and rightfully so. I have a real hard spot in my heart, not because of what happened to me, but what happens to a lot of people and a lot of institutions with the NCAA's Gestapo-type tactics. They put people in the defensive position of trying to prove themselves innocent, instead of actually having factual data. The NCAA goes on rumor and innuendo.

"I'm not claiming that I'm cleaner than the driven snow. I was a kid that, like a lot of other kids, could be prostituted very easily. And I was prostituted, though not to the same degree by Auburn as I was by the other universities that recruited me. Probably the two worst violators of the rules of recruiting when I came along were Alabama and Georgia. What they did I think was take the heat off themselves and put it on everybody else by feeding the NCAA all kinds of rumors.

"Nevertheless, the thing that really hurts is the fact that my parents, who had meager means, and my in-laws, who had meager means, made sacrifices to provide certain things for us that we were later charged with having received above and beyond a normal scholarship. That really hurt. I'm not claiming I didn't receive things; it's just that the items they zeroed in on, the fact that there was a Tuskegee appliance dealer that was struggling because of a boycott and I bought some appliances at a good price, that my parents paid for or my in-laws paid for, that I should be penalized and Auburn should be penalized for — that is ridiculous. And they made a big issue out of a boat which I was dumb enough to buy. I kept it for three months. My dad helped me with the down payment on it. We sold the damn boat, but they made a big issue out of it that Auburn had bought a boat. Auburn didn't buy a boat for me. And the same thing with an automobile. My wife's parents had bought her a car when she was sixteen-years old and it just so happened that on her eighteenth birthday they replaced the car that they had given her on her sixteenth birthday. And so all of a sudden we're driving around in a new car; it's her car, and they're saying that Auburn gave it to me. They did not. They did not pay one penny toward it.

"The NCAA investigator came to the apartment that I rented in Auburn; he never gained entrance to the place, yet he wrote this report about things that were in there that were not in there. He came under the subterfuge of being an encyclopedia salesman. My wife didn't even let him in. He portrayed us as having all these luxury items.

"My son was born with club feet, so Auburn is a warm place in the summer when I had to report. A window air-conditioning unit was bought to put into this apartment that we had rented. We rented the apartment because there were some real good friends of ours who lived in the same complex that had held it for us. It was a small apartment complex off campus. These friends of ours wanted us living next door to them and we secured the apartment through them. And we got the air conditioner. The investigator came and talked to my dad. He said, 'Mr. Fuell, who paid for the air conditioner?' My dad said he paid for it. When they interviewed me separately they asked me the same question and I said I paid for it. They said our stories didn't jive. Well, actually my dad had paid for it; he gave me the money to pay for it. That's how ludicrous it was. You never get a chance to clarify these things; they just put it down as conflict in statement.

"Walter Byers at that time, it was obvious he wanted this notch in his belt. Bernie Moore, who was the SEC commissioner, and his investigation exonerated Auburn of any wrongdoing, but then Walter Byers came to Atlanta. The SEC was going to stick by their guns, that was the word we were getting, and then Walter Byers comes in and I don't know what he did or what kind of pressure he brought on the SEC, but they went ahead and went along with the ruling. I know Auburn got a raw deal.

"I never got a day in court. I appeared in person, made myself available, but they would not hear me. The only time I saw them was in passing in the hotel lobby. That's the reason I label it as Gestapo, because if you don't give a person an opportunity to confront his accusers face-to-face then you're in a Gestapo-type atmosphere. I was in the hotel lobby in Atlanta when I heard about the SEC decision. I went back up to my room and broke down."

As hard as it was to take at the time, Fuell said the SEC's ruling to ban him from conference athletics may have put his life on a better course. "I was struggling at Auburn. I don't think I would have had the opportunity to play at Auburn. I might have been a second or third stringer. I'm just speculating. You never know what you're going to do until you're confronted with it. I was always a competitor so it wouldn't have been because I wasn't trying.

"I went on to Mississippi Southern and had a pretty good athletic and academic career there. I made little All-American when I first went there. They got university status my senior year and I made honorable mention All-American at the university level. I had other honorary things in school. I was a pre-dent student. I never pursued my dental career but I was awarded for being the outstanding pre-dent student. I was the president of my graduating class. I was a big man on campus there. I probably would have never achieved the same success at Auburn as I did at Southern."

After graduating, Fuell played several years of football in the Canadian pro league.

"Looking back on it, we are all faced with adverse conditions. We're basically not judged by the cards we're dealt, but how we play them. I'm still with an aerospace company. I'm enjoying a good career. But when I start reflecting on it, it's still tough."

Fuell remembered Jordan as someone to lean on during the crisis.

"I think Coach Jordan and his whole staff were very supportive of me. It came across to me that they really cared about what was happening to Don Fuell and that meant a lot. My opinion of Coach Jordan is that there's not a more classy individual, more knowledgeable about football and people, that I've ever known. He was a great man.

"They started recruiting me in about '55. Coach Jordan was the guy who was impressive. His style was so great. He would never dress down or get in someone's face on the sidelines. If he had a

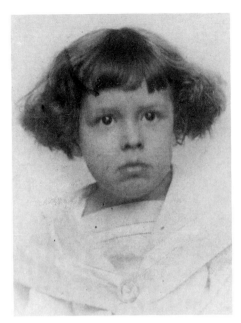

Jordan grew up in Selma, Alabama, the son of a railroad worker. His passion was sports, and he was Selma High School's first four-sport letterman. He is shown below, third from left in the top row, with his high school football team. Many of his teammates remained lifelong friends.

In addition to being a campus leader, Jordan was also an excellent athlete at Auburn from 1928-1932. As a sophomore he led the Southern Conference in scoring as a sharp-shooting basketball forward. He was a reserve center on the football team until his senior year, when he moved permanently into the starting lineup. Again, the friendships Jordan forged on the playing fields remained with him for life.

In 1936, Jordan was an assistant football coach under Jack Meagher at Auburn. He is shown here with fellow coaches Jimmy Hitchcock (l) and Boots Chambless in Havana, Cuba, at the Rhumba Bowl.

Jordan was an assistant under Meagher (to Jordan's left, above) before he was nominated as Auburn's head coach by a screening committee (below) that included old friends Hitchcock and Bo Russell.

In 1951, Jordan had a partner on the Plains in old friend Jeff Beard (above) and many great assistant coaches, including Hobbs, Waller, Bradberry, Senn, Lorendo, Eaves and McGowen. Joe Connally is not pictured.

By 1957, Jordan had guided Auburn from the bottom of the conference to the top of the nation. Shown above is his 1957 staff, including newcomers Atkins, Dooley and Herring. Below, Jordan accepts the National Championship trophy from AP Sports Editor Ted Smits.

Jordan was immensely popular in Auburn as he and his players fraternized well with both "town and gown." Above, Jimmy Phillips visits President Ralph Draughon and alumnus Roy B. Sewell at Homecoming, 1958. Jordan (below), riding a long winning streak, smiles to the crowd at the 1958 "Beat Bama" pep rally.

Jordan was well-loved by young men of all ages. He enjoyed time at home with son Ralph, Jr. (above). By 1964, Auburn's football fortunes were coming back to earth, but the affection the student body held for Jordan was still out of this world.

Jordan had twenty-two All-Americans during his twenty-five years at Auburn, but none more spectacular than Tucker Frederickson and Jimmy Sidle (above) and Pat Sullivan and Terry Beasley.

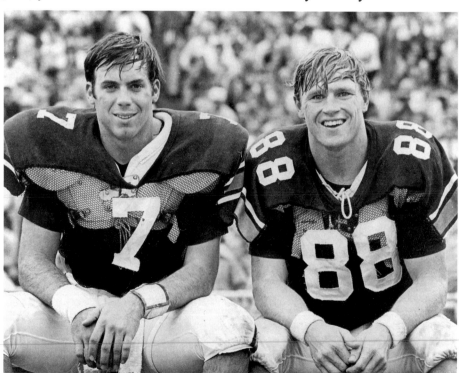

Jordan felt great pride in Pat Sullivan winning the Heisman Trophy in 1971, as he and Sullivan considered it an award for both the team and for Auburn. Late in his career Jordan pointed out that although Alabama had won more national championships, Auburn had the Heisman in its trophy case. The awards dinner also gave Jordan an opportunity to trade one-liners with one of his all-time favorites: movie actor John Wayne.

Pat Sullivan, in addition to rewriting the college football record book, was considered by his coaches and teammates to be "a coach on the field" and never lacked for confidence or grace under pressure. Recruited out of Birmingham by Gene Lorendo, Sullivan never seriously considered playing anywhere besides Auburn. He said the "greatest honor" of his life was playing under Jordan. The two remained close until Jordan's death.

Terry Beasley was the best of the many fine athletes who were on the receiving end of Pat Sullivan's passes. Beasley was recruited hard by Alabama, but finally decided that he, like Jordan, relished the role of the underdog and wanted to help Auburn rebuild as a Southern football power. He did that and more as part of an All-American career in which he used speed, strength, and tremendous pass-catching innovation to set a number of SEC records that still stand.

Jordan often spoke of "oft-forgotten" heroes like James Owens (above right), Auburn's first black football player, and Gardner Jett, whose steady kicking gave Jordan his sweetest victory.

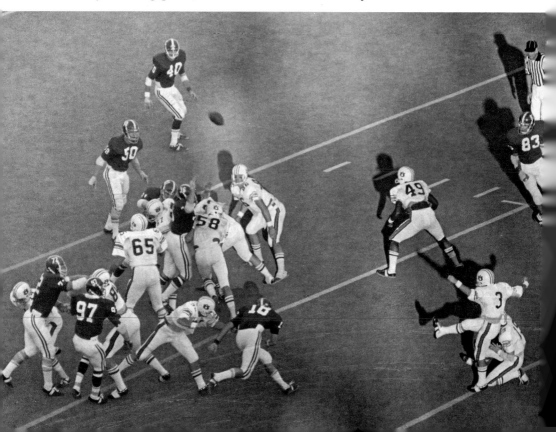

Bryant and Jordan were friends, though they did battle year after year. Below, Jordan leaves the field after his final home game in 1975.

problem with a player or coach he'd call them into the office and he'd do it behind closed doors. And he called me in a couple of times because I stepped on my you-know-what like any prima donna will. He was always trying to be positive. He would congratulate people in public, his whole style was in a positive manner instead of a negative manner. I'll take a guy like Shug Jordan any day."

Jordan, to his death, scratched his head over the probation. "There was fragmented, circumstantial evidence and it was vindictive," he said. "With the courts like they are today, that would probably end up in the Supreme Court...I know it knocked us perhaps out of four big bowls and it cost Auburn a lot of money."

Beard later said, "The more I got into it, the madder I got. I knew it was an injustice. I fought it so hard that the case was widely publicized. Maybe if I'd kept my mouth shut it wouldn't have attracted so much attention."

A day after the SEC decision Jordan sought to get back to business. "As far as Auburn football is concerned, we'll be making every effort to have the same good football team that we have had for the past five years."

But Don Fuell's case was one Auburn people would never forget.

13

"And catch a few terrors in between"
●●

The powers-that-be of the SEC had snatched away Don Fuell, and the reason still wasn't clear to Jordan, his staff or Fuell's teammates. The Fuell story concluded ten days before the opening game of the 1958 season. Fuell, saying the SEC had convicted him without a hearing, sought a court decision to overturn the SEC ruling that kicked him off the conference playing grounds. But Circuit Judge J. Russell McElroy of Birmingham said his court had no such jurisdiction, regardless of the merits of the case.

Five days before the opening game, Jordan said, "Frankly, since our (second) probation...our team, the school and the alumni appear to be closer and stronger than ever before."

If the formula for a second consecutive national title called for revenge, then Jordan welcomed the ingredient. But he knew it would take more. Auburn, winner of fourteen games in a row, led off everybody's hit list. While the 1957 title chase had in fact caught the players by surprise at mid-season, Jordan felt his 1958 team had to approach the season unwilling to settle for anything less. The staff drove this message into the players' heads during the tough pre-season workouts.

"All anybody talked about that fall was winning the national championship," said Ed Dyas, who was a 195-pound sophomore fullback in 1958. "The coaches told us, 'You've got to make the sacrifice.'"

Auburn had lost five starters from the 1957 team — end Phillips, tackle Preston, guard Baker, halfback Hoppe and fullback Atkins. But the 1957 squad had tremendous depth, having fielded two excellent units. The new first teamers for 1958 were familiar names — tackle Jeffrey, guard LaRussa, end Simmons, halfback Rawson and fullback Robbs. They joined returning starters Wilson at end, Smith at guard, Burkett at center, Wester at tackle, Lorino at halfback and Nix at quarterback. The second team also fielded great talent, though some of it was young. The second group included sophomores Dyas and tackle Ken Rice, both future All-Americans.

Auburn had recruited Dyas heavily out of Mobile since his junior season at McGill High School, which was Dooley's prep alma mater. Jordan visited Dyas on a construction job as the youngster assisted his dad. "He acted like he was going to pick up a hammer and a saw and start working with us," Dyas said of Jordan. "But we couldn't let him do that." Dyas picked Auburn over Alabama, Georgia, Tulane and Notre Dame.

Rice had played for Bainbridge High School in southwest Georgia. As a high school freshman Rice weighed 160 pounds and stood 5-6. When he graduated from Bainbridge he was 265 pounds and had grown eight inches to 6-2. He lettered in four sports. He was not only the biggest player on his football squad, he was also the fastest. He played fullback and linebacker his last two seasons in high school after playing on the line his sophomore year. Georgia Tech, Alabama, Florida State and Auburn all wanted him, but Auburn had the inside track.

Sam Williams was the backfield coach at Rice's high school. Williams had played high school ball for Auburn freshman coach McGowen when McGowen coached Eufaula High School. Williams told McGowen to come and have a look at the big boy. McGowen didn't go to watch Rice play football, but rather basketball. "He could stand flat-footed and dunk the ball," McGowen said. "I knew he had something going for him."

Rice, impressed by Jordan, McGowen and the blossoming program, chose Auburn. Jordan offered Rice the option of playing fullback or on the line.

"Where you want me to play is where I'll play," Rice said.

"I would like you to play tackle, but you can play fullback if you would like to try," Jordan said.

"I'll play tackle," Rice replied.

The brief exchange resulted in major consequences as Rice became the best tackle in America and the most sought-after lineman by the pros.

Twice during his freshman season Rice quit the team and went home. McGowen went and brought him back. "Coach McGowen came down and explained to me what I was passing up," Rice said. "The first time wasn't too hard. The second time was a little more difficult, but he impressed upon me the education I was giving up that none of my family had been able to afford or take advantage of."

"He was a home boy," McGowen said. "I'd look up and he was gone. I'd call Sam (Williams) and Sam would say 'Yeah, he's here, come on.'"

Jordan instructed the coaching staff to knock fifteen pounds off of Rice's frame. He became even quicker. He was the fastest lineman at Auburn. The freshman team's weekly scrimmages against the 1957 national champs honed Rice's skills. He learned fundamentals under line coach Connally. He learned toughness in the spring and fall drills prior to the 1958 season. Rice recalled that line coach Senn ran a practice drill called "bull-in-the-ring." All of the linemen stood around one man in the middle and Senn called out names and numbers to attack the middle man.

"We'll quit when I see blood," was Senn's favorite expression.

Something else pushed Jordan in early fall to perfect his 1958 team. The Tennessee opener would be on national television. It had been arranged prior to the NCAA penalty and the NCAA let it stand. Because of the first probation's no-television penalty, only those people sitting in the stadium had witnessed Auburn's climb to the top in 1957. Jordan wanted the country to see why Auburn had won the national title, why six SEC teams failed to score on Auburn, why Auburn had won fourteen games in a row.

On September 27, fans nationwide came to respect Shug Jordan and his football team. Auburn, ranked number-three behind Ohio State and Oklahoma going into the game, put on one of the greatest defensive shows in college football history. Auburn held Tennessee to minus-thirty yards total offense and no first downs. Auburn beat the Vols 13-0 before forty-thousand fans at Legion Field.

Jordan and Herring had seemingly anticipated every play Tennessee ran. They noticed that when Tennessee's tailback cheated out and over a step in the single wing he received the snap and ran around the short side. Herring told tackle Wester to charge straight up field whenever he saw the tailback line up in that manner.

"They ran it five times and Cleve hit the tailback for a five-yard loss every time," Herring said.

Line coach Senn's "tackle shuffle" had worn down the Vols. Senn rotated pairs of tackles throughout the game, including starters Wester and Jeffrey and backups Rice, Teddy Foret and Leon Myers.

Following the game, Herring turned a few heads when he said the defense had a ways to go. "We're not as good on defense as we were last year," he said. "We made a lot of mistakes that we've got to iron out."

Rawson and Lorino scored the Auburn touchdowns, both coming in the second half. Nix executed eye-opening fakes and pitches during the two touchdown drives. Fullback Robbs strained a ligament but sophomore Dyas carried the load impressively in his varsity debut.

Auburn beat Chattanooga and knocked off Kentucky, 8-0, in Lexington to stretch its winning streak to seventeen games and climb to number-two in the nation. But the following week Bobby Dodd's Georgia Tech, a six-point underdog, tied Auburn 7-7 at Grant Field. Nearly 45,000 fans witnessed the end of the winning streak. Auburn led 7-0 at half, having driven sixty-one yards primarily on the running of fullback Dyas, who was now starting in place of the injured Robbs. Dyas scored from the two and Nix kicked the extra point. Auburn dominated possession of the ball in the first two quarters, running forty-three plays to Tech's nineteen, but Tech kept punting itself out of trouble.

Late in the third quarter Tech's Fred Braselton brought the Yellow Jackets back. He intercepted a pass and ran it to the Auburn thirty-six. Brasleton then completed several passes, including one that was deflected by linebacker Dyas but which Tech's Jack Rudolph caught at the two as he fell to the ground. Braselton carried for one yard and then ran it again for the touchdown. It was the first rushing touchdown recorded against Auburn since the Alabama game in 1956. The extra point tied it, 7-7, which is how the game ended. Auburn outgained Tech 262 yards to 129, and held Tech to only fifty-eight yards rushing. Jordan didn't lament over the outcome. "We played a fine football game," he said.

Auburn fell to fifth but rebounded to fourth after beating Maryland, 20-7. The Tigers then nipped Florida, 6-5, in Gainesville. Auburn scored on a 63-yard drive in the second half with Nix completing three passes. At the tail end of the drive Jordan sent lanky junior quarterback Richard Wood into the game. Wood immediately tossed a fourteen-yard completion to Leo Sexton to the Gator ten, and followed with a scoring strike to Joe Leichtman.

A Florida field goal cut the lead to 6-3, and then Florida drove fifty-seven yards on two passes and threatened to go ahead. The second completion covered forty-two yards with Wood making the tackle on the two-yard line. On the ensuing play, guard Smith, on his way to the Outland Trophy, forced a fumble and Jimmy Pettus recovered. Two penalties forced Auburn back near its goal line and Jordan instructed quarterback Kern to take a safety. Auburn held on to the 6-5 margin.

Auburn drubbed Mississippi State, 33-14, Georgia, 21-6, and Wake Forest, 21-7, to improve its record to 8-0-1. Auburn went into the Alabama game ranked second in the nation behind fellow conference powerhouse LSU, led by All-American back Billy Cannon.

Auburn had defeated Alabama four games in a row by the combined score of 128-7. But Bear Bryant was the new kid in town and had driven the Tide to a 5-3-1 record, more wins than the three previous years combined under Whitworth. Auburn's vaunted defense had allowed just fifty-four points going into the game, but

Alabama had only given up sixty-one. Auburn scored in the second quarter and early in the final period to lead, 14-0. But Alabama put a scare into the Tigers and cut the lead to 14-8 with a long drive in the final period. Alabama got the ball back on its own twenty-seven with 3:24 left and drove the ball again. The Tide just missed a score when Tiger defensive back Lorino knocked a long pass out of the hands of an Alabama receiver on the goal line. Alabama's drive stalled at the Auburn twenty-seven.

The 1958 Alabama game sent a clear message to Jordan and Auburn: no more cakewalks over the Tide. The emphasis of that message only intensified over the following decades.

Auburn finished the season 9-0-1 and ranked fourth in the nation. LSU, coached by Paul Dietzel, won the national championship and conference title with a 10-0 regular season mark and beat Clemson 7-0 in the Sugar Bowl. The LSU staff had visited Auburn's spring practice prior to the season, just as Auburn had called on national title holder Oklahoma in the spring prior to Auburn's 1957 championship season.

Once again Jordan and Herring's defense led the nation in fewest total yards allowed per game at 157.5 (twenty-four yards more than in 1957) and in fewest yards rushing per game at 79.6 (twelve yards more than the previous year). The defense gave up sixty-two points on the season compared to twenty-eight in 1957.

The offense, for the second time in three years, led the conference in total offense with 319 yards per game. Quarterback Nix led the conference in individual total offense with 965 yards (682 passing and 283 rushing). He completed forty-nine of ninety-eight passes as Auburn opened up its offense somewhat, at times running out of the Wing T formation, which featured a wingback and a split end. Auburn never lost a game with Nix at quarterback.

Zeke Smith made All-American at guard as a junior and won the Outland Trophy, which honored the nation's best interior lineman.

Herring recalled that Smith's ability often shunned conventional technique. Jordan told Herring several times during the season that Smith was "running around the block" during his rush. But

Smith kept making tackles in the backfield so Jordan dropped the subject. "If the guy comes to block you on your left shoulder, you're supposed to fight through that way," Herring said. "Hell, ole Zeke was fast enough he'd go inside and catch the guy back of the line of scrimmage."

Junior center Burkett also made All-American. Burkett, Smith, tackle Wester and end Wilson made first team All-SEC.

It had been another remarkable year for Jordan and Auburn, though it would never be quite this good statistically for Jordan again. In the previous five years his teams had compiled a 49-11-3 record. They had gone twenty-four games without losing. Herring commented, "It was a great time with great players, and great men, too."

Jordan's popularity soared throughout the state and region. In eight years he had become Auburn's greatest football coach ever. Adults and kids encircled him on the field long after each game vying for an autograph. Had his two undefeated teams competed in more than the one game on national television during the 1957 and 1958 regular seasons, and played before millions on television in two major bowl games, Jordan's national stature would have grown even more. Certainly in the coaching community, following the 1958 season, the Jordan name was on par with a Neyland or a Wilkinson or Army's Red Blaik. And Jordan was still two years shy of his fiftieth birthday.

But then his teams stumbled. The 1959 and 1960 teams, still on NCAA probation, produced 7-3 and 8-2 records, respectively. The 1961 and 1962 teams were eligible for bowls but their respective 6-4 and 6-3-1 marks didn't attract any invitations. Suddenly cross-state rival Alabama not only surpassed Auburn as the state's supreme team, but became a national power. The Associated Press ranked Bryant's Tide number ten in 1959, number nine in 1960, number one in 1961 and number five in 1962. Auburn's only ranking during those four years came in 1960, at number thirteen. But what really cut to the bone was that Alabama shut out Auburn four years in a row, and beat Auburn by embarrassing 34-0 and 38-0 tallies in 1961 and 1962.

When Auburn was climbing to the top, its chief big-game rivals had been Georgia Tech, Tennessee and Georgia. Alabama had always been an important game because of the in-state excitement, but Alabama's program had been down. Now, with Bryant's emergence and the Tide's rise, coming on top of back-to-back Auburn probations that many Auburn people suspected Alabama promoted, Auburn football teams toiled each season with an anxious eye toward the year's finale.

Several factors came to a head to cause the turnaround. The main reason, of course, was Bryant himself. He brought to Alabama a reputation as a program builder and a win-at-any-cost coach. His first team, Maryland, had a 6-2-1 record in his only season there. He coached Kentucky to a 60-23-5 record in eight years, including a conference championship in 1950. He turned around Texas A&M's program in two years and during his four years there produced a 25-14-2 mark, including a number-five national ranking in 1956 with a 9-0-1 record. Bryant's success at Texas A&M hadn't come without cost. The NCAA put his program on probation in 1955 and 1956. Bryant admitted he had told the Aggie alumni to match the competition during the recruiting season.

Also, Bryant understood the Alabama football tradition. He was part of it. He had played end on the 1934 national championship team that beat Stanford in the Rose Bowl. Alabama's favorite son had returned home with a ten-year contract in one hand and a suitcase of bonus money in the other. Bryant also assumed the title of athletic director in addition to head coach, which didn't go unnoticed by Jordan.

Bryant didn't disappoint his zealous followers. He turned Alabama into a powerhouse almost overnight. Recruiting had a lot to do with it. Bryant signed his contract in early December, 1957. The recruiting season was already in full swing, but Bryant still landed some great prospects. That class, which included quarterback Pat Trammell, won the national title in 1961.

Jordan, in addition to some good luck with unheralded prospects such as Zeke Smith and Jackie Burkett, had been signing mostly prospects he knew were all-conference material, but those numbers nosedived when Bryant entered the picture.

Accusations flew as the state became a recruiting battleground. Auburn people accused Bryant of operating with a recruiting slush fund arranged and channeled by Tide alumni. Jordan recognized Bryant's recruiting prowess, and asked freshman coach McGowen to give up his coaching duties and become a full-time recruiter. McGowen obliged and maintained the position for eight years, until he left the staff in 1965.

McGowen said Bryant was an excellent recruiter, especially in that "he knew how to talk to a prospect's parents, to a prospect's girl friend and to the prospect himself, which pretty much covered it." McGowen also said, "Bryant knew more about cheating than anybody in the business. Whether he cheated or not, I don't know. But if anybody was cheating, he knew how to do it."

McGowen added, however, that "a lot less cheating went on than was talked about. I was in that stuff seventeen years and I never offered a recruit anything to change his mind to go to Auburn. I'm sure some people from Auburn did some things. But I didn't see how you could control and discipline people that you had broken the law for to come over to your side. Alabama did a few things we didn't do. It wasn't that big of a deal. They did it on a regular scholarship basis. It didn't fit the SEC rules and regulations, but they did it."

Bryant's arrival also coincided with Auburn's probation. That Auburn was ineligible for several bowl games probably hurt recruiting less than the nasty stigma of not playing by the rules, deserved or not, which opposing recruiters always mentioned to parents. Auburn signed the strong freshman class of 1957 when it thought it was coming off probation. The NCAA hammer came down again in spring 1958, which meant that most of the freshman class of 1958 had already signed. Auburn had to tell recruits following the 1958 season that they would be ineligible to play in a bowl game until 1961.

Jordan said the probations "undoubtedly cost some athletes." Bradberry said the probations "really hurt recruiting." McGowen said Auburn "adjusted pretty well, but Bryant's reputation made an awful lot of difference."

If the coming of Bryant and Auburn's probations comprised two parts of the mix in Auburn's noticeable decline, the third part was simply the time-honored axiom that all football programs that go up must come down.

"We couldn't overcome the problems you have when you've gone twenty-four straight games without getting beat," Bradberry said. "We had some good football players in 1959, but we really were not ready for the season like we were when we were hungry. It really happens to you in some degree. You don't know it's happening, but it does."

Fullback Dyas, beginning his junior year, recalled that in the fall preseason practice the coaching staff didn't work the entire squad, particularly the seniors, as hard as in the previous two seasons. This slight "letting up," along with a thinner depth chart, would bring Auburn back down to earth in 1959.

The season would be remembered for three heartbreaking losses. But going into the opening game against Tennessee in Knoxville, Jordan for one felt he had the horses to beat anybody. Indeed four of the starters — Smith, Burkett, Rice and Dyas — had already made All-American or would in the next two years. Wood had accumulated experience at quarterback during the previous season. Foret was an experienced tackle. Rawson was a veteran halfback. The Associated Press ranked Auburn number three going into the opening game.

"We had the best football team, I thought, in the history of Auburn," Jordan said. "The Saturday before we played Tennessee, at our dress rehearsal as we always called it, I told my coaches this is the best Auburn team we've had. And I'll be damned if we didn't go to Knoxville and play a sorry Tennessee team. Bowden Wyatt had scrimmaged them the day before, and they were the most bedraggled looking folks I've ever seen. But they beat us three to nothing and broke our long streak."

"Tennessee didn't have a team worth a toot," Dyas said. "We

had talent. But we went up to Tennessee, it was ninety degrees and in the first quarter it was over. We hadn't worked hard enough during preseason."

Dyas rushed for seventy yards, most of it on his own. Auburn averaged twenty pounds more per man than Tennessee, but the Vols had been eyeing this encounter ever since the previous season's embarrassment on national television. Before forty-thousand at Shields-Watkins Field, Tennessee won 3-0 kicking a 25-yard field goal in the third quarter. Billy Majors, the younger brother of Johnny Majors, rushed for eighty-seven yards. Auburn never moved the ball inside the Tennessee twenty. Tennessee intercepted four Auburn passes.

"After that game, we came back and you talk about brutal," Dyas said. "The coaches beat the hell out of us."

Auburn easily won its next two over Hardin-Simmons and Kentucky, and then traveled to Grant Field in Atlanta to play fourth-ranked Georgia Tech. Auburn won in typical low-scoring fashion, 7-6. The Tigers drove seventy-one yards in the third quarter, mostly behind the blocking of guard Smith. Sophomore quarterback Bobby Hunt scored on a six-yard run. A Dyas extra point was the difference. Tech missed a late 28-yard field goal.

Following the contest, Jordan praised the play of Zeke Smith, Jackie Burkett and Ken Rice. "All three played to perfection...great games by three boys who played their hearts out," Jordan said.

Sports Illustrated recognized Rice as its Lineman of the Week.

Auburn appeared to be starting another winning streak as it beat Miami, Florida and Mississippi State to go 6-1 on the season. Going back to the latter half of the 1956 season, Jordan's Tigers had won a staggering thirty of its last thirty-one games. But Auburn lost its next game, 14-13, to Georgia in new Sanford Stadium in Athens. At the end of his coaching career, sixteen years later, Jordan reflected, "What you remember as you look back is hard to put in a sentence. You remember those tough games you lost. They keep popping up and coming back and sort of haunt you. Like the loss to Georgia in 1959."

One of Jordan's mentors, Wally Butts, was in his next-to-final season as head coach of Georgia. His Bulldogs had lost only to South Carolina and were undefeated in conference play with Auburn and Georgia Tech left on the schedule. Auburn had only the one loss to Tennessee, which of course was a conference game, with Alabama coming up after Georgia. If Auburn had beaten Georgia and Alabama it would have at least tied Georgia for the conference title with a 6-1 league mark.

Sanford Stadium packed in 54,000 as Auburn jumped ahead 6-0 on two Dyas field goals of forty and forty-three yards. Georgia took the lead 7-6 late in the third quarter on quarterback Charley Britt's 39-yard punt return for a touchdown. But with 7:30 left in the game, and Georgia punting, Georgia blockers backed into the punt. Auburn recovered the ball on the Georgia one-yard line. Quarterback Bryant Harvard scored the touchdown and Dyas's PAT made it 13-7 Auburn.

Auburn's defense held and Auburn regained possession on its own thirty-nine. But Georgia end Bill Herron tackled the Auburn quarterback and caused a fumble. Junior All-American guard Pat Dye recovered on the thirty-four with 3:35 left. Junior Fran Tarkenton entered the game at quarterback for Georgia and quickly completed a pass to Fred Brown for a first down at the Auburn nineteen. Tarkenton then connected with Don Soberdash for nine yards to the ten-yard line. On second and one, Tarkenton threw incomplete, and on third and one completed the pass but Auburn dropped the receiver for a three-yard loss back at the thirteen. With time nearly gone, Tarkenton drew up the final play in the dirt in the huddle. He told left end Herron to block to a count of one-thousand-and-four and then run for the left corner of the end zone. Tarkenton took the snap, rolled right, faked a pass down the middle and then saw Herron a good three steps clear of the Auburn defender. Tarkenton threw perfectly and Herron caught the ball over his left shoulder on the goal line for the score. The extra point gave Georgia the 14-13 win. Georgia beat Tech the following week to win the SEC title, beat Missouri in the Orange Bowl 14-0 and finished fifth in the nation.

After the game, Jordan, with his trademark "good sport" demeanor, said, "If we had to lose, I am glad it was Wallace Butts who beat us." Inside, the loss was killing Jordan. The season represented Butts's last hurrah and in four years he would be embroiled in the famous Butts-Bryant betting scandal, from which both men were exonerated.

A bowl game was on the line for Alabama when it tangled with Auburn to close the season. The Tide played like it, doubling Auburn in yardage, 260-131, and shutting out the Tigers, 10-0. Alabama players carried Bryant to midfield to meet Jordan after the final horn. The *Montgomery Advertiser* reported, "After a short meeting in the center of the field of confusion, Jordan was seen wiping a tear from his cheek."

Jordan knew he had lost the momentum.

Auburn continued to put up All-American players. Senior Zeke Smith repeated as All-American and tackle Rice made All-American as a junior. Dyas made second team All-SEC.

While the football season didn't meet great expectations, the football program, under the guidance of Jordan and athletic director Beard, continued to flourish. Beard, who had worked hard to lure Tennessee back on the schedule in 1956, negotiated a home-and-home deal with Georgia, with Auburn hosting for the first time in 1960. Until the 1959 game in Athens, the two teams had played in Columbus for the past thirty years.

Though Bobby Dodd was determined that his Georgia Tech teams would never play Auburn outside of Atlanta, Auburn's football fortunes demanded that Dodd give in. Beard and Jordan insisted that Tech play Auburn every other year in Birmingham. Tech played Auburn in Birmingham in 1960, which was the first time the two teams had not played in Atlanta since 1904.

And, despite missing out on a lot of money from the two NCAA probations, Auburn gathered the funding to enclose the south end zone of Cliff Hare Stadium and added ten-thousand seats, increasing capacity to 44,500.

After announcing his retirement in the spring of 1975, Jordan said, "My only disappointment is that I haven't brought more SEC titles to the school. We've had so many opportunities it is hard to count. But when you start off with Tennessee every year, wind up with Alabama, and catch a few terrors in between, it just isn't a piece of cake."

Jordan may have been thinking back to the 1960 season when he made that comment. Auburn lost its opener to Tennessee in Birmingham, 10-3, and lost its closing game to Alabama, also in Birmingham, 3-0. In between Auburn reeled off eight straight wins, finished 8-2 and ranked number thirteen in the nation.

Dyas set an NCAA record by converting thirteen field goals (in eighteen attempts). Jordan had never considered the field goal to be a major offensive threat, but in 1959 the NCAA had widened the uprights five feet to 23 ft., 4 in. Dyas, who had kicked extra points in high school, had kicked four field goals in 1959.

Most of Dyas's field goals set up or delivered Tiger victories in 1960. He kicked a late 28-yard field goal to beat Kentucky, 10-7. His 37-yard boot in the second quarter was the difference in Auburn's 9-7 win over Georgia Tech in Birmingham. He kicked two in Auburn's 20-7 victory over Miami. His 31-yarder beat Florida 10-7. He broke the NCAA record with his eighth and ninth field goals of the season against Mississippi State, and also scored two touchdowns in Auburn's 27-12 win. He saved his best for Georgia, booting three goals in a 9-7 win at Auburn before the largest crowd (46,000) to ever witness a football game in the state. His final boot, a 25-yarder, came with less than a minute remaining in the game. Dyas also rushed for 110 yards that day.

But during the following week's win over Florida State, Dyas got knocked out of bounds, hit the bench and broke his helmet and his upper jaw bone, which required surgery. He could kick, but Jordan didn't allow him to play against Alabama, a major factor in Auburn's 3-0 loss. Dyas made All-American and finished fourth in the Heisman Trophy voting, at that time the closest an Auburn player had ever come. Baltimore of the NFL and San Diego of the AFL drafted Dyas, but he chose to pursue a career in medicine.

Senior tackle Rice made All-American for the second year in a row. Both the Buffalo Bills of the AFL and the St. Louis Cardinals of the NFL selected Rice as their first pick. Rice chose Buffalo and played professional football for seven years.

With his size and swiftness, Rice epitomized the 1950s era of the big Jordan lineman. His talent was best shown in one play against Georgia his senior year. Dyas had just kicked the field goal to put Auburn up 9-7 late in the game. On the ensuing kickoff Rice raced down the field, hurdled one Georgia player, knocked another one over, ran over the blocker in front of the returner and tackled the return man deep in Georgia territory.

In the immediate years ahead, Jordan and Auburn would long for the days when the Ken Rices of the world came to Auburn to play football.

14

"They won't even let you pray up here"
• •

Jordan's football program moved into a period of transition and sputtered for much of the 1960s, particularly after 1963. Certainly Jordan fielded some great players and hard-knocking competitive teams that on any given Saturday could beat anyone. And there were some great wins and upsets during these leaner years. But except for the 1963 team, Auburn lost its status as a national power for most of the decade.

From 1961 through 1968, only the 1963 team won more than six regular season games. Suddenly Auburn seemed to be losing a lot of the close ones. Jordan experienced his second losing season as Auburn's head coach in 1966. His job became a subject of discussion. Critics described his brand of football as old-fashioned and out-of-touch. Four of his original assistants since 1951 — Eaves, Senn, Bradberry and McGowen — had departed the staff for various reasons by 1966. Herring, a member of the staff since 1953, was also out by 1966.

Meanwhile, Bryant's Alabama won national titles in 1961, 1964 and 1965, and dominated the series with Auburn. As Jordan struggled to pull his team out of the mire, his health failed him. In the summer of 1968 doctors diagnosed him with prostate cancer.

But much of that was yet to come as Auburn prepared for the 1963 season. That year would be the last great hurrah for the Jordan coaching staff that, in a few short years, had taken Auburn from the dumps to being the best program in the nation.

The two previous seasons, 1961 and 1962, had provided some fireworks, but Auburn lost seven conference games while compiling 6-4 and 6-3-1 records. The high point of the 1961 season came in the opening game. Auburn beat Tennessee in Knoxville 24-21, rallying from a 21-7 deficit. The season took a nosedive the following week when Kentucky beat Auburn 14-12 in Auburn. Jordan's teams had won thirty straight games in Cliff Hare Stadium, dating back to a loss to Mississippi State in 1952. Auburn also lost to Georgia Tech 7-6 and to Mississippi State 11-10, meaning that Auburn lost three games by a total of four points. Alabama's national championship team beat Auburn 34-0.

Off the field, the highlight of 1961 came before spring practice, on January 31, when a 6-2, 202-pound fullback out of Hollywood, Florida named Tucker Frederickson accepted a scholarship to play football for Auburn. Jordan was at Frederickson's side when the handsome lad signed. Jordan knew he had notched a good one, but Frederickson's performance at Auburn went beyond even Jordan's imagination. Many Auburn fans remember Frederickson as the best all-around football player in Auburn history. Jordan, near the end of his forty-year coaching career, stated, "Tucker was the greatest athlete I ever coached."

Indeed, Frederickson was the last of the two-way stars, excelling as a running back and as a defensive safety. Even in 1964, when separate offensive and defensive teams came into the picture at Auburn, Frederickson continued to play both ways.

Jordan and the Auburn coaching staff never saw Frederickson play in high school. "Back then we were looking for certain things in a kid," said recruiting coach McGowen. "How he handled himself. What his attitude was. We didn't always see a kid play." Had the Auburn staff seen Frederickson play they no doubt would have been impressed. Frederickson scored seventeen touchdowns and rushed for more than one-thousand yards his senior season at South Broward High School.

Auburn, badly in need of talent since Bryant's arrival at Alabama, first heard of Frederickson in a newspaper clipping sent to ends coach Lorendo. The article quoted a prep fullback from Hollywood as saying that if he had his choice he'd go to Auburn. Recruiting coach McGowen made some inquiries and flew down to visit the boy and his family, stopping off first at the father's office. McGowen discovered that the boy's father and uncle were veterinarians. They wanted the boy to study veterinary medicine at Auburn. McGowen visited the boy and his mother at their home and found out that Mrs. Frederickson wanted her son to remain in the state so he would be closer to home.

"He was a good-looking kid." McGowen said. "He didn't say too much." McGowen read the boy's scrapbook and returned to Auburn.

Auburn invited Frederickson to visit the school and a trip was planned early in 1961. Frederickson recalled his initial meeting with Jordan. "It was January and the weather was a little tough. I was supposed to land in Columbus, but ended up landing in Montgomery. It was a Friday night and I got in late. I must have pulled into Auburn with Dick (McGowen) at about eleven o'clock. The athletes were living in Graves Center then and Bobby Hunt was going to take care of me. Coach Jordan was there. He was very much a gentleman, well dressed. After all the introductions Bobby suggested we go out and take a ride around town. I said I needed to change my shirt. I grabbed my suitcase and threw it on the bed. I opened it and there were five bottles of whiskey in it. I looked up and Coach Jordan was looking at me. Bobby started laughing and I said, 'Guys, you won't believe this, but this is not my bag.' Somebody had the same kind of luggage and had taken mine."

Jordan gave the situation a quick once-over and he, too, let go with laughter.

McGowen made a second trip to Hollywood. "My next-door neighbor, Jimmy Greene, was dean of the vet school," McGowen said. "I conned him into flying down there with me. We went to the Fredericksons' house and went out to eat; they talked vet medicine. Tucker's daddy said that vets out of Auburn could jump into the work right away, while vets from other schools required more training. He wanted Auburn real bad."

The University of Florida attempted to pull Frederickson into the Gator camp until minutes before he signed with the Tigers. Auburn's veterinary school was the deciding factor for Frederickson.

"Physically he's the best there's ever been at Auburn," McGowen said. "Tucker was fast, big, strong, smart, everything you dream of."

He was also good looking. Women went crazy over him.

Jordan always held brief Sunday morning workouts to see if any post-game aches required attention and to keep the players from lounging around in bed all day. Every Sunday morning a half-dozen women talked their husbands into bringing them out to meet the dashing football star.

"The rest of the players went in after the workout, but Tucker had to stay out and talk to the husbands and meet their wives," McGowen said. "We'd introduce him. The women just had to see him."

Frederickson found his way into hot water now and then off the gridiron, such as the time he and some teammates drank a few beers and drove a car through some chicken houses.

"It was mostly too-typical jock stuff," Frederickson said. "Whenever I had problems I had to go see Coach Jordan and that was something I didn't enjoy. He was like going to see your father when you did something wrong."

But Jordan also called Frederickson into his office during the course of a season to talk about any problems the team might be having. Frederickson was captain of the 1964 squad.

"Shug was very much an overseeing coach," Frederickson said. "He was the guy who dealt with the problems when they weren't dealt with at the lower levels. Some head coaches have to get into all levels of the game. That's not the way Shug did it."

Frederickson, playing at 220 pounds most of his Auburn career, delighted fans with his blistering blocks and pad-popping tackles. Plenty of enemy helmets flew off following big hits from Frederickson's safety position. "He was probably the most devastating safety man that's been in the SEC, ever," Bradberry said.

He dished it out as a ball carrier as well, playing halfback most of his career until late in his senior season when he played fullback. Frederickson's post-season honors proved his versatility. He won the SEC's Jacobs Trophy as the conference's most outstanding blocker in 1963 and 1964. He made first-team All-SEC in 1964 as a defensive back, while earning All-American honors at fullback.

Auburn's glory season during Frederickson's stay came his junior season in 1963 as the Tigers wound up fifth in the nation and played in the Orange Bowl. On offense, Frederickson spent much of his time blocking for junior quarterback Jimmy Sidle, another big boy at 6-3, 220. Sidle was a star in football and track at Banks High School in Birmingham. Sidle and Frederickson weighed as much as or more than any starting Auburn lineman that year. Etched in the minds of 1963 Auburn fans is the image of Frederickson and Larry Rawson, a 200-pound fullback, rolling out as blockers in front of Sidle who either passed or ran the ball. Bradberry called it the power run/power pass series. Sidle led the conference with 1,712 total yards (1,006 running, 706 passing).

Auburn fans had a good glimpse of Sidle and Frederickson their sophomore year in 1962. Sidle led the team in rushing with 398 yards on 6.5 yards per carry. He platooned at quarterback with Mailon Kent. Sidle completed sixty-two of 136 passes and Kent connected on fifty-nine of 121 attempts. They combined to make Auburn the conference leader in passing yards per game with 151.

Sidle didn't start his first varsity game in 1962, but he played a major role in a 22-21 win over Tennessee in Birmingham. Tennessee led 14-0 but a Woody Woodall field goal cut the lead to 14-3. Jimmy Burson returned a punt seventy-four yards for a touchdown to make it 14-9. Auburn took the lead 15-14 when Sidle ran for fifty-two yards and then passed for a six-yard touchdown to end Howard Simpson. Tennessee went back ahead 21-15 but Auburn drove fifty-seven yards with Larry Laster scoring from the one. Woodall's extra point, moved back fifteen yards because of a penalty, proved the final and decisive point. Sidle completed eleven of twenty-one passes for 118 yards.

Auburn won its first five games in 1962, but only one of its final five and finished 6-3-1.

Forecasters expected Jordan to field a competitive team in 1963, but few of the experts predicted Auburn to be a national power. The Tigers carried the element of surprise going into the season and took advantage of it. Sidle gained control of the quarterback position when Kent, a fifth-year senior, sustained a knee injury prior to the opening game. George Rose, a wingback, joined Sidle, Frederickson and Rawson in the backfield. Other starters included left end Simpson (215 pounds); right end Bucky Waid (195); left tackle Jack Thornton (200); right tackle Bobby Walton (215); left guard Steve Osburne (200); right guard Bill Van Dyke (200); and center Mike Alford (210).

Auburn won its opener over Houston, 21-14, then traveled to Knoxville to play Tennessee. For the third year in a row, and the second time in Knoxville, Auburn spotted Tennessee a substantial lead, this time twelve points, before rallying to win 23-19. Jordan gained tremendous satisfaction in beating the Vols in this manner. The close encounters stimulated the series and for many years it remained the first big game of the season for both teams, often with conference title ramifications.

In 1979, several years out of coaching, Jordan reflected on the rivalry as another Auburn team prepared to invade Knoxville.

"You know the old predictions by the coaches and press back there in the mid-'30s that Auburn and Tennessee would never be a drawing card, well all of a sudden we are right here on the threshold of 85,000 people that are coming from those caves and mountains and glens and river bottoms and from Auburn and all over the states of Alabama and Georgia, and they're concentrating on Knoxville, Tennessee to sit there and watch this classic. And that's what it's become — a classic.

"Of course we added fuel to the flame with some of our comments through the years. We kept reminding our football players that Tennessee really looked down their nose at us. They didn't even want to play us. Then I always had some comment to make. They have that blue tick hound, Smokey, and Smokey would come out there with his little orange blanket on and the cheerleaders would say, 'Smokey, there's ole Shug.' And Smokey would look at me and growwwwl. Then the Tennessee walking horse would come trotting around and nearly run over you.

"And you know the Auburn side of the field is the side Tennessee dresses on. All during my twenty-five years we always knelt down in a huddle and we'd say the Lord's Prayer. I thought it was a representative prayer, regardless of whether you were Catholic, Jewish, Protestant or what have you. We'd be right in the middle of the Lord's Prayer and here'd come the Vols running right out the chute and running right through our huddle, which prompted me to say, 'Hell, they won't even let you pray up here.'

"Of course there for a while with Sidle and Frederickson we'd spot Tennessee two touchdowns. People would say, 'Well ole Auburn's down two touchdowns but it's about time they started coming back. And most of the time we would."

Sidle and fleet-footed halfback Rose starred in the 1963 comeback before 35,000 rain-drenched fans in newly-named Neyland Stadium.

Auburn cut a 12-0 deficit to 12-9 at half on a safety and a Sidle-to-Rose touchdown pass of eight yards. Tennessee stretched the score to 19-9 late in the third quarter, but Auburn drove seventy-seven yards and scored with thirteen minutes remaining in the game. The touchdown came on another Sidle-to-Rose pass of eight yards. Sidle got the ball away with Tennessee's All-American guard, Steve DeLong, all over him. The score cut the lead to 19-16.

The Tigers began the winning drive on the Tennessee forty-three with six minutes left. Sidle carried two times down to the twenty-eight. A penalty moved it back five yards. Sidle then connected with Simpson for twelve yards and Frederickson ran for three yards and a first down at the eighteen. After an incomplete pass, Sidle ran to the two. A penalty on Tennessee pushed the ball to the one. Sidle scored from there to give Auburn a 23-19 lead with just under four minutes left. The defense, paced by Frederickson, held the Vols scoreless the rest of the way. On the day Sidle rushed for ninety-eight yards and threw for eighty-five yards on eight completions.

"Coach Jordan was always a methodical type," said Rose, who coached for Jordan from 1972-1975. "His thing was if you knocked 'em off the line and didn't make mental mistakes, you had a good chance of winning the football game. And it worked.

"The thing that stands out about the Tennessee game was that they still ran the single wing. It looked like they were pulling everybody on the offensive line. They were trying to drive the ball down our throats and we were trying to drive the ball down theirs. It really was three yards and a cloud of dust."

Sidle and Frederickson each scored a touchdown in a tight 14-13 win over Kentucky. After beating Chattanooga easily, Auburn whipped Georgia Tech in Atlanta, 29-21. Sidle ran for a touchdown and passed to Larry Rawson for another score. Frederickson scored on a 25-yard run.

Auburn shut out Florida 19-0 to go 6-0 on the season. But the next week Mississippi State beat Auburn 13-10 in Jackson. The Bulldogs, coached by future Jordan defensive coordinator Paul Davis, won it on a 36-yard field goal by Justin Canale with twenty-two seconds remaining. Auburn had led at half, 10-3, with Sidle running forty-seven yards for a touchdown and Woodall kicking a 30-yard field goal. Prior to Woodall's field goal, Sidle had passed to Simpson for forty-seven yards to the State thirteen-yard line. Malfunctioning scoreboard lights made it look like only six seconds remained in the half, so Jordan sent Woodall in to kick for the three points. There were really forty-six seconds remaining and Auburn could have gotten off one or two plays and possibly scored a touchdown, which might have been enough for the Tigers to win the game. Jordan shrugged off the mistake by saying Auburn might have fumbled or thrown an interception and not even gotten the three points. Jordan showed little disappointment over the loss, stating after the game, "I'm just as proud of this Auburn team as I have been on other days when we won." Sophomore Bill Cody played a great game at linebacker for Auburn.

The Tigers rebounded with wins over Georgia and Florida State, and came into the final game of the season with an 8-1 record, a number-nine national ranking and an unofficial bid to the Orange Bowl, whose officials said the bid was Auburn's unless the Tigers embarrassed themselves against Alabama. The Tide came into the contest with a 7-1 record, ranked sixth and had secured a similar agreement with the Sugar Bowl.

Legion Field held 55,000 fans on an extremely windy day as Auburn won, 10-8, and broke a four-game losing streak to the Tide.

Jack Thornton, who was a starting sophomore tackle for Auburn, recalled, "The papers had come out during the week and said Coach Bryant had found a weakness in Auburn's defense, basically referring to me. I was the only sophomore. The first three plays of the game were run straight at me. I never will forget Coach Bryant on his show Sunday night apologizing to me."

Bryant apologized because Thornton, with the support of his mates on defense, greeted the Tide running backs with a stiff message and proceeded to rough up junior quarterback Joe Namath. Defensive coach Herring turned the line loose on Namath while defensive back Rose and safety Frederickson patrolled the secondary.

"I stayed in front of Namath's face about all day," Thornton said. "Our line had kind of a duel going that afternoon, with each side trying to get to Namath first." Thornton was so pumped up that the sophomore once nailed Namath late and drew a flag. Thornton, Frederickson and end Simpson all had big games on defense.

But the story of the game was the play of backup quarterback Mailon Kent. The fifth-year senior had played very little during the season due to a knee injury. Strained ligaments forced Kent to wear a cast for several days. He required several more weeks to reach playing speed, by which time Sidle was leading the nation in rushing and Auburn was undefeated. Kent remained on the bench.

Three weeks prior to the Alabama game, Jordan had all but prophesied Kent's heroism. "Kent has always been a natural leader at Auburn," Jordan said. "When he was a freshman it was obvious he had the poise and leadership qualities to be a fine quarterback. He seems to be over the injury and it's certainly comforting to know Mailon is on our side when we need him."

Jordan needed Kent and his poise following Auburn's second play of the game. Sidle was hit hard and forced to leave the game. "Coach Bradberry wanted to call time and let Sidle catch his breath," Kent said. "But Coach Jordan didn't want to call time out so he grabbed me and sent me in."

On third and nine at the Alabama forty-four, Kent sparked Auburn with a twelve-yard completion to Bucky Waid for a first down at the thirty-two. Frederickson carried for seven yards and Rawson ran for three and a first down. Frederickson rushed for four more, Kent gained two and Frederickson ran for two to the fourteen. On fourth and two Jordan opted to kick the field goal. Auburn hadn't scored on Alabama in four games and Jordan recognized a psychological lift when he saw one. Woodall converted from thirty-two yards and Auburn led, 3-0.

Alabama threatened late in the half, but Auburn defensive end Simpson stripped the ball loose from Namath as he prepared to pitch out and Simpson recovered on the Auburn seven to kill the threat.

Alabama committed another major turnover in the third quarter when its punt returner picked up and dropped a dribbling punt. Simpson again recovered, this time at the Alabama seven-yard line. Fullback Rawson lost a yard on first and goal. Then Sidle threw incomplete. Jordan and Bradberry sent Kent into the game with a play.

"We had put that play in (for the Alabama game)," Kent said. "We looked at film and saw that the defense they were in really put them in a strain. It was a play that put pressure on the end. Tucker would flare around and circle into the end zone. If the end came up to take me I would throw it and if he didn't I would run the ball."

Kent rolled right and the defensive end committed toward him. Kent connected with Frederickson for an eight-yard touchdown pass. The extra point made it 10-0 with five minutes left in the third quarter. Alabama's Benny Nelson ran eighty yards for a touchdown late in the third quarter, and Namath's run for the two-point conversion made it 10-8. But Auburn's defense didn't lapse. Namath completed only four of seventeen passes for forty-three yards.

Following the game Jordan showed great emotion as he rode his players' shoulders to midfield to meet Bryant. The Alabama coach hesitated, stepped back and saluted up at Jordan.

Jordan gave Kent the game ball and praised Simpson for playing the best game of his career. Jon Kilgore's ten punts had maintained field position for Auburn.

The Orange Bowl was Auburn's first bowl appearance since the 1955 season because of the two probations. It represented Jordan's first major bowl game as a head coach.

Auburn fell to Nebraska 13-7 as the Cornhuskers jumped out early and held on. Quarterback Dennis Claridge scored on Nebraska's second play of the game on a 68-yard trap play off tackle. Two Auburn defensive backs collided as they were about to nail Claridge just past the line of scrimmage. Nebraska led 13-0 at half. Auburn cut the lead to 13-7 on a thirteen-yard touchdown run by Sidle. Auburn threatened deep in Nebraska territory late in the game, but turned the ball over on downs at the eleven-yard line when a fourth and four pass fell incomplete.

Auburn finished the season ranked fifth in the nation behind number one Texas, Navy, Illinois and Pittsburgh. Alabama was eighth. Ole Miss won the conference title with a 5-0-1 mark, and finished seventh in the country. Sidle made All-American and finished seventh in the Heisman Trophy vote. Navy quarterback Roger Staubach won the prestigious award. The *Nashville Banner* named Sidle the SEC's Most Valuable Player. Sidle made first-team All-SEC. Frederickson and Simpson made second team. Fullback Rawson made third team as did linebacker Cody and guard Van Dyke.

With Sidle, Frederickson, Thornton, Cody and Kilgore among twenty-eight lettermen returning for the 1964 season, Jordan dared to think about a second national title. Instead he began the three most frustrating years of his head coaching career at Auburn.

15

"We were going down hill"

Jordan was jolted late in 1963 when his ends coach and head scout, Joel Eaves, accepted the position of athletic director at the University of Georgia. Eaves was a mainstay from Jordan's original staff and had played a key part in rebuilding the football program. Going back much farther, Jordan had recruited Eaves out of high school and had coached him as a freshman in 1933. The two men had been friends for thirty years.

Eaves, also head coach of the Auburn basketball team, had grown dissatisfied with his situation at Auburn. Jordan preferred that Eaves commit to football. But Eaves's first love was basketball. He had established himself as a great roundball coach, having guided Auburn in 1960 to the school's only conference championship. His "Auburn shuffle" offense was known nationwide. In fourteen seasons he had won 214 games and lost just ninety-nine for an impressive .684 winning percentage.

Another factor in Eaves's decision to step off the playing field and into administration may have been a heart attack he suffered during the 1962-1963 basketball season.

A month later Eaves hired Auburn freshman coach Vince Dooley as head football coach of the Bulldogs. Dooley had assisted Eaves with football scouting for several seasons. Dooley could also talk a good game of basketball with Eaves as Dooley had been a roundball star in high school. Their friendship began when Dooley played freshman football at Auburn in 1950.

188

Jordan was apparently perturbed — for a while — that Eaves hadn't communicated with him about the Georgia situation. But Jordan rarely welcomed changes in his staff. Once he became comfortable with an assistant coach's role in his system, Jordan moved on under the assumption that the assistant was there to stay. When an assistant indicated a desire to seek a coaching position at another school, Jordan's blessing wasn't automatic. The situation could tug on Jordan's unusually strong sense of loyalty. It could nick at his comfort zone.

Georgia's summoning of Eaves and Dooley to rebuild the Georgia football program further developed the peculiar Auburn-Georgia relationship that began when Jordan served as an assistant coach under Butts and that deepened when Jordan picked four former Georgia players to serve as assistants on his first staff at Auburn. Later, former Auburn athletic director Lee Hayley, who played end for Jordan and served as an assistant coach, became associate athletic director under Dooley. Georgia All-American guard Pat Dye reached the pinnacle of his career in the 1980s as head coach and athletic director at Auburn, where he turned the ailing Tiger program around and won four SEC titles in seven years.

The shakeup in the coaching staff didn't dampen Jordan's optimism going into the 1964 season, however. Many experts picked Auburn to win the SEC. *Sports Illustrated* tapped Auburn to win the national title and featured a painting of Sidle on the cover of its college football preview issue. The headline on the cover proclaimed 1964 "The Year of the Running Back." The headline of the article inside the magazine added "...And Auburn Runs The Most." *SI* picked Ole Miss fourth and Alabama to finish sixth in the nation.

The article stated, "Although Auburn is first a college and a college town, it is, in its atmosphere and its interests, more like Green Bay, Wis., the home of the Packers, than almost any other campus town in the U.S."

A Pittsburgh Steelers scout said Auburn had more potential professionals than any team in the country. He said Sidle was going to be another Paul Hornung. He said Frederickson could be a first-round pick at any of five positions — halfback, fullback, tight end, cornerback and safety.

Jordan said, "Our 1964 football squad has as much potential as any we've fielded here. We have experienced depth, team speed, size and strength."

What the 1964 team lacked was luck. In the second quarter of the opening game against Houston, Sidle had just thrown a pass when a Cougar player grabbed his right arm and slung him out of bounds. Sidle landed on the point of his right shoulder and tore the rotator cuff. He never threw effectively again, which rendered his powerful rollout option ineffective. Later in the season Sidle moved to tailback. There's no telling what greatness Sidle would have achieved had he escaped injury his senior season. He was certainly a candidate to win the Heisman Trophy and repeat as All-American. Auburn appeared destined to at least equal its performance of 1963 and perhaps even surpass it. The Sidle injury, in terms of statistical ramifications, was the most devastating in Jordan's twenty-five years as head coach.

Auburn beat Houston 30-0 and nipped Tennessee 3-0 on a 42-yard field goal by Don Lewis. But the win over Tennessee revealed Auburn's sudden lack of firepower on offense. Kentucky shut out Auburn 20-0 the following week.

Tackle Thornton, on his way to making first team All-SEC his junior season, said, "It was a situation of 'Well, what do we do now that Sidle is hurt?' We kind of floundered before we got adjusted to giving the ball to Tucker a lot."

Auburn beat non-conference foes Chattanooga and Southern Miss, but lost to Georgia Tech, 7-3. Tech had dropped out of the conference prior to the season. Auburn also lost to Florida, 3-0. Auburn's record was 4-3 and the Tigers had scored a total of three points in three conference games.

Jordan opted to shake up the team prior to its final three games against Mississippi State, Georgia and Alabama. The NCAA had gradually loosened substitution rules to the point that many teams began fielding separate offensive and defensive teams instead of rotating first and second teams that played both offense and defense.

Thornton recalled the somewhat historical moment when Jordan called the team together and told them of the change.

"Coach Jordan said, 'Some of you are going to offense and some of you are going to defense.' When he started naming who was going where on the practice field, I was elated that I was going to defense. Coach Jordan was probably the last coach in the SEC to go over to two-platoon football."

Thornton immediately liked it because he remained fresher throughout the game. The big difference, he said, was not having to run fifty-yard wind sprints covering a punt and then having to remain on the field and be ready for the ensuing snap of the ball. One Auburn player who continued to go both ways was Frederickson.

Jordan and Bradberry, searching frantically for a solution to their offensive woes, moved Frederickson from halfback to fullback and Sidle to tailback in the I formation with a tight wingback. Tom Bryan moved in at quarterback.

The idea of Frederickson playing fullback had been talked about since Frederickson's freshman year, as he had played fullback in high school. During one of Frederickson's freshman games, former star Auburn halfback Jimmy Fenton noticed that Frederickson ran much better straight ahead than he did cutting laterally as required of a halfback. Fenton told Jordan that Frederickson was a natural fullback. In Fenton's opinion Jordan remained almost bullheaded about keeping Frederickson at halfback.

Jordan later offered an explanation. "I'm afraid we played Tuck out of position at tailback until his last three games. Trouble was, our regular fullback was not fast enough for tailback. Those are the toughest decisions a coach has to make and live with."

"I was much more comfortable at fullback," Frederickson recalled. "The connotations of a fullback are more of a straight-ahead power runner and that's what I always was. Fullback was always a position that had plenty of people at Auburn. But that last year we were desperate, nothing was happening, so I was moved to fullback."

Auburn beat Mississippi State 12-3 with the new platoon arrangement and with Frederickson at fullback. Frederickson gained fifty yards on thirteen carries. He also played fifty minutes of the game as the only non-platoon player. Quarterback Bryan ran for eighty-five yards. Against Georgia, Frederickson gained 101 yards on fourteen carries as Auburn won 14-7. He ran twenty-four yards for a touchdown. He played all but six minutes. Jordan said, "Frederickson played the best game he's ever played for us."

Auburn went into its final game hoping to spoil Alabama's undefeated season, but the Tide prevailed, 21-14, and eventually won the national championship. Auburn dominated the statistics — nineteen first downs to ten, 187 yards to 134, seventy-two offensive plays to forty-three — but Alabama made the big plays.

Alabama scored first when it recovered a botched Tiger snap on a punt in the end zone. Auburn took a 7-6 lead into intermission on a Frederickson three-yard touchdown run and an extra point. But Alabama's Ray Ogden returned the second half kickoff 107 yards for a touchdown. Alabama stopped Auburn inside the ten-yard line in the third quarter and proceeded to stretch its lead to 21-7 on a Namath touchdown pass. A Bryan-to-Sidle pass of sixteen yards accounted for the final score of the game.

Frederickson gained 117 yards on twenty-two carries to close out his career. "I think Tucker Frederickson was the best football player within three-thousand miles of Birmingham," Jordan said following the game.

Frederickson said, "The last game against Alabama when I played fullback was my best time offensively my whole time at Auburn."

The loss dropped the Tigers' record to 6-4 and so disappointed the players that they voted not to accept a bid to a minor bowl. Frederickson, captain of the team, remembered, "Coach Jordan came back to the team and said 'Do you want to play?' and the team said no. Everybody was really down. I for one voted against it. We didn't want to go play again after beating Alabama all over the field and they wound up going to play for the national championship."

For a remarkable third time in eight years, Jordan and Herring's defense led the nation in allowing the fewest total yards per game (164.7). The defense did a lot of stunting and shifting to keep opposing offenses off balance. Thornton, for example, who was extremely aggressive and quick, frequently moved from tackle to linebacker on the wide side of the field. Thornton, Frederickson and linebacker Cody made first-team All-SEC on defense.

Just as it had named Sidle the conference's most valuable player in 1963, the *Nashville Banner* picked Frederickson as the SEC's MVP in 1964. The Birmingham Quarterback Club and Atlanta Touchdown Club each named Frederickson the SEC's best back. Frederickson also made All-American at fullback and finished sixth in the Heisman vote. The top Heisman vote-getters included some great ballplayers in addition to Frederickson. Notre Dame quarterback John Huarte won the award. Jerry Rhome of Tulsa, Dick Butkus of Illinois, Jack Snow of Notre Dame, Craig Morton of California, Steve DeLong of Tennessee, Brian Piccolo of Wake Forest, Namath of Alabama and Gale Sayers of Kansas also made a run for it.

The New York Giants picked first in the NFL draft and selected Frederickson. He played seven years with the Giants at fullback.

The hangover from the disappointing 1964 season lingered into the next year. Criticism of the offense grew, much of it directed at offensive coach Bradberry. But Jordan put tight controls on what the offense could do.

"He liked the pass okay but he knew you could lose by the pass," said George Atkins, line coach at the time. "He used to have set rules. From the goal line to the thirty-yard line, no passing. You just run the ball and run certain fundamental plays. If you had to punt, that's fine, the punt is the best play in football. It moves them back. Then you play defense."

Atkins said that after reviewing film and grading players on Sundays, the coaches usually worked up a rough game plan on Monday with certain plays to be run against certain defenses. The coaches also kicked plays out of the game plan. They presented their recommendations to Jordan on Tuesday. He chiseled away at the play selection even more.

"We had certain plays going in that he would strike out, more than you can imagine," Atkins said. "He'd make sure we were doing certain things with the running game. When we got into a situation we either had to do this or that. But it got too restrictive. He tied our hands on a lot of things."

The Tigers put more points on the board in 1965, but the defense on the season gave up the second-highest point total a Herring defense had ever allowed. This made for some wild ballgames during a roller-coaster year. Auburn finished runner-up to Alabama in the conference race, but stumbled against non-conference opponents and completed the regular season with a record of 5-4-1.

Thornton, a senior tackle, played one of the best games of his career against Tennessee in Knoxville. He intercepted two passes. Both times Tennessee quarterback Charlie Fulton tried to throw out in the flat over Thornton, but Thornton blocked one and caught it coming down and snared the other in mid-air. His second interception came late in the final period at the Vol thirty-five with Auburn trailing, 13-6. Auburn drove and a three-yard pass from quarterback Bryan to Hank Hall made it 13-12. Auburn lined up to go for two and the win, but a delay of game penalty forced the Tigers to kick the game-tying extra point.

Auburn then beat a highly-regarded Kentucky team 23-18. Kentucky started three All-Americans — quarterback Rick Norton, halfback Roger Bird and tackle Sam Ball. The Tigers beat Chattanooga 30-7 to give Jordan his hundredth victory as Auburn's head coach. He had lost forty-three. Jordan quickly suffered two more defeats against non-conference teams, including a dismal 3-0 loss to Southern Mississippi. But the ensuing win over Florida, 28-17, was truly one of Auburn's finest under Jordan.

Florida came into Auburn ranked seventh in the nation with a 4-1 record. Five Gators, including junior quarterback Steve Spurrier, would make various All-American teams at the end of the season. Spurrier was a year away from winning the Heisman Trophy. Cliff Hare Stadium held a homecoming sellout crowd of 46,000.

Florida, as many expected, led 10-0 at half. But in the Auburn dressing room Jordan surprised his coaches and players with his bubbling enthusiasm. "We got 'em just where we want 'em now," he said. "We're going to unleash our attack now!"

Auburn cut the lead to 10-7, and then went ahead when senior linebacker Bill Cody intercepted a Spurrier pass and ran twenty-nine yards for the touchdown. The extra point made it 14-10 Auburn.

Florida regained the lead, 17-14, with 11:36 left in the game, but Auburn quarterback Alex Bowden found receiver Freddie Hyatt for a 69-yard touchdown pass and Auburn was back on top, 21-17.

Deep in its own territory, Florida attempted some razzle-dazzle. Spurrier moved to flanker and Harmon Wages came in at quarterback. Nobody was fooled when Wages took the snap and passed to Spurrier. He fumbled and the ball squirted around until Cody fell on it in the end zone for the touchdown to clinch the game for Auburn. *Montgomery Advertiser* sportswriter Sam Adams called it "one of the greatest victories in Auburn football history."

Auburn beat Mississippi State, 25-18, and edged Georgia, 21-19. The Tigers went into the Alabama game 5-3-1 overall, and 4-0-1 in conference play. A win over Alabama would have given Auburn the SEC title as Alabama had lost the opening game of the season to Georgia. But Auburn's Cinderella story caved in as the Tide won handily, 30-3. Alabama went on to beat Nebraska in the Orange Bowl and win the national title for the second year in a row and third time in five years.

Auburn's 5-4-1 mark was good enough to receive a bid to the Liberty Bowl in Memphis where Ole Miss beat Auburn 13-7.

Tackle Thornton and linebacker Cody made All-American their senior seasons. Thornton credited Jordan with motivating him toward an all-star career. Like so many of the players, Thornton considered Jordan a second father. Thornton recalled when the Lion's Club held a dinner in Thornton's honor in his hometown of Washington, Georgia. Jordan was the guest speaker. A freakish snow storm blew up, but Jordan drove over even though it took him several hours to maneuver the treacherous roads. Thornton was forever grateful.

The situation appeared grim for Jordan after the 1965 season. Buck Bradberry, head of the offense, and Hal Herring, in charge of the defense, both left the staff. They were instrumental in Auburn's climb to national prominence in the 1950s.

Bradberry was under pressure because many people believed the offense was too conservative as compared to some of the other schools that had opened up their attacks. Bradberry also recognized that his career in coaching may have peaked. He had interviewed for the head coaching job at a couple of major schools, including Florida when Ray Graves was hired.

Bradberry felt his connection to the Don Fuell case and the subsequent NCAA probation may have hurt his chances to gain a head coaching position at a major school. He wasn't interested in becoming a head coach at a small college. When a position as the associate director of the Auburn Alumni Association became available, Bradberry took it. He worked there for ten years under executive secretary Joe Sarver, who was Jordan and Beard's traveling companion during the early years. Bradberry later succeeded Sarver as executive secretary and led the alumni group to sensational fund-raising heights.

"I had three children in school. We had been settled in Auburn for fifteen years. I would still be close to Coach Jordan," Bradberry said of his career move.

Still, Bradberry's departure from the staff grieved Jordan. Their friendship went back to Jordan's years as an assistant at Georgia. When Bradberry's playing days ended, he stayed on to assist the Georgia freshman team and also assisted Jordan with scouting duties. Jordan saw Bradberry's potential early on and frequently questioned him about his coaching philosophies and techniques. When Jordan took the Auburn post in 1951, he asked Bradberry to join him.

While the two parted professionally, they maintained their close friendship until Jordan's death.

If one factor was singled out as the main reason for Auburn's success in Jordan's first fifteen years as head coach, it would be the defense. Herring's units were consistently among the nation's best and were in fact the very best at fewest yards per game for three seasons — 1957, 1958 and 1964. Alabama's Bryant, upon learning of Herring's departure, commented, "We won't have to worry about scoring on Auburn again."

But Herring's defense had one of its worst years in 1965. Some critics suggested that opponents had simply caught up to Herring's pro-style game plan. Following the season Herring apparently became restless with his position. Jordan had nothing better to offer him and Herring was out. He joined the staff of the Atlanta Falcons and coached defense for several years and later coached for the San Diego Chargers. He eventually became athletic director at DeKalb College in Georgia.

The departure of Bradberry and Herring meant that only Lorendo and Connally remained from Jordan's original staff in 1951. McGowen, the recruiting coach, had resigned early in the 1965 season to enter private business. McGowen had served under the previous head coach, Brown, as a recruiter and then became coach of the freshman team under Jordan. When Bryant came to Alabama, Jordan moved McGowen to full-time recruiter. Jordan had coached McGowen as a freshman in 1937.

Line coach Shot Senn had also left the sidelines. Ken Rice, the All-American tackle, described Senn as a "real tough little ole nut, just as tough as nails." If Auburn's spring and fall workouts had resembled boot camp, Senn was the gritty drill sergeant. He'd make two linemen go at each other in a blocking drill until both collapsed. "Give me two more over here while these two are getting up," Senn would snap. Senn had played on the Auburn line with Jordan in 1930 and 1931.

Suddenly Jordan found himself having to rebuild his program. Going into the 1966 season the coaching staff included Lorendo, Connally, Atkins, Bobby Freeman, Claude Saia, Jerry Elliot, Lee Hayley, Sam Mitchell, Bill Oliver and freshman coach Tom Jones.

What Jordan and his staff needed to turn it around were lots of good players. Bradberry recalled the situation when he left the staff.

"We were going down hill. We were getting into real bad troubles. We were really having a hard time getting football players. Bryant could wave a wand and get football players."

Some Auburn people suspected Bryant was waving more than a wand. An Auburn assistant coach said he visited the home of a boy after an Alabama recruiter had been there, and the prospect was still wide-eyed over a financial offer. Another Auburn assistant claimed to have taken to Jordan an Alabama football letterman's admission — on tape — of receiving illegal inducements. Jordan supposedly said this wasn't his operational style and refused to use the information against Alabama.

Also during this period Auburn appeared to have the upper hand in luring an all-star prep running back from the state of Alabama. But an Auburn assistant coach who was involved in recruiting the youngster said Alabama made the running back an offer too good to refuse. According to the coach, the athlete, while playing at Alabama, said somewhat apologetically to him, "You know where my heart is." The coach responded, "Yeah, but I know where your body is." Bryant stated that Alabama always adhered to the spirit of the rules.

By 1966 Bryant had something else to offer recruits. Jordan said, "It's true that Alabama has a big advantage over everyone else in the South in recruiting. When you find a fine high school prospect, he more often than not will say, 'I want to go to Alabama. I want to play on a national championship team. I want to go to a big bowl.' It's hard to overtake that prestige."

Also, Auburn no longer had a lock on the best preps in Georgia. Dooley was pulling a fair share of them into Athens.

Early in 1966, Jordan hired Bill Oliver to coach the defensive secondary. Oliver had played defensive back on Bryant's first national championship team at Alabama in 1961. Oliver was head football coach at Guntersville High School before coming to Auburn. Jordan liked the way Oliver had handled the high-pressured recruitment of his quarterback at Guntersville. Despite a University of Alabama background, Oliver had showed no bias and allowed the quarterback to make his own decision, which was to attend Auburn. Jordan's former assistant, Bradberry, also highly recommended Oliver.

As the winter workouts began, Jordan asked Oliver to stand back and size up the players for a couple of weeks and report his observations to Jordan. When Jordan called Oliver into his office and asked him what he thought, Oliver said he was appalled at the limited number of athletes and the overall slowness of the team. The next day Jordan called a staff meeting and said it was time to find some football players.

Jordan not only wanted to turn up blue chip recruiting a level, he wanted to begin basically a mini-recruiting program of walk-ons and unheralded prep players. He thought that if Auburn could lure dozens of these players to the practice field, surely two or three would surface as major college football material.

Buddy McClinton, a defensive back out of Lee High School in Montgomery, intended to walk on at Auburn in the fall of 1966. McClinton's size, a mere 5-7, 150, had run off all of the major schools and he wasn't interested in playing small college ball. Tom Jones, Auburn's new head freshman coach, had been the head coach at Lee and he knew McClinton possessed what it took to play in the SEC. Jones convinced McClinton that walking on at Auburn would be worth his while in the long run. Meanwhile Jones was trying to convince Jordan to go ahead and give McClinton a scholarship. Jordan finally agreed to do so the day before McClinton was scheduled to report as a walk-on.

McClinton would make All-American at safety his senior year in 1969 and first team All-SEC his junior and senior seasons. He was also an academic All-American. Oliver said McClinton had tremendous awareness on the field which, combined with his desire, overcame any size disadvantage. McClinton hit the weights and the chow line hard when he arrived at Auburn and by his senior season had grown to 5-10, 195.

Linebacker Mike Kolen also came to Auburn in 1966. But unlike McClinton, Kolen was recruited by Auburn, Alabama, Georgia and

Tennessee. He had starred for Berry High School in Birmingham and up until his senior season at Berry had been an Alabama fan. But when Kolen visited Auburn he liked the friendliness and down-home attitude he found in the football program. Also, Kolen's mother had ties to Auburn. Right after Alabama swamped Auburn 30-3 in the 1965 game, Kolen informed Sam Bailey, the man recruiting Kolen for Alabama, that he was bound for Auburn. Bailey could only smile and wish Kolen well. Indeed Kolen did well, making first team All-SEC his junior and senior seasons in 1968 and 1969, and going on to a successful pro career with the Miami Dolphins.

Kolen recalled of his initial impression of Jordan, "He seemed more like a statesman than a football coach."

The one thing Auburn recruiters could guarantee a prospect or a walk-on was a legitimate chance to play. Depth just wasn't there. Gusty Yearout's situation was a perfect example. He played offensive guard in 1965, middle guard in 1966 and linebacker in 1967.

"Anytime you do that, a kid doesn't get as much experience and really learn all he can at that position," Yearout said. "But we were going through some transitions. Alabama was beating us bad at recruiting. The coaches were filling in the gaps."

The position shuffling didn't seem to hinder Yearout. He made second team All-SEC in 1966 and first team all-conference as a senior in 1967. In fact Yearout was one of the few shining stars of Auburn football in the mid-1960s.

Yearout had walked on as a freshman in 1963 after playing linebacker and tight end at Ramsay High School in Birmingham. He made the freshman team, then coached by Dooley, and earned a scholarship going into the 1964 season. An injury set him back.

"I was limping around and the coaches were harder and harder on me," Yearout said. "So I quit the team. I don't guess I was real mature."

Later in the 1964 season Yearout met with Jordan about returning to the team.

"I made a mistake. I want to come back," Yearout said.

"You can come back, but you don't have a scholarship," Jordan replied. "You've got to earn it again."

Yearout won his scholarship for a second time and by the middle of the 1965 season was starting at offensive guard. The staff then moved Yearout to middle guard as part of a 5-2 defense. When Paul Davis became defensive coordinator in 1967 he moved Yearout to linebacker in a 4-4 defense.

Poor recruiting in previous years and the transition in the coaching staff combined to push Auburn adrift in 1966. Jordan experienced his second losing season in sixteen years as head coach. Auburn went 4-6 and was 1-5 in conference play, beating only Mississippi State, 13-0. Non-conference wins came against weaklings Chattanooga, Wake Forest and TCU. Alabama beat Auburn 31-0 en route to a 10-0 regular season mark. Alabama clobbered Nebraska 34-7 in the Sugar Bowl to finish with a perfect record, but still finished third in the nation, behind Notre Dame and Michigan State, who were undefeated but had played each other to a 10-10 tie.

Alabama fans complained of "Notre Dame favoritism" in the rankings. Auburn fans wished they had similar problems.

Had Jordan coached beyond his times? The question began to slip into football discussions among Auburn people during the dismal 1966 season. In November a meeting of influential alumni was held in Birmingham to discuss Jordan's position. Auburn President Harry Philpott, who had come to Auburn from the University of Florida in 1965, recalled, "there was a body of alumni that felt he (Jordan) had aged so he was no longer capable of doing the job they wanted to see done...I made it clear at the outset of the meeting that this (firing Jordan) was not in any way a matter for consideration."

Philpott added, "We had not been, as I analyzed it, doing as good a job in recruiting as we should. I think really we had the same recruiters among the alumni that we had had for twenty to twenty-five years. This was one of the things I suggested to Coach Jordan we needed to do and that was bring in a younger group and some who were much more closely tied in to the players and the state."

Jordan later said, "I remember we had a 4-5 record going into the Alabama game and someone decided to call a meeting in Birmingham about what they were going to do with me. Dr. Philpott, who was also invited to the meeting, was very protective of me and I am very thankful for that.

"Now I caught wind of the meeting long before it took place and arranged for some of my friends to keep me informed. So, prior to the game with Alabama, my managers kept in touch with some people at the meeting. One minute a boy would run up to me and tell me that I was in; the next minute I would hear that I was out."

Jordan of course kept his job. Two losing seasons in sixteen years was hardly grounds for firing him. But the focus of the meeting was not lost on Jordan. He recognized that Auburn's style of football, both offensively and defensively, had to change with the times.

16

"I'm tired of being good old Shug"

●●

The 1966 season had been Jordan and Auburn's first losing year since 1952. Jordan's familiar coaching ranks had been decimated. In the spring of 1967 Jordan hired Paul Davis as defensive coordinator. That fall, at the beginning of the football season, Jordan named Davis assistant head coach. Jordan's close friend from Montgomery, Billy Thames, had convinced Jordan that at age fifty-seven he needed a right-hand man.

Jordan asked Davis over the telephone to join his staff. He had tracked Davis down in Atlanta, where Davis was interviewing for a job with the Atlanta Falcons.

"Are you interested?" Jordan asked.

"I'm looking for work," Davis said.

Davis was well known in conference coaching circles. He had been the head coach at Mississippi State the previous five seasons, his best year coming in 1963 when the Bulldogs went 7-2-2 and beat North Carolina State in the Liberty Bowl. That was also the year State gave Auburn its only regular season loss, by the score of 13-10, as Davis's defense shut down Sidle and Frederickson most of the game. The Associated Press named Davis SEC Coach of the Year. But Davis couldn't consistently match that performance and his overall record was 20-28-2 when he left State following the 1966 season. State won only two games that year, while Auburn won only four. Auburn's only conference victory in 1966 came at Davis's expense by the score of 13-0.

"It was probably the sorriest game there ever was," Davis said. "Coach Jordan was in trouble and I was in trouble. It was a bad year for both of us."

Davis, raised in Knoxville, had coached defense and kicking throughout his career. As a young coach he attended the clinics of Tennessee head coach Bob Neyland. He played high school ball in Knoxville and played varsity football as a center at Ole Miss. He coached high school and junior college football for several years in Mississippi, was an assistant at Memphis State, coached in the Canadian professional football league and served as an assistant coach on defense at Georgia prior to accepting the top job at Mississippi State.

While Davis and Jordan had become friends during conference meetings, Davis had grown especially close to Alabama's Bryant. Bryant frequently had his airplane land in Starkville to pick up Davis en route to a meeting of head coaches. Prior to accepting Jordan's offer to come to Auburn, Davis phoned Bryant to tell him he was going to take the job.

Davis quickly found out that Jordan let his assistants do most of the coaching. "That was the greatest thing about him," Davis said. "He'd come into a staff meeting and you knew who was boss. He'd give the whole philosophy of what he wanted and then he'd leave."

Davis, whose boxer's face always stood out on the sidelines, said one reason he so enjoyed his years at Auburn was Jordan's wry sense of humor. For example, Jordan seldom questioned Davis about the defense, but did comment once on problems at the strong linebacker slot. "I can't believe we've got a position I don't believe Jesus Christ could play," Jordan howled.

Among the more riotous exchanges Davis ever witnessed occurred on the new artificial turf at Grant Field in Atlanta. Prior to a game with Georgia Tech, Jordan and Davis were smoking cigarettes on the new carpet. A security guard informed them that smoking wasn't allowed on the playing field because it might damage the turf. Jordan nodded, but he and Davis continued to smoke. The security guard made a second visit during the first half with a similar

request. The two smoked on as four Auburn fumbles and an intercepted pass allowed Tech to take a 7-0 halftime lead. Jordan and
Davis were finishing their last cigarette before heading in when the
security guard made his third appearance.

"Coach, I've asked you real nice," the frustrated guard said.
"You can't smoke on this astro-turf."

Annoyed, Jordan snapped, "Let me tell you something. I know
more about astro-turf than you do or any Georgia Tech coach does.
We've had forty yards of it at Auburn now for three years."

"You mean you're not going to cooperate?" the security officer
asked.

"Cooperate!" Jordan shrieked. "Hell, we've fumbled four times
and thrown an interception! What more cooperation do you want?"

While Jordan was quick with a good line, there were times when
his disciplinary actions were anything but funny. Davis remembered when a player was arrested for driving under the influence
following a minor car accident. The incident occurred on a Saturday
night after a football game. Jordan had gone to Atlanta following the
game and didn't hear about it until Davis told him on the practice
field on Monday.

"Damn, he threw a fit," Davis said. "He went and grabbed that
boy and ran him off the football field right then and there. The boy
never did come back."

In the spring of 1967 Jordan told Davis to run whatever defense
he preferred. Davis had installed the split four or 4-4 defense at
Mississippi State. He proceeded to put it in at Auburn and ran it all
of his nine years with Jordan. The 4-4 defense was a building block
setup in which each individual had a specific role. If any player
didn't maintain his position the entire defense began to crumble

"I was raised on the Tennessee wide tackle six," Davis said. "The
split four was pretty much the same thing, only you're playing
linebackers instead of tackles over the ends."

Davis spent a week at Notre Dame with defensive coordinator
John Ray, who also ran the 40 defense. Notre Dame had won the
national title in 1966.

Davis encountered a pleasant surprise when he stepped on the practice field that spring in 1967. He was shocked at the abundance of sophomore talent on defense such as McClinton, Kolen, Sonny Ferguson, Don Webb and David Campbell, in addition to veterans Yearout and Charlie Collins. "I couldn't understand why everybody was so worried because I felt like we had a good football team," Davis said. "Everybody was worried about whether or not we were going to beat Chattanooga in the first game. I said we if we can't beat Chattanooga we *are* in trouble."

Assisting Davis on defense were secondary coach Oliver, ends coach Sam Mitchell and interior line coach Joe Connally. Davis specifically coached the linebackers.

While the defense received a facelift, the offense totally changed its composition. Jordan, answering his critics, had placed the offense on the shoulders of ends coach Gene Lorendo because he knew Lorendo favored the passing game.

"Coach Jordan was basically an old-fashioned kind of coach," Lorendo said. "He liked two tight ends and a full house backfield. But we didn't have the personnel for that. My philosophy was if we spread them out and showed them the pass, we could still run the ball. He would listen to you and if you could convince him, he'd let you do it. But you better have results or you're going back to his way. You couldn't ask for more than that."

Lorendo, assisted by line coach Atkins and backfield coaches Bobby Freeman and Claude Saia, definitely got results. For the next five years Auburn lived by the pass. In 1967 Auburn scored 237 points during the ten-game season, compared to 104 points in 1966. Only the 1953 and 1954 Jordan teams had scored more. Auburn had not scored more than forty points in a game since 1962, but surpassed that figure three times in 1967.

Loran Carter started at quarterback as a junior in 1967. He led the conference in total offense with 1,372 yards, all but sixty-five of them by passing. His leading receiver was Freddie Hyatt, who caught thirty-four passes for 553 yards and six touchdowns. Hyatt's two best games were against Kentucky and Mississippi State. In Auburn's

48-7 win over Kentucky (a team that had beaten Auburn the previous season), Hyatt caught three passes for 104 yards and two touchdowns. In a 36-0 whipping of Mississippi State, Hyatt caught eight passes for 138 yards and three touchdowns.

The win over State sent Auburn into its final two games against Georgia and Alabama with a 6-2 record overall and a 3-1 conference mark. Tennessee had beaten Auburn in Knoxville in the second game of the season, 27-13. But the offense, which was averaging nearly thirty points a game, suddenly went sour and scored only a field goal in the final two games. Georgia knocked Auburn out of the conference race with a 17-0 shutout in Athens. Then Alabama beat Auburn 7-3 in Birmingham in the memorable affair in the mud.

"I didn't lose the game. They took it away," Jordan groaned afterwards to his friend Billy Thames. He referred to the officiating, which he felt gave Alabama its only touchdown.

More than 71,000 turned out for the game at Legion Field. It was played in heavy rains, gale-force winds and on a mud-wrecked field. Auburn missed three opportunities to score in the first half. Twice Auburn went for the score inside the ten-yard line on fourth down, but was stopped at the two and at the six. "We wanted seven points and had every reason to feel we could score," Jordan later said in defense of his decision to go for it. Auburn also missed a 35-yard field goal. Alabama, 7-1-1 going into the game and bound for the Cotton Bowl, never threatened in the first half.

Auburn finally scored with 10:33 left in the third quarter on a John Riley 38-yard field goal to go ahead, 3-0. But early in the fourth period, at the Alabama 31, Auburn failed to get away a punt following a bad snap exchange and Alabama took over on its own 46. Two running plays moved the ball to the Auburn 47. On third and three, quarterback Kenny Stabler ran right on the option, faked the pitch, cut inside between Auburn defenders and tracked forty-seven yards through the mud for the touchdown. The extra point made it 7-3, which was how the game ended. Auburn ran up thirteen first downs to the Tide's four and accumulated 216 yards on offense to Alabama's 176.

"The best team out there today lost," Jordan lamented. "We played too well to lose."

Stabler's run became a point of controversy in the days following the game. On his weekly television show Jordan commented about the block that sprang Stabler. "I wonder if number 84 thought he was on defense, because he made one of the finest tackles on Yearout I have ever seen," Jordan said. Linebacker Gusty Yearout was the senior captain of the Tigers.

Two days later Jordan refused to let the play rest. At the Selma Quarterback Club meeting he said, "I'm tired of being good old Shug. I'm going to say it as I've seen it."

Yearout described the play. "I knew what they were going to run because when they ran the option they'd split out their tight end — who I would line up on — three or four yards. I told the defensive end I was going to go inside. When I went inside I was right in Stabler's face. I was going to make the tackle. The tight end fired out and missed me. I'm on top of Stabler and the tight end just wraps both arms around my legs and I went down."

Yearout was certain a penalty flag was to be found somewhere in the muck. He went to the umpire and asked him where the flag was. "He said it wasn't his call," Yearout said. "I said, 'Well, whose call is it?' He said the man on the line. So I ran over to that official and asked him where the flag was. He said, 'You didn't get tackled.' I know both of them saw it."

While Jordan's post-game comments reflected his disagreement over the call, Yearout also felt Jordan was coming to his aid. "Some people thought Coach Jordan was making excuses," Yearout said. "He never said this to me, but I think he was defending me. I was supposed to make the play. I didn't, but not because I wasn't prepared to make the play."

The game marked the eighth time in nine years Alabama had beaten Auburn. The loss gave Auburn a 6-4 record, far better than expected in preseason forecasts, but nevertheless frustrating when compared to what almost was.

Hyatt made All-American at end. Yearout made first team All-

SEC on defense. Tackle Collins, defensive back McClinton and linebacker Robert Margeson earned second team honors.

The following season, 1968, was very similar to 1967. Carter shattered his own passing records, completing 112 passes in 248 attempts for 1,487 yards and fourteen touchdowns. He found another all-star end in Tim Christian, who caught forty-seven passes for 623 yards and seven touchdowns.

After eight games the record stood at 6-2 and the offense was averaging twenty-six points a game. The losses came to non-conference foes SMU and Georgia Tech. Two big wins had come against Miami and Tennessee. Auburn beat highly-ranked Miami 31-6 in Auburn. Davis's defense, paced by senior tackle David Campbell and linebackers Kolen and Bobby Strickland, held the Hurricanes to a humiliating minus-85 yards rushing. Carter completed fifteen of twenty-eight passes for 274 yards and three touchdowns. Christian caught seven passes for 151 yards and a touchdown.

But the most memorable win of the 1968 season occurred at night in Legion Field in Birmingham. Auburn, with a 5-2 record coming into the game, beat undefeated and fifth-ranked Tennessee, 28-14. The game was part of a day-night doubleheader, with Alabama defeating LSU 16-7 during the afternoon. The spectacle showcased to the nation the college football frenzy in the state of Alabama. The afternoon and evening games drew 67,000 and 69,000, respectively.

Sports Illustrated wrote, "There is a fine Gothic gloom to rainy November days in Birmingham. Clouds hang low on the earth and make a clammy, gray shroud, which nearly obscures the fiery furnaces in the city's vast landscape of steel mills and ironworks. It is easier, however, to dim the flames of Birmingham than to dull its passion, which, on any November day, is football...It was on this day that Birmingham was going to lay lasting claim to being The Football Capital of the South."

Following the four-hour break between games, Auburn jumped on the Vols, 21-0, with twelve minutes still remaining in the first half. Mike Currier scored all three Auburn touchdowns, running for one and catching two Carter passes. Tennessee cut the lead to 21-7 at intermission on a touchdown pass by quarterback Bubba Wyche, and made it 21-14 on another Wyche touchdown throw in the third quarter.

Auburn never mounted an offensive drive in the second half and made only one first down in the final two stanzas, but on the first play of the final quarter Auburn put the game away. Carter threw a strike to end Tim Christian for a 49-yard score to put Auburn ahead 28-14. Tennessee couldn't regain the momentum as Auburn defenders Kolen, Strickland and Campbell maintained the pressure on Wyche. The win improved Auburn's conference record to 4-0.

But as had happened in 1967, Georgia and Alabama turned thumbs down on the Tiger season. Georgia, which won the conference title, beat Auburn in Auburn, 17-3. And Alabama beat Auburn for the fifth consecutive year, this time by the score of 24-16.

The 6-4 record was good enough for an invitation to the Sun Bowl and Auburn responded with a 34-10 win over Arizona. Auburn intercepted eight passes with McClinton stealing four and returning one for a touchdown as he was named Most Valuable Player.

Auburn finished the season ranked number sixteen in the nation, one spot above Alabama. Campbell made All-American and first team All-SEC. Kolen and McClinton also made first team all-conference on defense while Christian and placekicker Riley made first team on offense.

Though not a great success, the 1968 season moved the Auburn football program several paces in the right direction. But for Jordan it had been a trying year. He knew he had cancer before the season began and he knew he would have to undergo an operation during the winter. He demonstrated great courage in carrying on as usual. But the illness and the mental exhaustion stemming from it were tough on the 58-year-old head coach.

On June 26, 1968, doctors at a hospital in Columbus, Georgia, had diagnosed Jordan with prostate cancer. A routine physical examination had led to the discovery.

"That was a frightening experience," Jordan said. "Sitting in bed while a panel of doctors comes in and tells you you've got cancer. I was overwhelmed. It took some time to absorb what I had heard. It was constantly on my mind. There was a depression that wouldn't go away."

Jordan was told the cancer was probably metastatic (spreading) and that he shouldn't plan on coaching during the coming season, if ever again.

Assistant head coach Davis remembered when Jordan called him and athletic director Jeff Beard into his office.

"He told us he had cancer," Davis said. "He was upset and we were, too."

"I'm going to resign and turn it over to Paul," Jordan said, glancing at Beard.

"You can't do that," Davis replied.

"That's what I'm going to do," Jordan said.

Davis went home and mulled over the situation. "What would Coach do?" Davis asked himself. "He doesn't have many hobbies. He'll die from not having anything to do."

Davis returned to Jordan's office that afternoon and pleaded with him to stay on as head coach even if the illness forced him to miss some activities. "Coach, if you have a problem, you don't have to worry," Davis said. "If Gene Lorendo and I can't run the offense and defense, you ought to fire both of us."

Jordan received a second evaluation at University Hospital in Birmingham. Dr. Sheridan Shirley reported to Jordan that the cancer was not spreading. Shirley put Jordan on medication and allowed him to coach through the 1968 season, with major surgery (radical prostatectomy) planned following the season. Jordan reported periodically to the Birmingham hospital during the fall. Jordan's cancer was well publicized and rumors ran the gamut. Some people said Jordan was dying. A sprained ankle and a noticeable limp during the season added to Jordan's physical problems and accentuated the dark news. Auburn University President Philpott received a note from a doctor who said he had sat up in the stands and observed

Jordan. The doctor said Philpott was cruel to allow Jordan to continue coaching; that even from the stands it was obvious Jordan had the deathly illness.

Surgery to remove the prostate was scheduled February 18 in Birmingham. "I was hanging on physically and somewhat mentally, too," Jordan said.

On February 7 Jordan's spirit received a boost when he was inducted into the Alabama Sports Hall of Fame. The First Annual Induction Dinner was held at Exhibition Hall in Birmingham. The first group of inductees included Jordan; Alabama's Bryant; former Alabama head coach Frank Thomas; former Alabama All-American end and Green Bay Packer great Don Hutson; another former Tide great, running back Johnny Mack Brown; Jordan's playing and coaching buddy, the late Jimmy Hitchcock, the triple-threat back who was Auburn's first All-American; former Auburn head coach Mike Donahue; and boxer Joe Louis.

Dr. Greer Megginson was a senior resident who treated Jordan during the operation in Birmingham. "It was like sitting down and talking to a guy you've known all your life," Megginson said of Jordan.

The evening before the surgery the doctors told Jordan that many patients who underwent the procedure experienced urinary incontinence (leakage) afterward.

"It's not going to happen to me," Jordan said pointedly.

"I hope it doesn't," Megginson said, smiling to himself at Jordan's declaration. "There are exercises you can do to try and prevent it."

Jordan, no doubt thinking of the tan khaki pants he typically wore on game day, said, "I'm not about to leave this hospital wet. I'm not about to go on Legion Field in front of 65,000 people with a wet spot."

Jordan never had the leakage problem.

The surgeon was at Jordan's side when Jordan came to following the operation.

"You're going to be able to coach again," the doctor said.

"Yeah, but am I going to live?" Jordan asked.

"Yeah, you're going to live."

"Hell, I can't die now — not with Pat Sullivan and Terry Beasley coming up."

Jordan departed the hospital cured of prostate cancer. Several weeks later an orderly, who had gotten to know Jordan during the coach's stay, and who was a big Auburn fan, told Megginson that Jordan had purchased several expensive suits from an Auburn alumnus in Georgia and given them to the orderly as a parting gift. A couple of days later Megginson, the chief resident, and the first-year resident, all three of whom had treated Jordan and all Alabama fans, were called into the hospital office. Jordan had sent them gifts.

"It was a nice little alligator type case, had a little Auburn symbol on it," Megginson said. "I said to the chief resident, 'The guy sent us an Auburn watch. That's really nice.' I figured since he gave this orderly eight-hundred dollar suits he'd give us a watch or something. I opened it up and it was this damn pack of Auburn playing cards, which I think was his little joke. He knew all three of us went to Alabama."

Jordan, who was always on the heavy side, lost twenty-five pounds during the ordeal. During spring practice in May, Jordan commented, "I'm not entirely recovered to full strength. When you go through the situation like I've been through in the last eleven months, you don't bounce out like Joe Louis or Jack Dempsey after the first two months."

But Jordan was at full speed by the beginning of the 1969 season. And he needed to be. He was about to embark on the ride of his life with a couple of youngsters named Sullivan and Beasley.

17

"Some Juicy Fruit and cotton in there"
●●●

The successful prostate surgery cast warm new sunshine on Jordan's career. When he left the hospital in Birmingham he had seven years remaining as head coach. Three of those teams — 1970, 1972, 1974 — finished nationally in the top ten. Three teams —1969, 1970, 1972 — beat Alabama. All but his final team in 1975 played in a bowl game. The success those teams experienced with vastly different compositions was a testament to Jordan's ability to adjust as a head coach in the late stages of his career.

While Jordan had opened up the offense in 1967 and 1968 with Loran Carter at quarterback, Auburn fans hadn't seen anything yet. The 1969-1971 teams, featuring quarterback Pat Sullivan and end Terry Beasley, played the most exciting football in the school's history. After the Sullivan-Beasley teams lit up the air with passing fireworks, the ensuing 1972 squad reverted with outstanding success to ugly, bone-crunching three-yards-and-a-cloud-of-dust football. Jordan also saw the new era of the black player enter his football program during his final years. In 1974 Jordan implemented the veer offense to capitalize on fast powerful running backs and Auburn remained a national power.

Also, perhaps because it was late in his career, Jordan seemed to grow even closer to many of his players. The six pallbearers at his funeral came from this period.

Jordan meant what he said to his doctor following surgery: that he didn't want to give up the ghost just yet with Sullivan and Beasley coming up to the varsity. Their performances on the freshman team at Auburn had lived up to their high school billings.

Jordan knew he had landed two great ballplayers in December 1967 when Sullivan and Beasley accepted scholarships to play for him. Dozens of schools wanted both players. They had both made the *Birmingham News* All-State first team. Sullivan, 6-0, 180 pounds, played for John Carroll High School in Birmingham. His senior year, while the team went just 4-5-1, Sullivan completed 113 of 211 passes for 1,382 yards and ten touchdowns. He also carried the ball eighty-five times for 681 yards. He kicked twenty extra points. In addition to his passing and running talents, Sullivan displayed the professional-like on-the-field confidence and maturity that would become his trademark at Auburn.

Beasley, 5-11, 180 pounds, with roadrunner speed and jackrabbit moves, caught thirty-one passes for 449 yards and six touchdowns his senior season at Robert E. Lee High School in Montgomery. He was named most valuable player — with six catches for sixty-one yards — in the final game of the season in which Lee lost to Lanier High School, 7-0. The Lee-Lanier game was traditionally a smaller Auburn-Alabama affair as sportswriters around the state predicted its winner.

Beasley was equally recognized for his performance in track. He was instrumental in Lee's winning the state track championship near the end of his senior year in 1968. He won the 100-yard dash, running it in ten seconds flat, and won the 220-yard dash with a time of twenty-two seconds. He had run a 9.7 100 a week earlier during the sectional meet.

The state meet, held in Auburn, came down to the final event, the mile relay, with Lee needing to finish at least third to take home the title. Beasley had never participated in the mile relay and had in fact showered and dressed after winning his two events. But the Lee staff summoned Beasley and asked him to run the third leg of the relay. When Beasley received the baton Lee was running fourth, but Beasley raced into the number two position and the anchor man on the relay team held the runner-up spot for Lee, which gave the

Generals the state title. For his outstanding effort, Beasley received the Wilbur Hutsell Award which recognized the meet's top performer.

Auburn had the edge on luring Sullivan from the beginning, while Beasley was up for grabs. Offensive coordinator Lorendo recruited Sullivan, having first seen him in action when Sullivan was a sophomore as John Carroll played Shades Valley. Sullivan's abilities stood out on the Catholic school team. "It was obvious Sullivan knew how to run the team," Lorendo said. "It's easy to pick out the good ones. After the game I went straight down to the field and introduced myself and met him and his parents."

Lorendo stuck close to Sullivan the remainder of the quarterback's prep career. The offensive coordinator attended one John Carroll game that was played in a rainstorm. Most of the other coaches and recruiters left at halftime, but Lorendo stayed to the end. "I looked like I'd been duck hunting for three days," Lorendo said. "I went down on the field to make sure Pat knew I'd hung in there. I told him, 'Pat, after all that rain, if you don't come to Auburn now...'"

Sullivan expressed some interest in Alabama and Notre Dame, but he had always leaned toward Auburn. "When you grow up in the state of Alabama, you're either an Alabama fan or an Auburn fan. I was always more of an Auburn fan," Sullivan said.

Jordan visited Sullivan in Birmingham early in Sullivan's senior year. They ate dinner and drove to an NFL exhibition game at Legion Field. The car overheated en route. "Meanwhile Coach Bryant had a police escort with all these sirens and they passed us," Sullivan recalled. "Coach Jordan looked at me and said, 'Well, Pat, you can either go in the limelight with him, or walk with me.'"

Sullivan said Jordan was straightforward and honest. "He never made outlandish promises that I was going to start and make all-conference," Sullivan said. Indeed Auburn signed six quarterbacks that year, including Sullivan.

"You're somebody we really need in our program, that we want in our program, and we're going to give you every opportunity," Jordan told Sullivan.

Sullivan announced he would attend Auburn two weeks before the signing date. "It felt right being around Coach Jordan," he said.

Bryant and assistant coach Clem Gryska had recruited Sullivan for Alabama. "Probably one of the hardest things that I had to do was tell Coach Gryska I was not going to Alabama," Sullivan said. "At that time you had unlimited contacts and you saw them weekly for a period of several months. You really developed a warm relationship with the people recruiting you."

"I knew if we got Pat we'd get some receivers, like Beasley," Lorendo said.

Alabama also lost the recruiting battle for Beasley, but not for lack of trying. During one of Beasley's trips to Tuscaloosa, Bryant invited him up to the top of the tower to observe a Tide practice. The Tide players were running sprints when Beasley noticed Bryant lifting his arms into the air. Suddenly the team charged the tower and gathered at its base, looking up in absolute silence at Bryant. The great coach said nothing for several minutes as he eyed each player. Then Bryant spoke: "Men, I believe you're beginning to look like the old Bama." The players went wild, hollering and beating on each other.

"It looked like they'd just won the national championship," Beasley said. "They almost killed themselves."

That same afternoon Bryant invited Beasley into his office. "I was shaking I was so nervous," Beasley said.

"Terry," Bryant began, "you're going to be an All-American, and we want you to be an All-American at Alabama."

Beasley smiled but didn't respond.

"Terry, what do you want to do when you're through playing football?" Bryant asked.

"I'd like to coach," Beasley replied.

"Then you can't go to a better school than Alabama," Bryant said.

Beasley recalled, "I told him I was still undecided and he said that was okay. He didn't ask me to give him an answer. Then I get out in the hall and guys are grabbing me, shaking my hand, saying,

'Hey, Beasley, great to have you with us.' And I hadn't said I was going anywhere. They just thought that I would automatically commit being in that kind of pressure situation."

Bryant also allowed Beasley to huddle with the Tide offense and listen in on the play calling during one practice. The Tide offense included quarterback Kenny Stabler and end Dennis Homan. Both players made All-American teams in 1967 and first team all-conference. Homan was Beasley's idol.

Auburn courted Beasley just as aggressively. Jordan put Tom Jones, head freshman coach and former Lee High School coach, on the job. Montgomery Auburn boosters Hilliard Peavy and Dave Poundstone assisted Jones. Jordan also played an active role.

"Coach Jordan made me feel at home," Beasley said. "He never put the pressure on me that other people did."

"Terry," Jordan said, "you'll be coming to Auburn for two reasons. Number one is to get an education. Number two is to play football. Anytime you want to talk, my door will always be open."

As the pressure became unbearable, Beasley sat down with his mother and asked her what he should do. She advised him simply to go where he would be the happiest during the next four years of his life. Her consultation seemed to ease Beasley's mind as he had tied himself into knots over wanting to please everybody.

Beasley was familiar with Auburn, having participated in several high school track meets on campus. He felt comfortable when he visited the school. The people were warm and friendly. Finally the idea of playing the role of the underdog appealed to him. "Alabama had beaten Auburn a few years in a row and I wanted to come to Auburn and beat Alabama," Beasley said.

Once Beasley indicated he wanted to play football for Auburn, the Auburn coaching staff advised him to visit some friends, stay low and out of reach of Tide recruiters. Anxious moments prevailed until Beasley signed the dotted line.

The Auburn staff thought it also had another first-team all-stater in the bag. Johnny Musso, a running back from Banks High School in Birmingham, had expressed interest in playing with Sullivan and showed all the signs of coming to Auburn. But Musso suddenly turned to the Tide.

On August 8, 1968, Sullivan and Beasley gave Auburn fans a sweet taste of what they could do as a passing combination. Sullivan threw four touchdown passes, three of them to Beasley, as the South squad beat the North, 27-7, in the Alabama high school all-star game. Sullivan's scoring tosses to Beasley covered thirty-one, twenty-eight and twenty-six yards. On the evening Sullivan completed nine of eleven passes for 147 yards. Beasley caught six passes for 113 yards.

Sullivan and Beasley and several other players, including Musso, worked together for two weeks at Banks High School in Birmingham prior to the game. Beasley had intended to stay in a hotel with money he had earned on a summer construction job. But Sullivan's parents wouldn't hear of it and they welcomed him into their home.

"We really developed some timing," Beasley said of the workouts with his new quarterback partner. "I told myself then, I've got confidence in this guy."

Musso, playing in the same all-star backfield as Sullivan, rushed for sixty-one yards on fifteen carries. The next time the three players were on the same team was when they were named to the South squad in the Senior Bowl following their final collegiate seasons.

Sullivan's performance in the all-star game came only several weeks prior to the beginning of freshman football practice at Auburn, giving him the edge over several other highly-touted prep quarterbacks Auburn had signed. Sullivan won the freshman starting job at quarterback, but the Auburn frosh dropped its opener to Florida, 54-17. Sullivan completed eleven of twenty-eight passes for 225 yards. Florida had recruited a great passing combination itself in quarterback John Reaves and end Carlos Alvarez, who would also put up some record numbers in upcoming seasons. Reaves and Alvarez starred in the Baby Gator victory, but Sullivan and Beasley would outshine them in their three varsity encounters, with Auburn winning all three contests handily.

While Auburn fans enjoyed the 1968 varsity team's potency on offense, with Loran Carter throwing for large chunks of yardage, they couldn't help but keep an eye on the Auburn freshman team. After losing to Florida, the Cubs won their four remaining games and averaged nearly thirty-six points in doing so.

Auburn beat Georgia 40-18 with Sullivan throwing two touchdown passes and running for two more. He passed for 137 yards and rushed for eighty-one. Beasley caught three passes for ninety-six yards, including a 46-yard scoring strike. Sullivan threw three more touchdown passes in a 37-14 win over Ole Miss, and ran for three touchdowns in a 30-7 victory over Mississippi State.

While the varsity team hadn't beaten Alabama since 1963, the freshman team hadn't defeated the Tide since 1962. It appeared that the Alabama frosh would add to its victory string as the Tide jumped out to a 27-0 lead over Auburn in Denny Stadium in Tuscaloosa. But the remainder of the game served as a blood transfusion to rejuvenate the Auburn football program.

With 5:43 left in the first half, Auburn took over on its thirty-three and drove sixty-seven yards in seven plays. Sullivan ran three straight times, for nine, eight and seventeen yards. He then threw thirty-three yards to wingback Daryl Johnson for the score to make it 27-7. A safety cut the lead to 27-9.

Late in the quarter Auburn had the ball on the Tide thirty-six. Sullivan faked a jump pass and then found Beasley who made an over-the-head catch for the touchdown. Alabama led at intermission, 27-15.

Auburn struck again early in the third quarter when Sullivan connected with Beasley on a 72-yard touchdown pass to shrink the lead to 27-22.

The Tigers got the ball back on their own twenty with eight minutes left in the third quarter. Punter David Beverly, on fourth and fourteen at the sixteen, kept the ball and ran for the first down to the thirty-two. The fourteen-play drive ended when Sullivan threw four yards to Jere Colley for a touchdown. Auburn led, 29-27.

Auburn then drove forty-five yards in four plays to score again. The big play was a Sullivan-to-Beasley pass for thirty-eight yards to the three-yard line. Beasley made a great diving catch beneath two

Alabama defenders who had gone up for the ball. Auburn ran it in for the touchdown and the extra point made it 36-27, which was the final score.

Sullivan completed thirteen passes in twenty-four attempts for 245 yards and four touchdowns. He also rushed for fifty yards in fifteen carries. Beasley caught four passes for 146 yards and two touchdowns. Alabama freshman coach Gryska, who had recruited Sullivan, could only long for the one that got away.

The late 1960s and early 1970s became the era of the passing quarterback in the SEC. Ole Miss had Archie Manning. Alabama had Scott Hunter. Florida had John Reaves. LSU had Bert Jones. Jordan thought the 1967 and 1968 teams were as wide open as his teams would ever be. But those teams were merely a flicker of the coming explosion.

The Sullivan-Beasley teams were a statistician's delight. They won twenty-five and lost five games in regular season play. They averaged 36.3 points per game in 1969, 35.5 in 1970 and 31.1 in 1971. The teams scored in the forties four times, in the fifties four times and in the sixties twice.

Sullivan started all thirty regular season games of his three varsity seasons and completed 452 passes in 819 attempts for 6,284 yards and fifty-three touchdowns. He also rushed for 559 yards and eighteen touchdowns. His 7.03 yards-per-play average during his career remains an SEC record. He also holds the SEC seasonal mark for 285.6 yards total offense per game in 1970. Sullivan's responsibility for seventy-one touchdowns and his 228.1 total yards per game remained SEC career records until 1992 when Florida quarterback Shane Matthews broke both marks. During regular season games Sullivan threw for more than two-hundred yards eighteen times and for more than three-hundred yards four times. He threw six touchdown passes that covered more than seventy yards, the longest to Alvin Bresler for eighty-five yards against Georgia Tech in 1970.

On the receiving end of four of those bombs — eighty, seventy-three, seventy-two and seventy yards — was Beasley. Beasley also started all thirty regular season games. He caught 141 passes for

2,507 yards (a 17.8 yard per catch average) and twenty-nine touch-downs. His twenty-nine scoring receptions remains an SEC record. His 83.9 yards per game receiving is also an SEC record. Beasley gained at least 100 yards receiving in ten regular season games.

"You can make a strong case that Sullivan and Beasley were the greatest passing combination in the history of Southern football, or in the history of football for that matter," Jordan said.

Their most memorable receptions came when Beasley sprinted down the field and Sullivan, with a long throwing stride, heaved the ball high and deep. Beasley would eventually bend his neck straight back, look up in the sky, follow the ball into his hands and arms and cradle it against his chest. It was similar to baseball great Willie Mays's back-to-the-infield chase and catch of Vic Wertz's deep smash in the 1954 World Series.

Beasley perfected the catch with hard work, not only with Sullivan but with any backup or freshman quarterbacks who were willing to toss to Beasley until dark. "Anytime you have to turn or stop your motion to catch a pass, it lets the defense catch you," Beasley said. "Over-the-head might make you speed up or slow you down, but you're still moving forward."

In a sense, the Sullivan-Beasley combination solidified Jordan's job. Alabama, having finally lost out on a quarterback to Auburn, and then having salt poured in its wound when it missed out on Beasley, proceeded to suffer through mediocre seasons in 1969 and 1970. Meanwhile the Sullivan-Beasley sophomore and junior teams vaulted the Tigers back into the national picture and beat Alabama both years. If Auburn had not signed Sullivan and Beasley and instead experienced the disappointing seasons that Alabama did, Jordan may have lost his job given that he had been on the ropes in 1966, had failed to win more than six games in 1967 and 1968, had lost to Alabama five straight seasons, and had created everlasting concerns over his health because of his bout with cancer.

Despite the success of the aerial attack, however, it wasn't an easy adjustment for the old-fashioned Jordan. Well into the 1971 season, the third and final year of the Sullivan-Beasley teams, Jordan commented, "Well, we're not controlling the ball anymore, but I'm getting a bit more adjusted to this new offense."

Midway through the 1971 season, with Auburn unbeaten and Sullivan and Beasley rewriting the record book, the offensive coaches met to discuss the plan for the upcoming game. Jordan was the last to arrive. When he came in he went straight to the blackboard and drew up a conventional offense with two tight ends and three running backs, the type of offense that won him the national title in 1957.

"What do you think about this?" he asked his assistants. "What would Tech do if we came out in this?"

The assistants glanced uneasily at each other. Finally offensive coordinator Lorendo spoke up. "They'd just beat the hell out of us," Lorendo said.

Jordan slammed down the chalk and left the room.

One of the keys to the success of the passing game was the protection the offensive line gave Sullivan. One day Jordan made his demands clear to offensive line coach George Atkins.

"I not only don't want him caught behind the line, I don't want him touched," Jordan said.

"They're not going to get to him," Atkins assured.

Atkins said the affection the linemen felt for Sullivan had much to do with it.

"When Sullivan came on he was like a coach on the field and all the coaches and players loved him," Atkins said. "He brought everybody real real close together. We thought we could beat anybody. Of course we couldn't because other people had more talent in some places.

"We worked real hard on trying to protect him. One year they got to him three times, one year five times. I used to explain to the linemen that the farther Beasley gets downfield, the quicker you're going to be coming out of the game. Back then we could punish the defense. We would hit them, reset, hit them again, pull off, hit them again. If we could keep them off four or five counts, that meant Beasley was downfield. I said to them that if you're the quarterback and you go back and set up and on one-thousand-and-two or one-thousand-and-three you get tapped, the next time you set up your mind is programmed, sending a message to your arm to get rid of the ball before one-thousand-and-three. But if you go back and release the ball on one-thousand-and-five and you haven't gotten tapped, that gives you the confidence to hang in back there and let the receiver open up. It was very tiring work, believe me. But they loved Sullivan so much they would do it."

Atkins's piercing eyes and no-nonsense manner also scared his linemen into performing. Some of the top offensive linemen during the three Sullivan years were centers Tom Banks and Spence McCracken, tackles Richard Cheek and Danny Speigner and guard Jimmy Speigner.

"Of course Coach Jordan always said it wasn't because of Sullivan's protection, it was because of his quick release," Atkins said. "Coach Jordan would always needle you in a nice gentle way."

Going into the 1969 season Jordan was growing tired of the press nagging him about Auburn's failure to beat Alabama. One reporter suggested Auburn's five-year string of losses was psychological. Jordan grimaced, probably not saying what was on his mind, and replied, "Alabama has won three national championships in the last several years and have beaten a lot of people. If they have a hex over us, they also have a hex over some other people, too. I don't think there's anything psychological to do with it."

Sullivan and Beasley started for the Blue team, which defeated the Orange 27-0 in the spring A-Day game before eighteen-thousand people. Sullivan was overthrowing some receivers but completed ten of twenty-three, four of them to Beasley for thirty-six yards.

Auburn had actually experimented with the wishbone during the spring, recognizing Sullivan's excellent ball-handling and running, and the speed and power in the backfield with Mickey Zofko and Wallace Clark. But Auburn possessed too much receiving speed and talent, and Sullivan's arm was too accurate to waste.

The fan anticipation created by two boys who had yet to play a snap in a regular season college varsity game was high, but Sullivan and Beasley delighted the fans for three years. Before the two had played their final down in 1971, youngsters all over the state of Alabama and throughout the South were wearing number 7 and number 88 jerseys and calling themselves Sullivan and Beasley as they ran backyard pass patterns.

On Auburn's first offensive play in the opening game of the 1969 season against Wake Forest in Auburn, Sullivan tried to hit Beasley with a long pass, but overthrew him as Beasley was breaking free at the 20-yard line. The crowd nevertheless stood and applauded the play. Wide-open football had come to Auburn. Two plays later Sullivan and Beasley made their first varsity connection, a twelve-yard gain. A late hit injured Beasley and forced him momentarily out of the game. This, too, was a sign of things to come, as defenders took their shots at Beasley throughout his career, and several times he left a game only to return and play sensationally.

Auburn scored first on a five-yard Sullivan touchdown pass to Ronnie Ross. Sullivan also scored on runs of twenty-one and nineteen yards as Auburn routed Wake Forest, 57-0. Beasley caught four passes for seventy-two yards, including a 42-yarder early in the third quarter.

Wake Forest was anything but a powerhouse, but the shutout indicated that Jordan and Paul Davis also fielded some talent on the defensive side of the ball with linebackers Mike Kolen and Bobby Strickland, and defensive backs Buddy McClinton and Larry Willingham.

Because the Sullivan-Beasley teams lost so few games in three years — countable on one hand in fact — Auburn fans remember the defeats as vividly as the victories. The first one came against Tennessee in the second game of the 1969 season. Auburn was playing its first game on Neyland Stadium's artificial turf, which later in the year Jordan referred to as a "Brillo pad" and said was a "disgrace to the SEC."

Jordan later recalled the loss to Tennessee. "It was the first time that we had played on artificial turf and of course Tennessee was well indoctrinated and adjusted to artificial turf. You know when a passer strides (on natural grass) and his front foot hits the ground, it slides just a little bit, two or three inches. But on artificial turf when he steps it sticks. So that threw Pat's body-lean backwards and he was overthrowing Beasley and Zofko and all that crowd and throwing them right into the hands of the Tennessee defenders who were lagging back."

Jordan also said Auburn had called Tennessee prior to the game and asked what kind of shoe it should wear on the carpet. "They gave us a particular brand and we bought 'em and went up there and found they wore a different type of shoe," Jordan said.

Sullivan, playing his first varsity game on the road, threw five interceptions, two of them in the first half, that set up a 14-0 Tennessee lead. The Vols led at half, 24-3. However, Auburn rallied in the third quarter and cut the lead to 24-16 on Sullivan touchdown passes to Mike Currier covering seventy and thirty-four yards. John "Rat" Riley's 35-yard field goal with ten minutes left in the game narrowed the score to 24-19. Auburn got the ball back in its own territory and Sullivan completed a twelve-yard pass to Beasley, but Beasley fumbled and Tennessee's All-American linebacker Steve Kiner recovered at the Auburn thirty-six. The Vols quickly took advantage with a touchdown pass to go ahead, 31-19, and then picked off a Sullivan pass and returned it to the Auburn one, and ran it in for the game-clinching score. During the day Auburn threw six interceptions, lost three fumbles, and played butterfingers with several punts.

"We won't be dropping punts and throwing interceptions like that again," a frustrated Jordan said after the game, remembering now that passing the football could lose football games as well as win them.

Sullivan completed twelve of twenty-four passes for 211 yards. "It wasn't a real pleasant experience, but it was a great learning experience," Sullivan said. "I tried to look at it from a positive side."

"I'll never forget that day in the dressing room," Jordan said. "I walked in expecting Sullivan to have his head in his hands, but he was going around the room talking it up to the other players."

Auburn blasted Kentucky and Clemson and nipped Georgia Tech before losing again on the road, to undefeated LSU, 21-20. Sullivan played his best game of the season, completing nineteen of thirty-four passes for 221 yards and two touchdowns. Auburn trailed 21-14 when Sullivan drove the Tigers ninety-five yards. A Sullivan pass to running back Mickey Zofko for fourteen yards made it 21-20 early in the final quarter. The extra point would have tied it, but a bobbled snap messed up placekicker Riley's timing and LSU blocked his kick. LSU held on to the one-point margin for the victory.

Sullivan and company rebounded the following week with a 38-12 win over highly-touted Florida. It was billed as a match-up between the passing combinations of Sullivan and Beasley and Florida quarterback Reaves and split end Alvarez. But the game is remembered for the nine Reaves passes intercepted by Auburn defenders, which is still an SEC record. Linebacker Sonny Ferguson picked off three and linebacker Strickland, cornerback Willingham and safety McClinton each stole two passes. Jordan and defensive coach Davis had altered their game plan for Reaves.

"We normally ran five men underneath man-to-man and played a two-deep zone," Davis said. "We were the first ones in the South to really run it. When Florida came in we changed and ran a zone defense underneath. Reaves kept thinking we were man-to-man underneath and he couldn't figure out what we were doing."

Secondary coach Oliver had assembled the nation's best pass defenders in 1969, including safety McClinton, an All-American that year, and defensive back Larry Willingham, who would make All-American in 1970. The Reaves-Alvarez combination provided Auburn's secondary with its greatest test. However, as McClinton said, the Auburn secondary faced the nation's best passing game every day in practice in Sullivan, Beasley and a half-dozen other excellent receivers.

"No question that Terry Beasley was the best receiver I ever played against," McClinton said. "We knew that in the upcoming game we would not see a receiver as great as Beasley or a passer as accurate as Sullivan."

Auburn's thirty-four interceptions in 1969 set a conference record. McClinton picked off nine and Willingham snatched seven.

McClinton said Oliver's strength was that he thought like an offensive coach and he taught the secondary to think with the quarterback. McClinton also said Oliver was excellent at studying and knowing the tendencies of the offense.

"Bill Oliver was a young guy," McClinton said. "We all related real well. It says a lot for Coach Jordan to have brought him in when he did, along with bringing in Paul Davis and Sam Mitchell. Basically, Auburn rediscovered defense."

Against Florida, Willingham, who was a speedster, lined up in front of Alvarez and stuck with the Florida star for ten yards no matter where he ran; then McClinton covered him.

While Reaves threw into coverage all day, Sullivan connected on twenty-two of thirty-nine passes for 218 yards and two touchdowns. He also ran for two touchdowns. Beasley caught three passes for forty yards, including one of Sullivan's touchdown throws.

Auburn pounded Mississippi State and beat Georgia in Athens, 16-3, to gain a bid to the Astro-Bluebonnet Bowl in Houston. The win over Georgia proved that Sullivan and Auburn could win in the conference on the road. It also broke a three-game losing streak to Dooley's Dawgs. The victory prompted Jordan to state the obvious: "This is the best team we've had at Auburn since the 1963 Orange Bowl team."

Sullivan wasn't on target throwing the football, hitting on only ten of thirty-four passes for 137 yards, but he still broke Loran Carter's school record for passing yardage in a season. The Auburn defense dominated the game, holding Georgia to 101 offensive yards. Tackle David Campbell, Strickland, McClinton, Kolen, and tackles Bobby Woodruff and Don Bristow all played well on defense. Georgia picked up ten first downs, but half of them came on Auburn penalties.

During the week prior to the game, Davis had told Jordan he thought Auburn could block a Georgia punt if Auburn went after it up the middle instead of from the outside. Jordan told Davis to go for it. The first time Georgia punted, an Auburn man would have blocked it but the ball went off the side of the punter's foot. The Auburn defender crashed into the punter for a roughing-the-kicker penalty. Two more times in the first half Auburn rushed up the middle, barely missed blocking the punt and was called for roughing. Finally Davis called for the outside rush on the next Georgia punt and for the fourth time in the first half an Auburn player roughed the kicker. Jordan walked over to Davis, "Dang it, Paul, this is getting ridiculous!" Davis gave up on blocking a Georgia punt and called for the punt return the remainder of the game.

Next up was Alabama, which was struggling with a 6-3 record. As anticipated, the game was an offensive showdown as Auburn broke its five-game losing streak to the Tide with a 49-26 win. Auburn racked up 541 yards of offense — 349 rushing and 192 passing. Sullivan completed thirteen of twenty-six throws and ran for fifty-three yards. He broke Travis Tidwell's single season total offense yardage mark at Auburn. Running backs Wallace Clark and Zofko combined for 191 yards running and five touchdowns. Alabama quarterback Scott Hunter completed thirty of fifty-five passes for 484 yards, still an SEC record for passing yardage in one game.

"That game meant so much to Coach Jordan," McClinton recalled. "Auburn had been second banana for a long time. He knew Auburn was going to win and win big. In previous years we had gone into the game a little uncertain, thinking there might be a little something missing. Not in 1969. Coach Jordan knew it."

Auburn took a 14-10 lead into halftime. Shortly before half, line coach Atkins, frustrated that the Tiger offense was floundering, burst in on a sideline conversation between Sullivan, Lorendo and Jordan.

"If you want to beat this bunch, run straight at 'em," Atkins blurted. "They can handle us from sideline-to-sideline. You've got the most powerful line you've ever had. You've got to go at 'em."

That's what Auburn did in scoring thirty-five second-half points. Alabama was hanging in the game, down 28-20, before Auburn blew it open. The most memorable play of the game came near its end with Auburn ahead 42-26. Punter Connie Frederick faked the punt and rambled eighty-four yards for the touchdown.

"We had noticed on film that their left end brush-blocked and dropped back on punt situations, so I thought I could run for good yardage," Frederick said. "I asked Coach Lorendo if I could try it; he said to use my own judgment. So on this particular play I checked the end man on that side and when he didn't come at me I just took off. Finally, Musso was the last man and I had just about run out of steam. But I got in with a little fake."

A reporter asked Jordan following the game how he intended to celebrate Auburn's newly-found domination of Alabama. "I am going to buy Mrs. Jordan and myself a box lunch, get on the bus back to Auburn with six or eight other people and eat cold chicken and potato salad," he replied.

Houston manhandled Auburn in the bowl game, 36-7. In the third quarter Sullivan received a shot of Jordan discipline.

"We were getting beat pretty good and we hadn't crossed midfield too many times," Sullivan said. "It was fourth and one on our thirty-six and coach sent a punter in. Well I sent him back out."

After Auburn failed to make the first down Jordan met Sullivan coming off the field and put his arm around the sophomore quarterback's shoulder.

"Pat, you didn't understand that I wanted to punt," Jordan said.

"Yessir, I understood, but I thought we should go for it."

"You sit your rear on the bench and don't get up until the game is over," Jordan ordered.

Auburn finished the season with an 8-3 record and ranked number twenty. Sullivan made second team All-SEC behind Manning of Ole Miss. He completed 123 of 257 passes for 1,686 yards and sixteen touchdowns. He rushed for 205 yards and seven touchdowns. Beasley, who also made second team all-conference, caught thirty-four passes for 610 yards and six touchdowns.

McClinton intercepted a school record nine passes and made All-American and All-SEC at safety. He set an Auburn record with eighteen career interceptions. McClinton remembered Jordan for his caring nature and his open-door policy whenever McClinton sought guidance and advice. "He was low key, but when he set those eyes on you, you got the message," McClinton said. "Even when he chewed you out in practice, you wanted to do good for him."

Banks at center and Kolen at linebacker also made first team All-SEC. Cheek at tackle and Frederick at end made second team on offense. Frederick caught thirty-two passes for 515 yards and five touchdowns. Strickland, Willingham and end Neal Dettmering made second team on defense.

The Miami Dolphins drafted Kolen following the season. One day Jordan called Kolen into his office and suggested that Kolen could help Auburn with recruiting in the Miami area, perhaps attend a prep game and do some scouting. Kolen said he would.

"You know what to look for in a high school prospect, Mike?" Jordan asked.

"I think I know what you're looking for and the credentials Auburn wants," Kolen replied.

"Well there are mainly three types of high school players," Jordan said. "The first type will get knocked down on the field and he'll crawl off to the sidelines and quit."

"I know we don't want that type," Kolen said.

"The second type, when he goes down, he jumps right back up," Jordan said. "But when he goes down again, he'll crawl off and quit."

"We don't want him either," Kolen said.

"The third type is raw bone tough," Jordan said with emphasis. "He'll get knocked down again and again but he'll get up every time and continue to give 110 percent."

"That's the type we want, right coach?" Kolen said.

"No," Jordan replied. "You find the guy that's been knocking him down."

This was the new Auburn. The Tigers led the conference in scoring with 36.3 points per game, and, for all of the attention given to the passing game, led the SEC in rushing with 224 yards per game. As good as the offense was in 1969, it was even better in 1970, and more people saw it. The addition of nearly seventeen-thousand seats in 1970 increased capacity at Cliff Hare Stadium to 61,261, which was forty-thousand more than when Jeff Beard became athletic director and Jordan became head coach in 1951. The Auburn athletic program was on the move. The previous year saw the opening of Memorial Coliseum, a 12,500-seat basketball arena. Jordan and his staff moved from Petrie Hall into offices in the six-million dollar coliseum, which also contained dressing and training facilities for the players.

After beating Southern Miss 33-14 in the 1970 opener, Auburn gained a measure of revenge against Tennessee with a 36-23 win in Birmingham. Tennessee led 10-0 but Sullivan hit Beasley with a 72-yard bomb for a touchdown to get Auburn back into the game.

"Our game plan was to control the ball, but Tennessee got after our running plays and kind of forced us to throw," Sullivan said. "We have this play called 58 OG. OG stands for out and go. We try to hit Beasley with the ball behind the cornerback and before the safety can get there. That was the first touchdown."

Sullivan completed seventeen of thirty-one attempts for 268 yards and led the team in rushing with seventy yards on seven carries. "A day like that sort of puts Mr. Sullivan in Archie Manning's class, doesn't it," Jordan said. "I've thought all along he belongs there."

Beasley caught five passes for 116 yards. Jordan commented, "I've never seen a player who worked as hard on every play in practice as Beasley does. And he works as hard at decoying as he does when he's supposed to be the primary receiver."

As would be the case for much of the season, Auburn's defense struggled and it was up to the offense to take up the slack. Jordan was generally patient with his assistants, but throughout the season he cornered Davis when the defense sputtered. "What are you going to do about it?" Jordan would grumble. There wasn't much Davis could do as injuries ate up the defense as the season progressed.

The biggest plus on defense to come out of the Tennessee game was the play of sophomore Mike Neel, who started at outside linebacker. Neel had received one of Auburn's final two scholarships in early 1969. He had played linebacker for Banks High School in Birmingham and was teammates with Musso and Willingham. Auburn was the only SEC school to offer a scholarship to Neel, who was a small linebacker at 5-10, 175 in high school. He played fifteen pounds heavier at Auburn.

Several weeks after the Tennessee game Neel encountered Jordan's wrath for the first time. Neel had twice blitzed untouched into the Georgia Tech backfield and attempted to cream the Yellow Jacket quarterback up high. Both times the quarterback ducked and Neel tackled nothing but air.

"I got to know Coach Jordan pretty personal when I came off the field," Neel said. "He was ready to have me executed."

Neel almost caught some Jordan flack prior to the Clemson game. After defeating Tennessee, Auburn rolled over Kentucky and prepared to do the same to feeble Clemson. During the week before the game, which was to be played at Clemson, Jordan grew concerned about the players taking Clemson too lightly. He rode them about being too loose and relaxed.

"He had a way like that," Neel said. "He'd get something in his mind that he was concerned about that would affect the team. He'd get big-time serious about it."

Jordan was worried because many of his players were sophomores and would be making their first varsity road trip, which could easily turn their attention away from the game. After the Friday afternoon workout, Neel was feeling good in the locker room and started to whistle. Suddenly Jordan hollered, "Who is that whistling?"

Neel shut up quickly and the rest of the players grew silent. Jordan walked through the locker room trying to pinpoint the guilty party. "Who was it?" he asked again. Everybody kept a straight face and nobody said a word.

Jordan warned, "If I ever catch that son of a bitch I'm going to run him up and down the stadium steps until he learns how to whistle."

Neel recalled, "I was so thankful that the senior guys didn't turn me in. It would have been all over."

Jordan needn't have worried as Auburn won 44-0.

Auburn followed with a victory over Georgia Tech to go to 5-0 on the season. But then, ranked sixth in the nation, Auburn lost a heartbreaker to LSU at Auburn, 17-9. Rain fell throughout the game and drenched the field. Sullivan threw for 217 yards, but tossed three interceptions. Beasley caught five passes for 134 yards.

LSU head coach Charlie McClendon commented, "A lot of players can run 9.6 on a track. But very few can run 9.6 pass routes. Beasley does."

Auburn rebounded the following week by murdering a respected Florida team, coached by Doug Dickey, 63-14 in Gainesville. Sullivan and Beasley had perhaps the best games of their careers. Sullivan completed twenty-one of twenty-seven passes for 366 yards and four touchdowns. Beasley caught seven passes for 176 yards and three touchdowns and also scored on a 34-yard end-around run. For the second year in a row the Auburn defense gave Florida quarterback Reaves fits.

Coming off the LSU loss Jordan could taste blood and late in the Gator game, with Auburn winning easily, Jordan did a slow burn when his defense lost the shutout.

"He always had a great sense of humor, but he could get on you when something was not going right on the field. He had a temper," Paul Davis recalled.

Davis said that secondary coach Bill Oliver, who usually sat in the press box, had asked Davis if he could spend the second half on the sidelines, as Auburn led 35-0 at intermission. Davis said OK.

Florida cut the lead to 35-7 with a Reaves touchdown pass in the third quarter. "Coach Jordan went down there and grabbed Bill," Davis recalled. "Coach thought Dave Beck (defensive back) was responsible for it. Bill said we were two deep and the flanker came down and cut inside and cut back outside. It wasn't Dave Beck's responsibility, it was another kid. Coach Jordan let it go at that."

Auburn led 56-7 when Reaves threw another scoring pass in the final quarter. "They ran the same pattern again for a touchdown,"

Davis said. "Coach Jordan went over there and jumped on Oliver, lost his temper completely. Bill didn't know what to say or do."

Oliver walked over to Davis when the storm subsided.

"Does he jump on you like this on the sidelines?" Oliver asked.

"Yeah, when something's going wrong that he don't think is right," Davis said.

Ends coach Sam Mitchell stepped in. "Bill, you just gotta do the two-step."

"What do you mean?" Oliver replied.

"Well, when something goes wrong like that and they score, we look at Coach Jordan and if he takes one step toward us we take two to get away from him."

"I'll tell you one thing," Oliver said. "I don't care if it's one-hundred to nothing at half, I'm going to the press box."

Oliver said Jordan apologized to him on the sidelines near the end of the game.

A 56-0 win over Mississippi State the next week proved costly as linebacker Strickland, the leader of the defense, broke his leg, and defensive end Bob Brown tore ankle ligaments and was lost for the season. With a bid to a major bowl on the line, Auburn lost its next encounter to Georgia in Auburn, 31-17. Georgia's running game chewed up the Auburn defense. Sullivan threw for 320 yards, but never found the end zone and threw two interceptions. Auburn settled for a bid to the Gator Bowl to play Ole Miss.

Jordan made the team pay for its lackluster effort. Losing to Georgia always grated on Jordan. Instead of giving the team Monday and Tuesday off, which was the normal procedure in previous seasons with the off-weekend before the Alabama game, he ordered them to report to the practice field on Monday afternoon.

"I understand there are some of you who don't want to go to the Gator Bowl," Jordan said. "I'm going to tell you, not only are we going to the Gator Bowl to play Ole Miss, we're going to beat Alabama in the process. I just want twenty-two of you. We're going to find out who wants to play."

Neel recalled, "Coach Jordan would get really angry with attitude. He was serious about pride and handling yourself without this give-up attitude that we had showed in the Georgia game. That Monday was by far the most awful day I've ever spent in my life. We went individual one-on-one tackling. It didn't matter if you were hurt. It didn't matter if you had played bad or played well against Georgia. We didn't match up based on size or position. It was whoever was next in line. It was brutal. It was bad, really bad."

"We knew we had to take them up to the next level to have a chance to beat Alabama," Atkins said.

The team scrimmaged relentlessly throughout the week running only basic dive plays, and didn't begin specific preparations for Alabama until early the following week. "It was a situation where I think our football players at first got very ticked off at the coaches and probably at each other," Sullivan said. "Then as time grew I think we bonded together and formed that unity and pride that helped us in the football game."

But big men do not knock heads for days on end without repercussion, and Auburn, already plagued by injuries, lost two more starters during the grueling workouts. Offensive tackle Speigner and center McCracken missed the final game. Meanwhile Davis found some bodies to fill the depleted linebacker corps in offensive end Ross, running back James Owens and defensive tackle Tommy Yearout. Sophomore Neel was the only experienced linebacker able to play.

In the south end zone of Legion Field the afternoon before the game, Jordan recalled Pearl Harbor to the players kneeling about him. He said it would have been easy for the American people to quit following the bombing, but quitting wasn't the American people's way. Someone always rose to the occasion.

The message was not lost on the Tigers but Alabama jumped ahead, 17-0. Beasley had been knocked cold following a reception on Auburn's first offensive series. The impact of his face on the turf caused his teeth to come through his lip. "They had to pull the lip down and get the teeth back in my mouth," Beasley said. "They said if I had it stitched up right then and got hit again, the stitches would tear more and leave more of a scar. They put some Juicy Fruit and cotton in there. Later I took about nineteen stitches in the lip."

Bits and pieces of the game would gradually come back to Beasley through the years.

"It was daylight when I got knocked out," Beasley said. "When I woke up it was getting dark and the lights were on in the stadium. I looked at the scoreboard and it was lighted up and said Alabama seventeen, Auburn nothing. I remember asking if something was wrong with the scoreboard."

After awhile Atkins walked over to Beasley. "You better tell Coach Lorendo you're ready to go back in," Atkins said.

Beasley, still groggy, went over to Lorendo and told the coach he was ready. Lorendo sized him up and felt the player was feeling a little too sorry for himself.

"No you're not ready, go sit down," Lorendo instructed, all the while watching Beasley out of the corner of his eye.

Meanwhile Auburn drove forty-four yards to make it 17-7. Sullivan completed passes of thirteen and fifteen yards, respectively, to fullback Harry Unger and end Dick Schmalz during the march. Sullivan scored from the one.

Beasley went to Lorendo a couple of more times asking to go in and Lorendo said he couldn't. Then right before halftime Beasley grabbed Lorendo's arm and shouted, "By God, coach, I'm ready!"

Alabama drove to the Auburn sixteen but Ross intercepted a Hunter pass at the five and returned it to the Auburn eighteen. Beasley entered the game with 1:27 remaining in the first half. In the ensuing drive he caught Sullivan passes of eleven, seventeen, eleven and twelve yards. With only seconds left in the half Jordan sent in Gardner Jett to kick a 26-yard field goal, which made the score 17-10 at intermission.

In the third quarter Dave Beck intercepted a Hunter pass and Auburn took over on its twenty-four. Auburn moved to its own forty-eight and then on the play of the game Beasley took a Sullivan handoff on an end-around, broke several tackles and darted forty-five yards to the Alabama seven.

Beasley recalled the lingering effects of the first-quarter blow to his head. "I was out of breath quicker. I was real nervous. It was a wonder I wasn't offside on every play. My body was literally trembling the whole time. I remember on the end-around play I really should have scored, but my balance was so off once my brain was jarred that the gravity pulled me out of bounds."

Sullivan ran for the seven-yard touchdown to tie the score at 17-17 with 8:35 left in the third quarter.

Alabama kicked a field goal to go up 20-17 early in the final quarter, but Auburn's Jett answered with a 37-yarder to tie it. Auburn got the ball back and drove sixty-four yards in five plays with a Sullivan-to-Robby Robinett pass of seventeen yards accounting for the score. Auburn led, 27-20.

Alabama, aided by a late-hit penalty on Hunter, drove eighty-three yards for a touchdown and made the two-point conversion on a Hunter pass to David Bailey to go back ahead, 28-27, with 5:18 remaining in the game.

Auburn returned the kickoff to its thirty-nine. Sullivan connected with Bresler for nineteen yards to the Tide forty-two, then threw to Zofko in the flat. He rambled thirty-six yards to the Tide six-yard line. Zofko carried to the three, and Clark ran it in for the touchdown with 3:56 left. Interceptions by Beck and Johnny Simmons iced the 33-28 win.

On the day Sullivan threw for 317 yards, completing twenty-two of thirty-eight. Beasley caught nine passes for 131 yards.

After the game Jordan said, "My hat's off to this team. Taking everything into consideration, this might be one of the best efforts by an Auburn team and coaching staff."

Sullivan shattered all kinds of records during the 1970 season. His 8.57 yards per play set an NCAA record. He led the country in total offense with 285.6 yards per game, still the best ever in the conference. He completed 167 passes in 281 attempts for 2,586 yards (nine hundred more yards than the previous season) and seventeen touchdowns. He ran for nine touchdowns. His responsibility for twenty-six touchdowns led the nation. He finished sixth in the

Heisman Trophy vote.

Beasley tied the NCAA record of 20.2 yards per catch. He caught fifty-two passes for 1,051 yards and eleven touchdowns. On all but six of his receptions he made a first down or scored a touchdown.

For the second year in a row Auburn led the SEC in scoring (35.5 points per game) and also led in total offense with 485 yards per game. Auburn topped the country in passing yardage per game with 288.5

Two of the greatest SEC quarterbacks ever, Sullivan and Manning, squared off when Auburn played Ole Miss in the Gator Bowl. Auburn won the slugfest 35-28 as Sullivan completed twenty-seven of forty-three passes for 351 yards and two touchdowns. Beasley caught eight passes for 143 yards and a touchdown. Manning, playing with a cast on his left arm, courageously passed and ran for 275 yards.

An emergency appendectomy forced Jordan to miss the game. Complications from the surgery would bother Jordan and require periodic treatment the remainder of his life. Paul Davis filled in as head coach.

The win and 9-2 season gave Auburn a number-ten national ranking, Auburn's first top ten finish since 1963. Nebraska, Notre Dame and Texas had finished one-two-three. Tennessee finished fourth and LSU came in seventh. Defensive back Willingham made most All-American teams and Sullivan and Beasley made one All-American team. Along with Willingham, Sullivan and Beasley, first team All-SEC players for Auburn were kicker Jett and linebacker Strickland. The Speigner brothers made second team on the offensive line.

Jordan suffered a big blow to his staff following the season when secondary coach Oliver departed for a similar position on Bryant's staff at Alabama. Bryant, who had sought Oliver's services for a couple of years, called Jordan and asked for permission to speak to Oliver. Jordan asked Oliver not to make any commitments until they talked after Oliver and Bryant had met. Bryant offered Oliver the job and before accepting Oliver conferred with Jordan, who said he would match and possibly top any financial arrangement Bryant had proposed. Oliver told Jordan his decision had nothing to do with money or any allegiance to Bryant and his alma mater, but that the step would broaden his knowledge of the game.

"It was like going to another library," Oliver said. Oliver found the decision an extremely tough one to make. He had begun raising a family in Auburn during his five year-stint. But who wouldn't want the experience of coaching under both Shug Jordan and Bear Bryant?

Oliver's defensive wizardry would help Bryant and Alabama win national championships in 1978 and 1979 and capture eight SEC titles in nine years from 1971-1979. Oliver's defense was the driving force in yet another national title for Alabama in 1992, this time under head coach Gene Stallings.

The 1971 season would be Auburn's best chance in many years to win a national championship. Sullivan was the early favorite to grab the Heisman Trophy. That Sullivan and Beasley would make everybody's All-American teams was a foregone conclusion. The frenzy became a nerve-racking situation. Jordan said he became so concerned about Sullivan and Beasley getting injured in preseason practice that he combed the field before each session and practically patted down the grass to make sure no holes ambushed his super-stars.

It was a long way from three yards and a cloud of dust.

18

"You're so right, Carl"

•••••••••••••••••••••••

Jordan completed his twentieth season as head coach in 1970. His popularity, attached to the success of the much-adored Sullivan-Beasley teams, had reached new heights and would continue to ascend through his retirement in 1975. Near the end of Jordan's career, and particularly after he was out of coaching, the word "legendary" was routinely associated with Jordan's name. One reason for his legendary status was his coaching longevity: young adults grew up having never known another Auburn coach.

In the popular mind, Jordan entered the realm of legend during the 1971 and 1972 seasons, when he fielded two of the most popular teams in the school's history. In 1971, Sullivan, who with Bo Jackson is the most popular player in Auburn history, won the Heisman Trophy and Auburn flirted with the national title. In 1972, Jordan's press-belittled team won ten games and blocked two punts to beat undefeated Alabama, 17-16.

Though Jordan's stature blossomed with age, Auburn people always felt they could reach out and touch him. Many Auburn people who never met him, who never even saw an Auburn football game in person, loved Jordan deeply. They perceived him as warm, intelligent, well-mannered, smiling and funny; as a family man who believed in the traditional American values. He made parents feel good about sending their children to Auburn during a stormy period on college campuses across the nation.

"I don't think we ever had a protest march at Auburn during the turbulent 1960s," Jordan said. "Maybe it's because of the pastoral setting around Auburn, the small town atmosphere of Auburn. I think things have been handled beautifully at Auburn to avoid situations like that. Now we have had some panty raids at Auburn, but I think the women encouraged it just about as much as the people that did the raiding."

Newspaper stories contributed to this public perception of Jordan. Indeed sportswriters treated Jordan warmly because he went out of his way for them. After a long day of preparation and practice for the upcoming game, Jordan went home, poured a glass of buttermilk and routinely returned calls from sportswriters well into the night. "Those people are as much responsible for building your program as anything you can do on the field," Jordan said.

But it was his television show that brought him into the family gathering on Sundays. He was the uncle everyone liked, coming by to say hello, and to talk a little football. But he never stayed too long, unlike some of the other relatives.

Jordan's show, "The Auburn Football Review," came on at five p.m. immediately following Bryant's show. Jordan first appeared on television in 1955. The show aired only on WSFA in Montgomery and was hosted by Leroy Paul. The next year it aired around the state with each station responsible for finding a sponsor. In 1957 Southern Bell came in as the statewide sponsor and, later as South Central Bell, remained the sponsor throughout Jordan's career. Paul hosted the show for six years and Earl Hutto hosted it two years. Carl Stephens, sports director at WSFA, became the host in 1963 and remained at Jordan's side each Sunday during football season for the next twelve years.

During one of the early shows, Stephens opened as usual with a statement about the game and introduced Jordan.

"Well, you're so right, Carl." Jordan responded.

Jordan repeated the line the next few shows, not because he planned it but because it's what popped into his mind. Some of Jordan's friends noticed it, however, and began to kid him about it. Then Jordan made sure he always said it at some point in the show and when he said it he nudged Stephens under the table.

"You're so right, Carl" became a household line. It became a bumper sticker. It appeared on homecoming floats. It was the first memory many fans had of Auburn football from their childhood.

Except for the last couple of years of Jordan's tenure, the show was produced live at the Montgomery station. Even when it was videotaped at one p.m. it was never edited before it aired. The studio used two cameras. The game was filmed with five cameras, which was state-of-the-art for the times.

Jordan always arrived an hour early to visit with the technical personnel, to look at game film and jot down notes for his opening remarks. He was excellent at knowing the names of players on both teams.

"He was easy to talk to," Stephens said of Jordan. "He never put any restrictions on what we talked about. Right before we started the show he always said, 'Just ask me any questions you want.'"

Stephens remembered that Jordan superstitiously made a point of exiting the building the same way each Sunday.

After almost every show, Jordan stopped by the home of his Montgomery buddy, Billy Thames. When Auburn hired Jordan in 1951 the word in Montgomery was that the influential Thames was the power behind the scenes. Thames enjoyed watching over Jordan and often advised him. Down through the years Thames bought Jordan wardrobes, including some of the khaki apparel and golf hats Jordan wore on the sidelines.

Thames also hosted the Jordan family at his house on Lake Martin. On several occasions Thames held weekend parties that brought together Jordan and Bryant. The two great coaches remained friends through the years and frequently kidded one another about their programs.

Late in his career Jordan joked that Bryant had copied him when Denny Stadium was renamed Bryant-Denny Stadium. This occurred in 1975, two years after Auburn's Cliff Hare Stadium became Jordan-Hare Stadium.

Thames also watched over Jordan's players. One Sunday evening following the television show in the early 1960s, Thames and Jordan were relaxing with a drink at Thames's residence when the phone rang. Thames answered and listened to one of Jordan's star players anxiously describe his predicament. Several players had traveled to Panama City, picked up some girls, gotten too rowdy and disturbed the peace. Police had escorted the player on the phone to jail. The player needed bail money and had called Thames for help. Thames gave the player the name of a local contact. Jordan shook his head in dismay when Thames relayed the conversation.

On Tuesday morning Jordan called the player into his office. "I don't know where you're going to get the money, but you better take it over to Billy Thames's house tonight."

Astonished, the shaken player asked Jordan how he knew about it. "I was there when you called," Jordan said to the snake-bitten star.

The 1971 season was a year for stars and the biggest star in all of college football was Pat Sullivan. Jordan called Sullivan the most complete quarterback he had ever seen. The Birmingham senior handled the double-pressure of the Heisman Trophy and leading his team toward a near-unbeaten season with tremendous grace. Additional pressure came to Jordan as well in having to deal with the Heisman Trophy, but by no means did Jordan view the award as a burden. He wanted the Heisman in the Auburn trophy case. Of course he felt Sullivan deserved the award; he also saw it as something Alabama didn't have and stated this numerous times in later years when reporters brought up Alabama's national championships.

The relationship between Sullivan and Jordan deepened during this memorable season. Jordan greatly respected Sullivan's maturity and leadership. "Off the field Sullivan is as fine a young man as I've ever been connected with," Jordan said.

Sullivan recalled, "Coach Jordan would come talk to me about the football team. Maybe use me for a sounding board. There were a few instances where I went by his home on behalf of the football team. Our relationship grew in that aspect, as far as player-coach, but it was more than that. When I won the Heisman and he and I went to the Heisman dinner, it was something I think he felt a great pride in, which he should have. The times I had to go to him to get permission to be away from the team a day or two because of the awards and trips, on those occasions we would sit and talk for a long while and I would ask his advice on certain matters. And then after the football season there were many times we visited either at his house or his office. We'd sit in his back yard. It was a special time. After I left Auburn it became a ritual to call and talk to him once a week."

In the spring of 1975, before Jordan publicly announced his retirement, Sullivan was one of a handful of persons that Jordan had told ahead of time.

The preseason media hype could have distracted the 1971 team, but Jordan's intense winter program of wrestling and weight-lifting didn't promote complacency. And the fallout from the 1970 loss to Georgia, when Jordan worked his players to the bone prior to the Alabama game, was still recent history. "The Alabama game we won was great, but Coach Jordan never forgot the loss to Georgia," said Mike Neel, a junior linebacker in 1971. "We talked about it through the spring. We focused on it."

Going into the season it was obvious that if Sullivan was going to win the Heisman Trophy and if Auburn was going to contend for the national title, good things would have to happen in two extremely tough road games against Tennessee and Georgia. That's exactly how it played out.

After crushing Chattanooga 60-7, Auburn invaded Knoxville to play the Vols in front of 63,000 fans in Neyland Stadium and before a regional television audience. Tennessee's only loss the previous season had been against Auburn when Sullivan had the great day in Birmingham.

The Tennessee game always fell around Jordan's birthday and in 1971 came on that day, September 25. Jordan turned sixty-one.

"Coach Jordan always pointed toward the Tennessee ballgame," Sullivan said. "That was the one you really tried to get your season going with. You had a new team, no matter how many people you had coming back, and you needed to win a big game early."

Auburn won 10-9, with Sullivan driving the team eighty-six yards for the winning score in the final minutes. Until then, on a blistering hot day, Sullivan's Heisman shot and Auburn's national aspirations appeared in double jeopardy.

Auburn trailed 6-0 at half as Sullivan played what he later called his worst half of football ever. He had completed only five passes in eighteen attempts for a meager twenty-five yards. Meanwhile Tennessee's All-American defensive back, Bobby Majors, had knocked Beasley cold as the star receiver attempted to make a catch. Tennessee kicker George Hunt had converted two field goals to account for the only scoring.

It didn't get much better in the second half. Auburn's Gardner Jett kicked a 28-yard field goal to cut the lead to 6-3, only to be answered by Hunt's 50-yard blast early in the final period to put Tennessee back up by six points, 9-3.

Sullivan and the offense finally drove the football early in the fourth quarter. Sullivan connected on two passes to Beasley and an eighteen-yarder to Dick Schmalz. When a Tennessee defender interfered with Beasley on a long Sullivan pass, Auburn had first and goal on the two-yard line. But on the next play Auburn fumbled into the end zone and Tennessee recovered.

Tennessee proceeded to make a time-consuming thirteen-play drive to the Auburn fourteen, which was well within Hunt's victory-clinching field goal range. But the Vols gave Jordan a birthday present when they coughed up the ball on a running play and Auburn linebacker Bill Luka recovered it with 6:07 left in the game.

"It was a situation where our football team had a lot of confidence," Sullivan said. "Even though we hadn't played very well, we didn't think we were supposed to get beat."

Terry Henley, a junior running back, recalled, "When Pat Sullivan came into the huddle you always had the feeling you were fixing to score. You could see the confidence bubbling out of him."

Sullivan said he wasn't thinking about the Heisman Trophy as he drove Auburn down the field, but everybody else was. He completed a pass to Beasley for six yards out to the twenty. He threw back-to-back bullets to Schmalz for twenty-three and twenty-two yards, with Schmalz leaping high for both grabs. At the Vol thirty-five, Sullivan passed to Beasley who darted to the sixteen. Sullivan connected with Schmalz again for another first down at the five. Fullback Harry Unger, behind a James Owens block, dove into the end zone for the touchdown. Jett's extra point put Auburn ahead 10-9 with 2:44 left.

Following the kickoff Tennessee drove to the Auburn forty-four, but linebacker Neel dropped the Tennessee ballcarrier for an eight-yard loss and the drive fizzled out.

Auburn players celebrated heartily on the field before the stunned Tennessee fans. Neel, at 5-10, ran and touched the crossbar in full gear. He would try but never be able to do it again.

Auburn methodically blew out its next six opponents. The first team offense rarely played an entire game. Beasley caught nine passes for 194 yards, his most yardage ever in a single game, in a win over Kentucky. He caught eleven passes, his personal best, in a win over Southern Mississippi. Sullivan threw for 281 yards and three touchdowns in a 31-14 win over Georgia Tech in Atlanta. Even more responsibility fell on Sullivan's shoulders as the Auburn running game had fallen off somewhat with the graduation of running backs Zofko and Clark. Zofko had also been one of Sullivan's favorite passing targets.

In what was billed as the biggest game in SEC history, Auburn, 8-0, traveled to Athens to play Georgia, which was 9-0. While national and conference championships possibly hinged on the outcome, Sullivan also needed a great performance to win the Heisman Trophy, which would be announced prior to the final game against Alabama. Cornell running back Ed Marinaro appeared to be running head-to-head with Sullivan for the award.

Beasley recalled Sullivan's leadership during the week of preparation for Georgia. "Sullivan really held us together," Beasley said. "All week I knew the pressure was building on him, but all he'd do was give us a big smile and go about practicing."

Running back Henley recalled the pregame atmosphere in Athens. "The electricity was the most unbelievable thing from the time we arrived in the city limits," Henley said. "People lining the streets, people driving by us blowing their horns and hollering. Good gracious, what a crowd!"

"I don't know if any Auburn team has ever been in a more hostile environment than Athens that day," Jordan said.

Royce Smith, Georgia's All-American offensive guard, had a poster on his wall on which a teammate had written: "If the world was ending tomorrow, your one wish should be that we are playing Auburn today."

Jordan felt the big advantage Auburn had over Georgia was speed, and that proved to be the difference in Auburn's 35-20 win. Auburn jumped out to a 14-0 lead in the first quarter. The first score was set up by a Sullivan-to-Schmalz pass of twenty-seven yards that Sullivan released after being hit. Schmalz broke a tackle after the catch. Sullivan connected with Beasley on an over-the-head reception for thirty-four yards for the second touchdown.

Georgia tied the game 14-14 but Auburn took the lead 21-14 at half on a fifteen-yard pass from Sullivan to Schmalz. Georgia scored in the final period to cut it to 21-20, but Auburn's Roger Mitchell blocked the extra point to maintain Auburn's lead.

The play that clinched the Heisman Trophy for Sullivan came on the first play after the kickoff. From the thirty, Sullivan zipped one to Beasley over the middle at the forty-three. Beasley bounced off a hit and sprinted for the seventy-yard touchdown.

Beasley felt severe cramping in both legs as he ran for the score. A few yards before crossing the goal line he lifted the ball high with his right hand. Jordan later advised Beasley that too many freak fumbles occurred when players celebrated a little too early. Beasley's one-handed display of the ball was not a spur-of-the-moment act. It was a gesture to his grandparents who were watching the game on television.

Auburn scored again on a Sullivan-to-Schmalz pass of four yards, giving Sullivan four touchdown throws on the day. Sullivan completed fourteen of twenty-eight passes for 248 yards. Beasley caught four for 130 yards and two scores.

In the locker room following the game, an exhilarated Jordan commented on Sullivan's chances to win the Heisman, "If someone else does get it, I'll bet he's Christ reincarnated." Suddenly Jordan gasped and held up a restraining hand. "Hold it. I'm a religious man and now I'll be up all night saying Hail Marys. Maybe I had better say that if someone else gets it, he'll have to be, ah, magnificent."

In the past Jordan had referred to two players as the greatest he had ever seen — Georgia back Charley Trippi and Auburn back Tucker Frederickson. Now he similarly praised his quarterback. "Sullivan is the greatest player I've ever been around," Jordan said. "He has withstood the test of time."

In the Georgia locker room head coach Vince Dooley said, "Sullivan was a super player having a super day. I know the other guy they are talking about, Marinaro. He is good. But Sullivan has got to win the Heisman."

Jordan said of one of his greatest days as a head coach, "It was Southern football in all of its glory in an Indian summer in all of its glory." He paused and added, "I feel a little poetic."

On Thanksgiving night two days before the Alabama game, the Downtown Athletic Club of New York City named Sullivan the winner of the Heisman Trophy.

Following the Georgia game, Auburn accepted a bid to play undefeated Oklahoma in the Sugar Bowl. Meanwhile the Orange Bowl matched up another pair of unbeatens, Alabama and Nebraska. Two of the four teams were destined for defeat prior to New Year's Day because Nebraska and Oklahoma were scheduled to tangle on the day of the Heisman announcement, and Alabama and Auburn, ranked number three and number five, respectively, were meeting two days later at Legion Field. In one of the greatest games of all time, number-one Nebraska beat number-two Oklahoma, 35-31.

The win over Georgia and the excitement over the Heisman Trophy had taken its toll on Auburn's emotions. All but one day of the team's preparation for Alabama, which had spanned as usual through an off-weekend, had taken place prior to the Heisman announcement. Several years later Jordan addressed the situation.

"I'm not trying to say winning the Heisman Trophy wasn't a great thing for Auburn and for Pat and the team, it certainly was," Jordan said. "But the question is did it take our mind off the Alabama game. I can remember leaving the Guest House in Birmingham and going out to get on the bus, and the alumni and friends were all around, and here we were about to play Alabama but there was no mention of Alabama. There wasn't that Tide-Tiger atmosphere. The talk was all about the Heisman Trophy. It's such a psychological, such an emotional game. No matter how hard the coaches fight at times and even the players to get themselves in the proper mental frame of mind, sometimes it's just an impossibility."

Alabama, which had gone to the wishbone prior to the season, ripped Auburn, 31-7. Johnny Musso rushed for 167 yards and two touchdowns. Alabama held the ball offensively for forty-two minutes to Auburn's eighteen. Sullivan, under a tremendous rush the entire game, completed fourteen of twenty-seven passes for 121 yards. He threw two interceptions in the second half which led to Alabama scores. The closest Auburn got in the contest was 14-7, when fullback Harry Unger took a Sullivan pitch and threw thirty-one yards to Beasley for a touchdown late in the first half. Beasley caught eight passes for 102 yards.

"We did not have a defensive plan that would work against the wishbone," recalled Neel, who started at linebacker. "The wishbone was a new offense in the SEC. All the problems it created for defenses were still novel for us. It was the kind of thing where defensive people had three or four responsibilities instead of one or two. It was extremely frustrating because it had nothing to do with attitude and effort. I only felt that way in two games in my entire career and that was Alabama and Oklahoma."

Oklahoma, also running out of the wishbone with quarterback Jack Mildren and running back Greg Pruitt, bashed Auburn 40-22 in the Sugar Bowl in much the same fashion. At half time, feeling totally helpless, Jordan uttered just one sentence to his players in the locker room: "I want you to go out there in the second half and remember who you are."

In between the Alabama game and the bowl game, Auburn had its day in the sun when Jordan and Sullivan attended the Heisman Trophy banquet in New York City. Seated with Jordan and Sullivan at the head table was actor John Wayne, a favorite of Jordan's. As Jordan finished his speech, Wayne put his arm around Sullivan and said, "Kid, you got a hell of a coach there."

When Jordan sat down, Wayne reached out for him. "Coach, you made a fine talk. You know, I may have a part in my next movie for you."

"Well, John, I come high," Jordan deadpanned.

Auburn finished the year a disappointing twelfth. Alabama, battered by Nebraska in the Orange Bowl, finished fourth. Sullivan and Beasley made everybody's All-American teams. Sullivan threw for 2,012 yards on 162 completions in 281 attempts and twenty touchdowns. Beasley, double-teamed all season, caught fifty-five passes for 846 yards and twelve touchdowns. Along with Sullivan and Beasley, first team All-SEC players from Auburn included defensive end Bob Brown and punter David Beverly. End Dick Schmalz, offensive tackle Danny Speigner, defensive tackle Tommy Yearout and defensive back Johnny Simmons made second team. Schmalz caught forty-seven passes for 647 yards and seven touchdowns.

Few people knew it, but following the Sugar Bowl Jordan and his family considered his retirement, with the Sullivan and Beasley era passed and age creeping up on Jordan. But the idea of leaving a major rebuilding task to a new coach didn't sit well with Jordan. He referred good-heartedly to the players returning for the 1972 season as "country bumpkins." He knew it was time for his football team to get back to basics. The more he thought about it, the more anxious he became to begin his twenty-second season as head coach.

19

"He was my daddy"
● ●

Just when Jordan had decided to carry on as head coach, a matter of great importance caused him to reconsider his future. Early in 1972 athletic director Jeff Beard told Jordan and President Philpott he was resigning after twenty-one years to spend more time with his wife, who was seriously ill.

Beard recommended to Philpott that Jordan be considered for the post. Jordan wanted it very much, and wanted to remain as head football coach, as well. That way he could groom a successor before he stepped away from coaching and still remain in charge of the total athletic program. Jordan figured he deserved the job after his life-long devotion to Auburn. Hadn't the University of Alabama done as much for Bear Bryant even before Bryant coached his first game for the Tide?

"What he wanted was the control an athletic director had," said Kenny Howard, long-time head trainer and Jordan confidant. "He didn't want the nuts and bolts of running it. He was going to appoint someone to do the detail and budgets. But he wanted the control."

Jordan's ambitions didn't mesh with Philpott's hard-line philosophy that the athletic director and head football coach should be two different jobs.

Philpott recalled, "Bear Bryant was athletic director and head coach. He never did anything much as athletic director. Sam Bailey, his assistant, did all the work. I think Coach Jordan felt that he could do the same thing; get somebody to do the athletic director details. I felt very strongly philosophically and administratively that we needed a full-time person as athletic director and told coach Jordan I would be glad to give him the choice of either being head coach or athletic director...Coach Jordan and I talked and he said quite frankly that football would be his main interest. He felt that with football producing most of the revenue for the athletic department, it should be preeminent in the whole program. All the other sports would be minor to it...I didn't feel at that time that he would have given the kind of emphasis to the other sports that I hoped he would have...So he made the decision he wanted to continue as head coach if he couldn't have both jobs. He nominated (Lee) Hayley to be athletic director."

Hayley succeeded Beard as athletic director in the summer.

"Coach Jordan was hurt worse than anything," said David Thames of Montgomery, who grew very close to Jordan as had his father, Billy Thames. The younger Thames told Jordan he was underestimating the power he had accumulated in twenty-one years as head coach; that if Jordan told the Auburn people he was going to resign and told them why, "they would kick Philpott out of there so quick it would make your ears turn around."

Only Jordan and Beard could really appreciate what the development of Auburn football had done for the overall athletic program and the university. A quick glance at Cliff Hare Stadium and Memorial Coliseum reminded them each day of how far Auburn had come. Most definitely Jordan believed the football program should be the feature attraction; to pretend that the other sports deserved similar recognition may have been politically correct, but it wasn't a true assessment of the situation.

But Jordan's love for Auburn dissuaded him from declaring open warfare on the administration, and his love of coaching and his immediate desire to rebuild the football team determined his response to Philpott's either/or proposition. Yet he felt the university owed him both titles. Thereafter, Jordan held a lower opinion of Philpott.

With bruised feelings, Jordan turned away from university

politics and put his heart into the 1972 football team.

"We had one play, Terry Henley up the middle," Jordan said. "What an outspoken, free-spirited, tough-minded competitor Terry Henley was."

"He was my daddy," Henley said of Jordan.

The Jordan-Henley relationship represented the very essence of the 1972 team, which finished 10-1 and ranked fifth in the nation. Almost from the moment Henley reported as a freshman in 1969, the head coach and player struck a father-son relationship. Henley's father was deceased and had previously been divorced from Henley's mother for many years.

Henley came to Auburn out of Oxford High School in Alabama. He didn't possess great speed, but he ate up yardage and played the game with tremendous zest. What Jordan soon found out was that Henley could become unruly both on and off the football field. What Henley needed, Jordan saw, both on and off the field, was discipline.

Jordan welcomed Henley into his home, heard the boy's griefs, pampered him and advised him. Jordan also called him on the carpet, scolded him and punished him; then felt lousy about punishing him, or felt frustrated because the boy wasn't getting the message; or grinned and admired the boy's addiction to living life to its fullest. Their relationship involved many memorable encounters.

Prior to the start of his senior year, in the fall of 1972, Henley reported to team picture day with long hair, though he had gotten a trim for the occasion. He was jostling with some of the other players when he noticed Jordan, who was standing at the goal post, motioning him to come over. Henley sprinted over in good spirits and greeted the coach. Jordan shook his head with disgust and grimaced at Henley.

"You're so full of it it's pathetic," Jordan said.

Henley hung his head and his enthusiasm vanished.

"You make me sick, Terry," Jordan continued. "You're undisciplined, not a team player. You haven't cut your hair by the rules like everybody else. I make the rules."

The tongue-lashing wounded Henley, but he didn't get his hair cut. He expected Jordan to say something else to him, but several days passed and the coach said nothing. Henley ran into Mrs. Jordan in the athletic complex. She told him Shug had come home visibly upset the evening he had ripped into Henley. She didn't usually ask him why he might be upset, but this time she did. Shug told her he'd had to get on Terry about his hair. Mrs. Jordan promptly informed her husband that Terry's hair looked nice, that he kept it trimmed and that the head coach should leave him alone about it.

"Has he said anything else to you?" Mrs. Jordan asked Henley.

"No ma'am."

"Good, he won't," she responded. "That's our secret."

Jordan was fanatical about haircuts, but a few years earlier he had decided he would set the trend for his players by loosening up and letting his hair touch his ears and collar. The fashion statement was shortlived because the hair agitated him so much that he was always picking at it.

Jordan called Henley to his office about another matter early in the 1972 season.

"Some of the freshman players are thinking about quitting and going home," Jordan said. "Some have lost twenty pounds because you won't let them eat at night."

"What do you mean?" Henley asked.

"They say you keep them singing and dancing," Jordan replied. "You've got to lay off of them a little. They say they're tired and give out because you get them up at two and three in the morning and make them take cold showers. They can't understand how you still go out and run the ball fifty times."

Another meeting between the man and the boy resulted from an incident involving sorority rush week just prior to the beginning of school in the fall. The freshman girls who wanted to pledge a sorority weren't allowed to speak during this period and some of the football players would park their cars and take pictures of the girls as they walked across a certain part of the campus. The handsome Henley approached a girl one day and asked to see her name tag. She started to run away. Henley's football mates encouraged him to pursue her. Henley ran after the girl and gently tackled her. The girl screamed for him to let her go, which of course he did.

The next morning Jordan called Henley into his office.

"I have to talk to you about a couple of things," Jordan said. "I hear you're harassing the girls during rush."

Henley started to explain that the incident was blown out of proportion, but Jordan cut him off.

"Don't start with that," Jordan said. "You're going to have to stop it."

Henley agreed and started to leave Jordan's office.

"Wait a minute," Jordan said. "I want to read you something."

Jordan pulled out a piece of paper. "I have this note here from Dean Cater," he said, referring to the women's dean. "It was hand delivered to me today. I want you to hear this."

One can only assume that at about this time Jordan was wondering if the likes of Rockne and Stagg and Warner had to address such steaming issues during their careers. Jordan read the letter: "One of your players, Terry Henley, allegedly tackled one of my girls..." The note went on to mention that the girl had sustained a bruise and stained her dress during the encounter.

Henley stood in disbelief, not at the note, which was probably true, but at the bureaucracy that now entangled him. "This is carrying this too far," Henley said. "I'll handle it."

Jordan managed a tiny smile. "I already handled it," he said. "I told Dean Cater you couldn't tackle anyone."

Jordan once found himself in the unenviable position of riding as a passenger in Henley's car. During an open weekend Henley's senior year, Henley requested of the coach to let him drive home to Oxford to see his younger brother, Mike, play a high school game. Since Auburn was recruiting Mike, Jordan decided to go. Jordan informed Henley that because of recruiting rules Jordan wouldn't be able to buy Henley a coke or hot dog or popcorn, and that Henley had to sit in the stands while Jordan sat in the press box.

They headed out on highway 431 with Henley behind the wheel. Jordan kept leaning over and looking at the speedometer. "How fast are you going?" he asked. "You need to slow down."

Henley slowed down but eventually picked up the speed and again Jordan leaned over and recommended that Henley slow it down. This happened a couple of more times.

As they neared Lafayette, Henley's speed was to the point that Jordan was forced to lean left and right as they took several curves. "The tires are kind of squealing, aren't they Terry?" Jordan inquired, growing more tense. "I'd sure hate to be thrown in the Lafayette jail."

"Don't worry, Doc Wheeler will get us out," Henley joked, referring to Dr. Nick Wheeler of Lafayette, who was a close friend of Jordan's.

Jordan, finally fed up with the uncomfortable situation and with the boy's lack of concern, sternly drawled, "Let me inform you that Doc Wheeler went to Europe today." Henley got the message.

An example of Henley's unpredictable nature on the field occurred during the 1970 Auburn-Alabama game. As a sophomore, Henley had averaged 6.6 yards per carry and rushed for 264 yards. A chunk of that yardage had come on a 78-yard touchdown run against Clemson. In the 1970 Alabama game Henley returned four kickoffs for 127 yards. Henley caught one of the kickoffs as he straddled the goal line. He was uncertain whether to down it in the end zone or run it out. Just when he had decided to down it, the referee told him he had to run it and Henley broke loose for a long return.

"What are you doing?" Jordan yelled as Henley returned to the sidelines. "I want to know what you're doing!"

"I thought I was in the end zone," Henley replied meekly.

Jordan responded, "I've told you four-million times to quit thinking. That's what they pay me for. You run, you react. You don't think."

Jordan and his assistants worked with Henley until he emerged as a dependable, steady running back. During spring training prior to Henley's sophomore season of 1970, during a scrimmage, Henley broke a couple of tackles at the line but was brought down in open field by a lone defender. On the sidelines Jordan held up his left hand.

"You knew something was fixing to come down when he held up his left hand," Henley said.

Jordan crossed the field and met Henley. "Terry, that was a good run, that was a good run," Jordan acknowledged. "But a GREAT back would be in the end zone tossing the ball to the official right now. That would be a GREAT back. We want to learn to be a GREAT back rather than just a good back."

Several plays later Henley made a similar run and confronted another one-on-one situation in the secondary. This time Henley broke the tackle, ran into the end zone and tossed the ball to the scrimmage official. Henley passed Jordan as he returned to the sidelines. Jordan smiled. "That's a GREAT back."

The way Jordan saw it, Henley needed two things: to toughen up as a running back and quit fumbling the football. A spring practice scrimmage in 1971 accomplished the first part.

Jordan instructed offensive coordinator Gene Lorendo to take the offensive and defensive teams down to the goal line for some serious work. On the first play, Henley took the handoff and angled into the hole off tackle. Lorendo jumped on him for creeping along and told the defense that Henley would run the ball the next twenty plays. The defense kept teeing off on Henley and Lorendo continued to ride him. A few plays later Henley spun, twisted, broke a tackle and ran into the end zone. "That'll teach him," Henley muttered to himself.

"Bring it back!" Lorendo yelled. "Let's do it again!"

Years later Henley and Lorendo recalled their exchange.

"He tells me I didn't do it the way he wanted me to do it," Henley said. "He tells me to do it his way and not my way. I got mad. I'm fixing to hit him. He kind of shoves a couple of players out of the way and grabs me. He dares me to hit him."

"He's looking for sympathy and he doesn't get back in the huddle," Lorendo said. "I said, 'What are you going to do, Terry, quit?' He clenched his fist. I said 'I wish you'd hit me, then I'd know you had some guts.'"

"He slung me around and says, 'Get in the huddle and do what you're told,'" Henley said.

"I tell him 'I'm either going to make a ballplayer out of you or I'm going to kill you or we'll both quit,'" Lorendo said.

"We do it ten more times in a row," Henley said. "Finally I don't make an inch and he says, 'That's the way I want it done right there.'"

"To this day he'll tell you that's what made him a ballplayer," Lorendo said.

Henley had learned toughness, but he was still fumbling. During his junior season in 1971, Auburn had won its first four games and was playing Georgia Tech at Grant Field in Atlanta. Henley fumbled the ball three times in the first half. One fumble came on Auburn's six-yard line and Tech cashed it in for a 7-0 halftime lead.

Jordan stood before his players in the dressing room during intermission. "We're behind 7-0, but the defense is playing good," Jordan said. "Offense, you're playing all right, except for Terry. Terry, stand up and tell them you're sorry for fumbling."

Henley hesitated because he wasn't sure if Jordan was kidding. Suddenly Jordan shouted, "Stand up and tell them you're sorry!"

Henley apologized to the team and played a great second half as Auburn won 31-14.

A few weeks later Auburn carried a 7-0 record into a home game against Mississippi State. During the contest Henley made a nice fifteen-yard run only to fumble it away on the Mississippi State twelve-yard line. He stalked to the sidelines and slung his helmet at the bench. Jordan strolled up and put his arm around the boy's neck. Jordan's clench was such that Henley was forced to look up into the stands, which was what Jordan was doing.

"Your mama here today?" Jordan asked.

"Yes sir."

"Granddaddy and grandma here today?"

"Yes sir, I think they're here."

"What about your brothers?"

"Yes sir, they're probably up there."

Jordan paused to scan the stadium. "What do you think they think of you right now?"

"What do you mean?" Henley asked.

"I mean what do you think they think about your fumbling?"

"I guess they're a little embarrassed," Henley replied.

Jordan tightened his grip on Henley's neck. "I want you to promise me and them you won't ever fumble again."

"I promise," Henley said.

Henley didn't fumble again, not during the remainder of the 1971 season, and not once during his senior year in 1972.

For three years Jordan had invested a lot of time in Terry Henley, and in 1972 he needed a return on his investment. Jordan and offensive coordinator Lorendo reviewed the experienced manpower returning on offense — tailback Henley, fullbacks James Owens and Harry Unger, tackle and co-captain Mac Lorendo and guard Jay Casey. It appeared to be slim pickings, but Jordan saw in those players the nucleus for an I formation. The key question was whether Auburn's offensive linemen could learn to block for Terry Henley up the middle. Jordan made sure that they could.

The 1971 team had lost 40-22 to Oklahoma in the Sugar Bowl on New Year's Day 1972. Two weeks after the game, Jordan revealed to his team what was in store for 1972. The routine in previous years was to begin winter workouts, which consisted of running, lifting weights and wrestling. But on this day one of the team managers came into the dining hall and informed the players that Jordan wanted them in helmets and shoulder pads in the stadium that afternoon. The same thought ran through each player's mind: "We just got through playing. We're going back at it again?"

The players gathered on the field in the afternoon and were horsing around, waiting for the coaches to arrive. Nearby was a seven-man blocking sled. Then a man appeared at the far end of the field and approached the team. Henley recognized him from the previous day as someone he and defensive back Johnny Simmons had seen at the athletic complex. They figured he was the father of one of the players. "He didn't have any neck; his ears grew out into his shoulders," Henley said.

The man reached the players on the field. "I'm Pat Morris. I'm the new offensive line coach for Auburn University. I've been instructed by Coach Jordan to teach you all how to block better than Oklahoma."

Morris told the team to form seven lines at the blocking sled. The linemen started forming lines. Henley stepped to the side.

"Where are you going?" Morris asked.

"I'm a running back," Henley replied. "I'm Terry Henley."

"I don't give a damn who you are, boy, you understand me. You better put your damn helmet on and line up in this line before I kick your ass all the way back to where you come from."

Henley, punter Beverly and placekicker Jett nearly knocked each other down trying to get into line.

The team worked the sled and blocked one-on-one up until the official spring training period. They practiced at the north end zone so they couldn't be seen from Haley Center, the tall classroom building in the middle of campus. The winter workout focused on technique as much as conditioning.

Meanwhile Jordan and Paul Davis's defense and kicking game appeared to be in excellent shape going into the spring. An all-star secondary included safety Johnny Simmons and sidebacks Dave Beck and David Langner. Defensive ends Danny Sanspree and Eddie Welch, and tackle Benny Sivley were all experienced and talented. Co-captain Mike Neel and Bill Luka had proven themselves at linebacker. The kicking game featured one of the best punters in the nation, David Beverly, and returned as consistent and cool a placekicker as there was in Gardner Jett.

Sportswriters apparently underestimated the defense and the kicking game; they didn't bother to estimate the offense. They picked Auburn sixth in the conference.

Jordan later acknowledged that the 1972 spring workout was the toughest spring since his first one in 1951. The set in his jaw and the determination in his eyes expressed to his players from the outset that it was going to be intense. Much of the time it was the first-team offense scrimmaging the first-team defense. Henley ran the ball over and over again.

"Everybody discovered neck collars," Neel said.

The only question mark on defense appeared to be at the inside linebacker positions. But junior Bill Newton and sophomore Ken Bernich stepped forward by the end of spring.

It was the stuff Jordan liked best. Hard-nosed football. A great block. A great tackle. A back lowering his shoulder, breaking off a hit and throwing a stiff arm.

By the end of spring it appeared Dave Lyon had won the starting position at quarterback. He was quick and handled the ball well. But during the final spring scrimmage a knee injury ended Lyon's career. The players went home for the summer not knowing who their quarterback was.

Before the season started, Jordan called Henley in Oxford and asked him to come to Auburn to talk about the quarterback situation. Jordan asked Henley whom he would feel most comfortable with at quarterback, the tall sophomore Randy Walls or junior Wade Whatley. Both were ball-control type quarterbacks and suited for Auburn's conservative attack. Henley said he could play in the backfield with either one of them.

"We're going to put the lead bell on Randy," Jordan told Henley. "If he can't do the job we'll take the bell off of him and give it to someone else."

The fall preseason practices revealed the team's toughness. Spats broke out during practice between the players. This "spit and fire" demonstration prevailed the entire season, Neel recalled, as Auburn players scuffled with opponents several times, and then banged up each other in practice between games. Neel required fourteen stitches in the mouth when a teammate busted his face mask several seconds after the completion of a play during practice.

A week before the opening game against Mississippi State in Jackson, Jordan said, "I think any team operates pretty well from an underdog position. I think this team wants to prove something to themselves — that they can win without Sullivan and Beasley. I believe we have that flaming spirit that can take you a long way."

On the day before the Mississippi State game Jordan emphasized to Henley that the offensive game plan would include only three or four plays and it was going to be all Henley.

"You think they'll write about me?" Henley kidded.

"They'll write about you if you live through it," Jordan replied.

Henley paid dividends for Jordan throughout the season. The Atlanta Touchdown Club named him the SEC Back of the Year. He led the conference in rushing with 843 yards on 216 carries. He scored ten touchdowns.

Auburn won nine and lost one during the regular season and ripped Colorado in the Gator Bowl, 24-3. The team became known as "The Amazin's."

"We had a lot of courage on that team," Jordan said. "They were well disciplined and they were in splendid physical shape."

The game that's most remembered from the 1972 season of course is the blocked punts drama against Alabama. But the game that sparked the Tigers was against Tennessee.

Auburn opened the season beating Mississippi State, 14-3. Henley gained 136 yards on twenty-two carries and scored on a three-yard run. Walls completed five passes for forty-one yards to officially announce the end of the Sullivan-Beasley era. The defense established its potency by holding State to ninety-eight yards rushing on forty carries.

Auburn then beat Chattanooga 14-7 with Henley rushing for 152 yards on twenty-two carries and scoring on runs of seven and twenty-nine yards. The 1971 team with Sullivan and Beasley had beaten Chattanooga 60-7. Auburn was 2-0, but still unranked. The lack of scoring caused Auburn to be a big underdog against upcoming opponent, fourth-ranked Tennessee.

On the Thursday prior to the game, Jordan told his players he would proudly take them anywhere to play anybody, including a Nebraska or an Oklahoma. On the day before the game, as the team prepared to board the buses for Birmingham, Jordan, sniffing a lack of confidence in the air, told them the only players he wanted on the buses were players who knew Auburn was going to win — not maybe win, Jordan said, but definitely win.

"We knew we were going to Birmingham to beat Tennessee," Henley said. "The man had told us we were going to do it."

Auburn did it, 10-6, before nearly seventy-thousand fans at Legion Field. One reason was because defensive coach Sam Mitchell impressed upon the defense that speedy and elusive Vol quarterback Condredge Holloway was not planning to pass when he dropped back, but intended to scramble with the ball. Mitchell was right. With this mindset the Auburn defense blitzed on almost every play. Auburn held Tennessee to eighty yards rushing on forty carries and 109 yards passing.

Midway through the first quarter, with the game still scoreless, Auburn took possession on its own nineteen-yard line. In sixteen plays the Tigers marched the length of the field with Henley picking up the final yard for the touchdown on the second play of the second quarter.

Henley carried the ball twelve times during the drive, including the final ten plays. His feat is one of the more memorable in Auburn football history. His consecutive carries began at the Tennessee forty-two. Auburn linemen Lorendo, Casey and Bob Farrier created the space for Henley to gain five, then seven and a first down at the thirty. He ran for two, then six and gained two more for a first down at the twenty. He carried two times for short yardage and Auburn faced a crucial third down. Jamie Rotella, the All-American linebacker for Tennessee, had stopped Henley on second down. As they rose from the pile, Rotella said, "Now you've got to throw. You thought you could run it all the way down."

The fiery Henley barked, "Jamie, we're going to run the same damn thing again, the same thing, Jamie." Auburn ran the same power play and Henley bolted for the first down to the nine. He then ran for eight yards to the one before scoring the game's only touchdown. Jett's extra point was all Auburn needed as the defense, paced by Sanspree, Bernich and Beck, stymied the Vols. Jett also kicked a thirty-yard field goal.

"It's mighty sweet to win when not a damn soul in the United States, including you gentlemen of the press, thought we could," Jordan said after the game.

Auburn had ended Tennessee's ten-game winning streak, and the following week snapped Mississippi's ten-game victory string. Auburn, having moved into the rankings to number seventeen after the Tennessee game, beat Ole Miss in Jackson, 19-13. Henley rushed for 150 yards on thirty-three carries. Ole Miss threatened in the final minute of the game inside the Auburn ten-yard line, but linebacker Neel blitzed and dropped quarterback Norris Weese for a nine-yard loss on third down. Linebacker Luka batted down a fourth-down pass to clinch the win, which was Jordan's 150th as head coach

Auburn moved up to number nine in the nation but didn't stay there long as undefeated and eighth-ranked LSU whipped the Tigers 35-7 in Baton Rouge. LSU quarterback Bert Jones threw for three touchdowns and ran for another. LSU humbled the Auburn defense with 477 total yards. Henley's one-yard touchdown run had cut the lead to 14-7 in the second quarter, but LSU scored again just before half and forced Auburn out of its ball-control offense. Henley, who had carried nineteen times for fifty-eight yards in the first half, carried only once in the second half. The loss to LSU gave Auburn a 4-1 record.

Jordan continued to express his optimism to the players rather than punish them in practice. He had not seen any letdown in effort and attitude during the LSU game. In the next outing Auburn fell behind Georgia Tech 14-0 but rebounded for a 24-14 win. While Henley rushed for forty-nine yards and scored a touchdown, Auburn discovered another capable tailback in Chris Linderman, who gained ninety-nine yards on eighteen carries. Bob Newton and Eddie Welch stood out on defense.

Henley scored three touchdowns and rushed for 105 yards as Auburn roughed up Florida State, 27-14. Linebacker Bill Newton left the game with a strained knee ligament that would render his playing status uncertain going into each of the remaining games.

Henley picked up where he left off the following week as he bolted forty-seven yards for a quick touchdown against Florida. He scored again on a pass from Walls and Auburn built up a 26-7 halftime lead before hanging on to win 26-20. Henley rushed for eighty-one yards in the first half, but a sprained knee forced him to miss the second half and also to sit out the following game against Georgia in Auburn. But Linderman rose to the occasion, scoring Auburn's first touchdown on a 47-yard run and rushing for 149 yards on the day. Eleventh-ranked Auburn beat Georgia 27-10. David Langner intercepted two passes to tie him with Dave Beck for the team lead with six. Following the game, Auburn, for the fifth time in Jordan's career, accepted a bid to play in the Gator Bowl.

Then came Alabama.

Nobody thought Auburn would be 8-1 and ranked ninth nationally as it prepared to play the Tide, though no one was too surprised that Alabama had won ten straight, was ranked second in the nation behind Southern California and was bound for the Cotton Bowl to play Texas. In fact, Alabama had already clinched the SEC title because it had played one more conference game than anybody else in the league.

After reviewing the films and combing the scouting reports, Jordan and defensive coordinator Davis saw only one weakness in this powerful Alabama football team: the kicking game.

20

"This team at the top of the list"

•••••••••••••••••••••••••••••••

A University of Alabama fan once asked Terry Henley why Auburn people kept talking about those blocked punts. "I'll make you a deal, pal," Henley said. "Y'all quit singing about the Rose Bowl and we'll quit talking about the kicks."

Indeed that improbable contest, which occurred on December 2, 1972, is the foremost of all Auburn victories. Had it happened against Tennessee or Georgia — with Bill Newton blocking two punts and David Langner returning both for touchdowns — it would still be remembered, but it would not have been as deeply felt in the Auburn heart. This one was against Bear Bryant and an undefeated Alabama team.

While the Sullivan-Beasley teams had done a couple of numbers on the Tide, those wins didn't completely heal the wounds inflicted by Alabama throughout the 1960s — when Bryant too quickly rebuilt Alabama and knocked Jordan and Auburn off the top of the hill; when Alabama won the national title in 1964 after preseason forecasts picked Auburn to win it with Sidle and Frederickson; when Snake Stabler ran for a controversial touchdown in the mud to give Alabama a 7-3 win in 1967. But Auburn's 17-16 win in 1972 ended the hurt. Shug Jordan knew this and basked in it. The 17-16 victory, like the entire 1972 season, was Jordan's masterpiece. His team won with an excellent kicking game and a stout defense. They won in the role of an underdog.

Just a few days before Auburn played Alabama in 1975, Jordan's final season as head coach, he sat in his office and admired a painting on his office wall of the first blocked punt. He rattled off the names of the visible Auburn players — Newton, Bernich, Roger Mitchell, Danny Sanspree. "And Langner standing over in the wings waiting," Jordan said. "I can see Gantt (the punter) and I can see the ball rolling around and it's eventually going to bounce up behind Gantt, and Langner's going to pick it up and go for a touchdown. The same thing happened the next possession of the ball by the same two people, the blocked kick and pickup, Newton and Langner. It's unparalleled in the history of American football. And what a great day, 17-16."

Alabama appeared to have gotten out all the kinks during its second year of running the wishbone in 1972. The offense, directed by quarterback Terry Davis and with the blocking of guard John Hannah and center Jim Krapf, both All-Americans, had scored 37.7 points per game and led the conference in offensive yardage per game with 425. Auburn had averaged 18.7 points per game and 280 yards of offense. The Alabama defense, though playing in the shadow of the offense, was giving up fewer yards per game than anybody else in the league at 225.

The statistic that many people overlooked, which showed it would likely be a tight, low-scoring contest, was the average number of points allowed each game by the two defenses. Alabama had given up 11.6 points per game compared to Auburn's 13.6.

As Auburn began to prepare for the game, defensive coordinator Davis approached Jordan. "I have never seen an Alabama football team as sloppy as they are in the whole kicking game," Davis said. "It's just not sound."

Davis and Jordan viewed game films and saw several instances when opposing players had reached the kicker but had simply missed the ball.

"I believe we can block a punt," Davis emphasized to Jordan. "I believe we can block an extra point and a field goal."

Davis intended to stick with Auburn's eight-man rush, but he felt an adjustment at the right time in the manner of the rush might force a breakdown in Alabama's blocking and allow an Auburn body to get on the football.

While Jordan and Davis liked their chances in the kicking game, they became aggressive with the defensive plan to stop Alabama's wishbone. The previous season the Alabama wishbone ran at will over the Auburn defense in the battle of the unbeatens.

"The one thing that the wishbone always took away from you was the ability to blitz or take chances because you had so much responsibility to spread between two or three people on the outside," recalled Neel, a senior linebacker in 1972. "But this time we had a very good plan against the wishbone. We were able to do some things."

Auburn threatened first in the game following a David Langner interception at the Alabama thirty-five, which he returned to the ten, but which a clipping penalty pushed back to the twenty-five. Henley carried three times for twenty-one yards and Auburn had first and goal on the four. But three running plays lost a yard. Jett came on to attempt what seemed like a sure 23-yard field goal, but the snap from center flew over holder Dave Beck's head and Alabama took over on the twenty-nine.

Alabama promptly drove seventy-one yards in fifteen plays and scored with 11:16 left in the first half. Roger Mitchell, who had blocked a big extra point in the 1971 win over Georgia, rushed in from left end and blocked this one. Alabama led, 6-0.

With just over two minutes remaining in the half, Alabama intercepted a Walls pass at the Auburn forty-one and returned it to the thirteen. The Auburn defense stiffened and Alabama settled for a 24-yard field goal by Bill Davis. Alabama led at intermission, 9-0.

Alabama seemed on the verge of putting the game away when it scored early in the third quarter. The Tide drove seventy-eight yards in ten plays. Davis kicked the extra point this time and Alabama led, 16-0. At this point Auburn's offense had made only one first down in the game.

Just prior to the end of the third period, following a long missed field goal by Alabama, Auburn began its only drive of the day.

Henley and fullback Rusty Fuller carried for a first down to the Auburn thirty-four. As the final quarter began, three running plays made another first down. Walls was dropped for a seven-yard loss as he set up to pass, but tailback Linderman carried twice for seven and fourteen yards for a first down on the Alabama forty-one. After Fuller gained a yard, Walls completed a pass to sophomore end Thomas Gossom for fourteen yards and a first down. But there the drive stalled and Auburn faced a fourth and eight on the twenty-four. Jordan made the decision to go for the field goal with 9:15 left in the game. He felt that his team, after it had come so far, didn't deserve to be shut out by rival Alabama. Three points would generate enthusiasm and cut into Alabama's momentum. Three points would still make it possible for Auburn to win the game with two touchdowns and two extra points. Even if Auburn went for it and scored the touchdown, it would still need two more scores — a touchdown and a field goal — to win the game. And converting a fourth-and-eight for a first down against this Alabama defense, though Auburn was finally moving the football, wasn't anything to bet on. It wasn't a difficult decision for Jordan.

When he sent kicker Gardner Jett in, some of the crowd expressed its disagreement loud enough to be heard. On the sidelines Jordan turned and looked back at trainer Kenny Howard. Jordan smiled and said, "They don't think we're gonna win, do they?"

Jett converted the 42-yard field goal to make the score 16-3.

Following the kickoff, Alabama chalked up three first downs. But on third-and-five quarterback Davis fumbled the snap and fell on it at midfield. Alabama was forced to punt with less than six minutes remaining.

Defensive coordinator Davis may have felt that Alabama's punt blocking was soft, but it had still been good enough to give punter Greg Gantt the time to get away some long ones. Gantt had led the league in 1971 with a 41.9 average. He would lead it again in 1972 with a 42.6 average and again in 1973 with a 48.7 average.

As Gantt dropped back to punt, Auburn put its standard eight players on the line, four on either side of the center. Alabama placed seven men on the line, including the center, put two up-backs just off the line of scrimmage, each between a guard and the center, and stationed a deep blocking back in front of the punter. Oftentimes when Auburn went after the punt, the third Auburn man from the outside (on both sides of the line) lined up in front of the offensive tackle. At the snap of the ball that Auburn player "jammed" or held up the tackle so he couldn't block out on the Auburn end (who was the second man from the outside), thus allowing the end to rush between the offensive tackle and the offensive end; meanwhile the very outside Auburn man rushed to the outside of the offensive end. This could create a two-on-one rush from the outside if the offensive tackle was neutralized.

But on the ensuing punt by Gantt, Auburn switched to another version of its punt-block rush. The third man from the outside lined up on the inside shoulder of the Alabama tackle. On the right side of the Auburn line this man was linebacker Bill Newton. On the left side of the line it was linebacker Ken Bernich. Both players were having the game of their careers and each were well into double figures in tackles. Newton had played much of the game head up on All-American center Jim Krapf. Newton wasn't even listed as a starter for the game because of a knee injury. As Newton and Bernich lined up on the inside shoulders of their respective offensive tackles, the fourth Auburn man from the outside on both sides of the line (or the two most interior men) stationed himself on the outside shoulder of the offensive guard. The intention was for this Auburn man to rush into the up-back hole between the offensive guard and the center, and decoy the offensive guard into blocking down on him, instead of blocking out on the third man from the outside — Newton and Bernich. If the offensive tackle did his job and blocked the second man from the outside, nobody would be left to block the third man from the outside.

It worked. The adjustment in the Auburn setup seemed to confuse the Alabama linemen. Both offensive guards failed to block outward and Newton and Bernich charged untouched between their respective offensive guards and offensive tackles. Newton dove and blocked the punt on the Alabama forty-yard line. Bernich was right behind him and probably would have blocked it if Newton hadn't. The ball bounded behind the punter into the hands of Langner at the twenty-five and he ran for the touchdown. Jett's extra point made it 16-10 Alabama with 5:30 left in the game.

Newton recalled, "I moved down on the inside shoulder of the tackle. In doing this they messed up their (blocking) calls. When the ball was snapped I got through. I saw Gantt catch the ball and as I was seeing everything develop I just timed myself to take the ball off his foot. I'm not being cocky in saying this, but I had it all the way."

Alabama received the kickoff and drove for two first downs to its own forty-two. Two running plays gained six yards and Alabama had third and four on the forty-eight. Only 2:10 remained in the game. Davis rolled right on the option and linebacker Neel nailed him for a five-yard loss.

"Coach Davis had called a stunt where the end and linebacker switch responsibilities," Neel said. Neel's role was to go directly after the quarterback. "It was the easiest play I ever made in my life. I ran right through there. Nobody touched me. All I had to do was tackle somebody who was just turning to look at me when I got there."

Gantt came back into the game to punt. Bryant had told him to move up two yards and just punch the ball down the field.

"They thought we had blocked the first one from the outside," Davis said. "But we blocked it from almost the middle. When they moved their kicker up, it helped on the second one."

Instant replay. The offensive guard failed to block out on Newton and instead followed the rush of the man on Newton's left into the hole between the offensive guard and center, where the up-back was already positioned to stop that man's rush. While the up-back and guard unnecessarily double-teamed this man, and the offensive tackle blocked the man to Newton's right, Newton zipped in and blocked the kick on the thirty-five. The ball hopped neatly into Langner's hands at the twenty and he raced to the end zone. Jett's extra point gave Auburn a 17-16 lead with 1:34 left. The offensive guard on Bernich's side of the line had corrected his error and successfully blocked out on Bernich and put him on the ground.

Newton said, "I went through a similar place which was between the tackle and the guard. I don't remember if anybody hit me or if I ran over anybody, but I know I wasn't hindered too much in going through the line. It developed again and I blocked the punt. I saw Langner score. I went over to the sidelines worn out and sat on the bench. Everybody was hooping and hollering."

Davis said, "You always try and develop a mistake in there. What tickled me was that Ken Donahue, Alabama's defensive coordinator, had really developed that punt rush himself."

"Both times I saw somebody getting through there ahead of me, so I knew they had a better chance to block it than I did," said Langner, who was the outside man on the right side of the line, the same side Newton came from. "I decided to run behind the punter. I figured if I were back there I'd have time to stop and pick the ball up and still probably get to run with it."

Neel's responsibility on the punts was to stay back and watch for the pass. "I remember the sound of the ball hitting a body," he said, "and then people screaming."

Following the kickoff, a Langner interception of a Davis pass killed the Tide's chance to rally and ended Alabama's perfect season and national title aspirations.

On the day Newton recorded twenty-two tackles, eleven of them unassisted. Bernich also made twenty-two tackles, ten unassisted. Neel was in on fourteen tackles, seven unassisted. Langner scored two touchdowns and intercepted two passes.

The Auburn defense, seemingly on the field all day, held Alabama to 251 total yards (175 yards below the Tide's game average), 235 of which came on the ground on sixty-five rushing attempts. Auburn gained but eighty yards on offense, with fifty coming on the ground in forty-six attempts.

Years later Newton said of his greatest hour as a football player, "It was somewhere that I just happened to be on a very beautiful December day in 1972. I was fortunate to be playing football for

Auburn."

Jordan said, "I like to think we out-smarted Bear on that one."

Several days after the game, Bryant said, "I have a hard time looking at people in the eye."

At an awards banquet in Birmingham following the season, while everyone waited for Bryant to arrive, Newton chatted with former Tide star Johnny Musso. Newton was to be honored for his performance in the Alabama game. Finally Bryant showed up, said hello to several folks and made his way over to Musso.

"Coach Bryant, this is Bill Newton," Musso said.

Newton stuck out his hand. "Coach Bryant, it's nice to meet you."

Bryant looked down on Newton, looked at his hand and grumbled, "Yeah." Then he turned and walked away.

Neel recalled that he received scores of letters following the game. "They weren't really writing to congratulate me, but just saying where they were when it happened," Neel said. "It's been that way ever since. Everybody can remember where they were when Kennedy was shot, when the man walked on the moon, and if you're from the state of Alabama, when Auburn blocked the punts."

The victory over Alabama moved Auburn to sixth in the country. Auburn rolled over thirteenth-ranked Colorado 24-3 in the Gator Bowl and finished number five. Alabama finished number seven following a loss in the Cotton Bowl to Texas. Southern Cal won the national title.

Henley, Lorendo, Sanspree and Beck made first team All-SEC.

"I feel like I played with the toughest, roughest players to ever strap on an Auburn football helmet," Henley said. "What a close-knit group we had. I think that was a tribute to Coach Jordan."

At the beginning of the 1972 season, Jordan had stated, "With all due respect to our opponents, and realizing it will take a superb effort on the part of all the players and coaches, we are not conceding anything."

After the Alabama game, he said, "In twenty-two years I have always hesitated to put one of my teams ahead of any of the others, but today I'm putting this team at the top of the list."

The Associated Press named Jordan the SEC Coach of the Year for the third time — a remarkable twenty years since his first such honor in 1953.

21

"Normal is what I say is normal"

Following the 1972 season, Jordan and his family again discussed his retirement. After all, he had been to college football's mountaintop in 1957, and then staged one of the game's great comebacks fifteen years later culminating with the Cinderella team of 1972. But Jordan felt like he was on a roll. He enjoyed it immensely. And his twenty-fifth year as head coach — a number that seemed almost magical to him — seemed right around the corner.

But 1973 proved to be an in-between year for Jordan's football team. Proven talent returned in Bernich, Newton, Langner and Sivley on defense, and center Steve Taylor anchoring a solid offensive line. But the nucleus from the I formation of the 1972 offense — linemen Lorendo and Casey and running backs Owens and Henley — had graduated. The 1973 offense lacked personality and scoring punch. Auburn failed to score more than ten points in five games. Injuries hindered quarterbacks and running backs the entire season.

Auburn won in lackluster fashion over Oregon State to open the season, and beat hapless Chattanooga, 31-0. But Tennessee broke a three-year losing streak to Auburn and soundly whipped the Tigers, 21-0, in Knoxville. It was the first shut out of an Auburn team since 1967. The loss also ended Auburn's eight-game winning streak.

The highlight of the season, and one of the finer moments in Jordan's career, came on October 6 during a ceremony preceding the Ole Miss game. Before the home crowd, Governor George Wallace, on behalf of the state of Alabama, honored Jordan by renaming Cliff

Hare Stadium as Jordan-Hare Stadium. Wallace stated of Jordan, "His honor, integrity, impeccable character and his coaching record make him a legend in his own time."

The following summer, as Jordan drove slowly past the stadium, the magnitude of the honor hit home. "I saw 'Jordan-Hare,' and it was startling to say the least. And unbelievable, if you will, to realize my name is up there with Dean Hare's." Jordan's thoughts turned back to those difficult days following World War II, when his career was in limbo at Auburn and he frequently sought the company and advice of Cliff Hare on the older man's front porch. Jordan became the only active coach in America to have a stadium named after him. During Jordan's era the seating capacity in the stadium almost tripled, from 21,500 to 61,261.

Auburn beat Ole Miss and won five of its first seven games, including a 7-0 shutout of Houston. But the Tigers lost three of four down the stretch. After another dismal offensive performance in the eighth game of the season, a 12-8 loss to Florida in Auburn, Jordan decided to change the offensive formation from the I to the veer.

"We didn't have the personnel for the I," Jordan said. "To change horses in mid-stream, which I don't recommend unless you're somewhat desperate, is unthinkable. But we had people like (running back) Secdrick McIntyre who had a lot of quickness, which the inside and outside veer is so dependent on. We didn't accomplish a great deal in 1973, but we were building the veer into our offense for the 1974 season with (quarterback) Phillip Gargis."

Bill Yeoman, head coach of the University of Houston, had introduced the veer, a triple-option formation that retained two wide receivers. The two running backs split and lined up shading the outside of the offensive guards. As the triple option began, one of the backs ran at the tackle slot and the quarterback moved to him while reading the defensive tackle. If the quarterback didn't hand off the ball, he moved out with the trailing running back and optioned run or pitch depending on the movement of the defensive end.

The veer worked like a charm the first time Auburn ran it in 1973, against Mississippi State. McIntyre, a freshman, gained 117 yards on twenty carries and scored three touchdowns. Auburn won, 31-17.

Auburn didn't look good as it lost its final games of the season to Georgia and number-one-ranked Alabama. Freshman quarterback Gargis received valuable playing time toward the end of the Alabama game and revealed potential as a strong option quarterback. Gargis, from Leighton, Alabama, had starred as a wishbone quarterback in high school at Colbert County High.

Auburn finished the regular season with a 6-5 record and played in the Sun Bowl. "We really didn't have a bowl team," Jordan said. Auburn lost to Missouri, 34-17.

One of the coaches responsible for implementing the veer in 1973 was freshman/junior varsity head coach Doug Barfield. Freshmen were eligible to play varsity ball by this time and the junior varsity consisted mostly of freshman players. The future of Auburn's veer depended on two of these freshmen, Gargis and McIntyre. Barfield and Davis traveled to North Carolina State to study the veer as run by Wolfpack head coach Lou Holtz.

Jordan had hired Barfield prior to the 1972 season. Barfield, who grew up in Grove Hill, Alabama, played quarterback for Southern Mississippi from 1953-1956. He coached in the high school ranks for eight seasons and joined the staff at Southern Miss from 1967-1969. He moved on to Clemson as offensive coordinator for the 1970 and 1971 seasons.

Barfield visited Jordan when the position as freshman coach opened. "He made me feel like he really wanted me," Barfield said of Jordan.

Barfield's main concern was that Jordan might retire in a year or two and a new head coach would replace Jordan's staff. Barfield asked Jordan how long he intended to remain as head coach. Jordan said at least four years, which turned out to be accurate. Barfield also asked if Jordan had already lined up a successor. Jordan said no.

Following the loss to Georgia late in the 1973 season, Jordan despaired over the plight of his program. His teams had produced some great seasons recently, but he felt the current year had set the program back. Meanwhile Bryant's Alabama was coming into the

Auburn game undefeated for the third straight season and was ranked number one in the nation. Alabama was also stretching its lead in the recruiting game. The situation would worsen if Alabama whipped Auburn, and that seemed a good possibility. Jordan needed to throw a wrench in Alabama's momentum and give Auburn's program a spark. He focused on the junior varsity game between Auburn and Alabama, which fell on the off-weekend before the varsity game.

Jordan called his staff together. "Things look bad," he said. He pounded his fist on the table and stared at Barfield. "We've got to win this game."

Barfield's junior varsity team won it, 17-3. Jordan wanted the game so bad he allowed six freshman players to participate who had seen considerable varsity playing time during the season and who would play in the upcoming varsity game against Alabama. McIntyre was one of the six. He scored on a two-yard touchdown run. Freshman quarterback Gargis, who would see playing time against the Alabama varsity, threw a five-yard touchdown pass.

"I was afraid not to win," Barfield said. "I thought my neck might have been on the line. Coach Jordan was a fatherly type and a Southern gentleman as people have often said, but he was also a fierce competitor. He could get really ornery when the time came."

Jordan felt good about the 1974 season with Gargis at quarterback, McIntyre and Mitzi Jackson as the running backs, and having run the veer in actual game conditions. McIntyre and Jackson gave Jordan as much speed in his backfield as he had ever had at Auburn. They also stood out in another way: both players were black.

The emergence of the black football player in the SEC represented yet another of the many, many developments Jordan witnessed and contributed to during his incredible association with college football. Jordan and his staff learned from the experience as it developed.

"They were good people thrown into a tough situation," said Thomas Gossom, a black wide receiver who played from 1971-1974. Most important to Jordan was that "race" remain a non-issue in

Auburn's football program.

Gossom became the second black player to start regularly at Auburn. Prior to Gossom, James Owens, a hard-working, blue-collar type fullback, had played freshman ball in 1969, established himself as a kick returner on the varsity in 1970, and developed into an excellent blocking back in 1971 and 1972. Gossom addressed Auburn's first black player as "Daddy Owens," out of respect for Owens breaking the football color barrier at Auburn.

After Gossom, Auburn signed Jackson prior to the 1972 season and signed McIntyre before the 1973 season. In 1974, Gossom, a senior, Jackson, a junior, and McIntyre, a 5-10, 195-pound sophomore, all put forth the most productive seasons of their Auburn careers. McIntyre, who played through the 1976 season, became Auburn's all-time career rushing leader with 1,996 yards, overtaking Fob James, and went on to play a season of professional football with the Atlanta Falcons. McIntyre started the tradition at Auburn of swift, big-yardage, pro-caliber running backs. The likes of Bo Jackson, James Brooks, Joe Cribbs, Brent Fullwood and Lionel James all surpassed McIntyre's rushing mark, but very definitely followed in his footsteps.

McIntyre played prep ball at Lee High School in Montgomery. The highly-coveted runner appeared on the verge of signing with Alabama, until Jordan visited him. "We're going to give you the ball. We're going to make you an All-American," Jordan stated.

McIntyre took to Jordan's great expectations, and he also appreciated Jordan's apparent indifference toward the color of his skin. McIntyre sensed that Jordan was his own man in the recruitment of blacks.

"I don't think anybody at Auburn had the guts to try and push Coach Jordan to do something that he didn't want to do," McIntyre said. "Coach Jordan said how it was going to be and that was the law. Coach Jordan didn't see black or white with me. I never sensed that. He was more of a friend to me than a coach. It was, 'Come here, son, this is what's going on.' As for some of the other coaches, I think it (race) was very prevalent at times. But it really wasn't a big deal for me as long as I could play."

Jordan's program wasn't immune from isolated racial run-ins between players. During McIntyre's freshman year a teammate told McIntyre that Auburn could "win without niggers." McIntyre restrained himself from going after the player.

"He didn't know my background. It was nothing for me to bust somebody in the mouth," McIntyre said. "Basically that's what I saw growing up. But I didn't want to resort to that. When I felt threatened I'd call my daddy and he'd say, 'Walk away from it if you can.'"

When McIntyre roomed with a white lineman, a few teammates chided the lineman for rooming with the black running black. The lineman responded, "Any of you think you're big enough to whip either one of us?" Nobody tried.

Gossom recalled a few scraps on the practice field as a result of racial tension, but said the worst kind of experience came when he and several white teammates gathered socially and somebody let the word "nigger" slip out.

"They'd all go to apologizing," Gossom said. "A lot of times I'd avoid big groups because I didn't want somebody I liked to slip up and say something that might cause some friction between us."

Gossom played high school ball at John Carroll in Birmingham, the same school Pat Sullivan attended. During freshman orientation at Auburn in the summer, Gossom walked into the athletic department and said he wanted to try out for the football team, a bold move considering Auburn's roster listed only one black player at the time and Gossom was an unknown. Gossom proved himself his freshman year and received a scholarship.

Though their situations created frustration at times, both McIntyre and Gossom departed Auburn with many white teammate friendships that continued through the years.

"Coach Jordan probably bent over backwards to make things appear to be equal," Gossom recalled.

Quarterback Gargis observed, "I don't think there was a racial bone in Coach Jordan's body as far as football was concerned. Everybody was treated as athletes, not black, not white. You work hard, you get a chance to play."

Jordan said, "I don't give a damn whether competitors are red, white and blue, green or even turquoise."

The most delicate situation Jordan confronted involving his black football players came in February 1974. Jordan had sensed a lack of determination, pride and poise on his team during the latter part of the 1973 season. It embarrassed him. He set about bringing everyone together by way of tighter discipline. "I decided at the start of our winter program we would get everything in ship shape," Jordan said.

The incident was over facial hair and Jordan's rule that forbid football players to wear beards, goatees, moustaches and muttonchop sideburns. Jordan encountered running back Jackson in the dorm and told him bluntly he needed to shave. Jackson didn't appreciate the order nor its tone and met with Gossom, McIntyre and a black running back named Sullivan Walker. McIntyre was the only one of the bunch who couldn't grow facial hair. The players felt Jordan's demand was unreasonable during the off-season, especially since grooming requirements had become lax for the basketball players. Word of the disgruntlement got back to Jordan and he scheduled a Thursday afternoon meeting with Jackson, Gossom and Walker.

The fourteen black athletes living in the athletic dorm — four football players, six basketball players and four members of the track team — quickly met to discuss the issue. The group decided that if the situation couldn't be resolved, the black track members as a show of support would boycott a weekend meet in Montgomery, and the black basketball players would skip their game Saturday night.

"Coach Jordan never liked having his back up against the wall," Gossom recalled. "Here was a man who started as head coach at Auburn in the 1950s and here were some kids with the nerve to test him over whether they had to shave or not."

At the meeting, Gossom said, "We really want to talk about it."

"Either yes or no," Jordan said.

"You're not giving us a chance," Gossom said. "If you put it like that we don't have much of a choice."

"You have a choice," Jordan replied.

"I guess we'd rather leave if we can't sit down and discuss it," Gossom said.

Following the meeting Jordan stated, "I met some unexpected resistance from three boys I've been very close to. I asked if they intended to comply with the regulations. They indicated their intention to defy, so I recommended to the athletic director they move out of the athletic dorm and remain on scholarship the remainder of the quarter and that their scholarships be terminated at the end of the quarter."

Jordan spoke separately with McIntyre. He emphasized that McIntyre had tremendous potential as a football player. "I want you to stay," Jordan said.

McIntyre said that because he couldn't grow a beard he didn't really have a reason to want to leave. But he could hardly stay behind as the only black football player left in the dorm. Jordan said he understood McIntyre's position.

"Don't make any crazy moves. Don't think about transferring," Jordan said. "Let's see if this thing will blow over."

McIntyre said, "Here was a man who had a special feeling for me."

When McIntyre returned to the dorm his black teammates were packing their cars. McIntyre didn't move his belongings out of his room but he jumped in his car and nervously drove home to Montgomery. He explained the situation to his dad, who couldn't believe what he was hearing. "You don't even have fuzz on your face, let alone talk about a facial hair problem," Mr. McIntyre said. "You're there for an education. You're not there for a popularity contest. If these other guys want to leave that's up to them."

The four football players quickly discovered that the black members of the track team and basketball team hadn't followed suit and were participating in the weekend events.

Jordan stated, "I have rules and regulations about hair. I've had that rule since 1951 and I am going to keep my rule. I think discipline is part of winning whether it is football or life. As long as I am head coach I am going to run this football team. I have treated all, blacks and whites, alike and will continue to do so."

Jordan told the press the situation did not involve McIntyre.

Jordan met again with Gossom and Jackson on Sunday and two days later with Walker. They agreed to obey Jordan's facial hair rule, and Jordan agreed to reinstate them to the squad and continue their scholarships. Jordan required that they live the remainder of the winter quarter at one of the student dorms and then move back into the athletic dorm.

Afterward, the athletic department established a haircut and facial hair rule for all of the sports teams, and also set living condition guidelines for the athletic dorm.

Defensive coordinator Davis recalled when he, Jordan and athletic director Hayley met to discuss dormitory rules. When Davis suggested that the head coaches of the other teams probably ought to be present, Jordan reacted angrily. "That was like slapping Coach Jordan in the face," said Davis, who of course hadn't intended his remark to be offensive. But Jordan didn't agree that the formation of basic disciplinary rules required an act of Congress, and he saw no reason why he shouldn't set down the rules himself.

Jordan later said, "The black coach at Florida A&M, Jake Gaither, who was well known all over the country and a marvelous fellow, was asked one time what kind of haircut he required his team to have. Jake said a normal haircut. They asked Jake what was normal. And he said, 'By God, normal is what I say is normal!' That's the kind of discipline I was raised with."

A couple of years after graduating from Auburn, Gossom saw Jordan at a bowl game in Birmingham. "I'll never forget, he pulled me to the side and gave me his phone number at home," Gossom said. "He told me I should always call him if I needed anything. I appreciated that more than anything that ever happened between us."

The facial hair controversy was long forgotten by the beginning of the 1974 football season. The team played as a unit and won nine and lost two in the regular season. Then it demolished Texas in the Gator Bowl and finished eighth in the nation.

Certainly McIntyre, Jackson and Gossom put the incident behind them. McIntyre rushed for 839 yards on 170 carries, a 4.9 yard average. He performed his best in big games. Jackson rushed for 525 yards. Rick Neel also rushed for 437 yards. Auburn set a school record for yards rushing per game with 280.6. Center Lee Gross and fellow offensive linemen Lynn Johnson, Andy Steele, Dave Ostrowski and Chuck Fletcher made room for the running backs. They didn't do much pass-blocking as Auburn threw only 104 passes, completing forty-three. Gossom caught nearly half of them, twenty, for 294 yards and three touchdowns.

Sophomore quarterback Phil Gargis was the straw that stirred the drink. Jordan, who always referred to Gargis as Phillip, admired the quarterback's hard-nosed, all-out brand of football. Jordan emphasized raw toughness throughout the season.

"I bet we saw *Walking Tall* ten times," Gargis said, referring to the movie about Sheriff Buford Pusser, who returned law and order to a small Southern town by breaking up illegal activities and people's heads with a giant wooden club.

"Let's walk tall and carry a big stick!" Jordan told his players over and over again.

Gargis not only played a mean game of football, but he boxed well, too. He participated in the school's boxing tournament. Jordan loved the sport of boxing. He related to people with physical prowess such as Gargis.

"I go into the ring and look out and Coach Jordan is sitting in the front row," Gargis said. "He's shaking his left fist for me to go get 'em. How could I lose the match with him sitting right there?"

Gargis won the match and the tournament. Occasionally Gargis fought outside of the ring as well. "If I was in the wrong, Coach Jordan would let me know," Gargis said. "But he was supportive when I wasn't at fault and it was a matter of my pride and honor."

While Gargis ran the veer on the field, assistant coach Barfield steered it from the sidelines. Jordan named Barfield offensive coordinator prior to the season.

As did the offense, the defense played exceptional football in 1974. Ken Bernich, a senior linebacker, and Mike Fuller, a senior safety, made All-American and first team All-SEC. The Birmingham Quarterback Club named Fuller the SEC's Most Valuable Back. Fuller, who had also made first team All-SEC as a junior in 1973, was one of the best punt returners in the nation during his career and the very best in the SEC. He set a conference record for yards per return with 17.7. He returned three punts for touchdowns in 1974. Fuller went on to a distinguished career in the NFL, playing eight years with San Diego and Cincinnati.

Senior defensive end Rusty Deen was Auburn's third player to make first team all-conference in 1974. Deen grew extremely close to Jordan and served as a pallbearer at Jordan's funeral.

Deen and Jordan first met when Auburn recruited Deen in 1970 as a lanky 6-foot-2 southpaw quarterback out of R.E. Lee Institute in Thomaston, Georgia. Jordan's assistant, Sam Mitchell, brought Deen to the Auburn athletic complex during the recruiting season. As Mitchell and Deen walked past Jordan's office, Jordan hollered from his desk, "Sam, who you got? Is that Rusty Deen?"

Deen couldn't believe that Jordan even knew he existed. Mitchell took Deen into Jordan's office and the aging coach told Deen he was also left-handed and the idea of a left-handed quarterback thrilled him.

Jordan then picked up a piece of chalk in his left hand and wrote "Rusty" on the blackboard. Jordan took the chalk with his right hand and, starting with the "n" in "Deen," wrote the last name backward. When Jordan finished, the first and last names looked like they had been written straight across with one hand. The writing exercise, on top of being recognized by the great coach, won over Deen in a hurry.

Jordan's hopes for a southpaw signal caller were shortlived. In the first freshman-varsity scrimmage of 1970, a crunching hit on Deen's shoulder ended his career as a passer. The following fall Deen moved to defensive end and added forty pounds, up to 215, under the tutelage of coach Jim Hilyer. Auburn redshirted Deen during the 1971 season. He played on special teams in 1972. He became a starter in 1973. But he nearly missed his all-conference season in 1974.

"Going into the spring of 1974 I was feeling sorry for myself," Deen said. "My neck was sore, my shoulder was sore. I thought I wanted to be drinking beer instead of practicing football. I went to Coach Jordan and told him I didn't feel like I wanted to take my fifth year."

Jordan asked Deen if football had become a drudgery.

"Yes sir, I guess so," Deen said. "It's not fun."

"Football never is fun in practice," Jordan said.

"I guess not," Deen replied.

"As you make up your mind, just think of this," Jordan said. "Auburn is going to be fine without Rusty Deen. But how is Rusty Deen going to be without Auburn?"

Deen recalled, "I thought, 'You sorry old buzzard. I wanted you to feel sorry for me and beg me to stay.' I was in full pads the next day."

Deen's affection for Jordan ran so deep that he gave his daughter the middle name of Jordan.

"Coach Jordan was a learned man," Deen said. "Everything he said was substance. He didn't try to be famous. He just wanted to win as many football games for Auburn as he could."

Going into the 1974 season Jordan's thoughts weren't solely focused on winning football games. His mother, Katie Jordan, had passed away earlier in the year at his brother Ned's home in Texas. She was buried in Selma at the age of eighty-five.

The 1974 team became the third Jordan team to win ten games, along with the national champs of 1957 and the "Amazin's" in 1972. Auburn's victory over Tennessee in the third game of the season confirmed speculation that this team played on another level.

Auburn had beaten Louisville 16-3, and murdered Chattanooga 52-0 prior to the UT game. For the first time ever Auburn was to play Tennessee in Auburn rather than Birmingham.

Jordan recalled somewhat sarcastically, "For a long time the contract between Auburn and Tennessee specified that the games would be played in Knoxville and Birmingham. Of course that contract was signed before Auburn was in a position stadium-wise to have the kind of crowd that the game was going to draw. It would have been a financial disaster. Why the game in 1974? Well Tennessee, out of our urging and out of the goodness of their hearts, said, 'We will come and see how it is.' Well, it wasn't very good for them. Some people threw oranges at 'em and hit one Tennessee coach. That's not really the right way to handle things, but it was such an unusual situation. So much had been written about the fact that Tennessee would not come to Auburn."

Before a standing-room crowd of 64,293 in Jordan-Hare Stadium, Auburn annihilated the Vols 21-0. Bernich, Deen, end Liston Eddins and their defensive cohorts held Tennessee to 153 yards total offense. Tennessee crossed midfield once. The Auburn veer meanwhile rushed for 268 yards. Jackson and McIntyre ran up and down the field, and reserve back Kenny Burks drove the final nails as he scored three touchdowns on runs of four, two and three yards.

Auburn beat Miami, Kentucky, Georgia Tech and Florida State to go 7-0 on the season. But once-beaten Florida knocked off the Tigers, 25-14, in Gainesville. Florida led 19-14 in the third quarter when Auburn drove to the Gator thirteen-yard line. On a halfback pass Mitzi Jackson threw a strike to an Auburn receiver in the end zone, but the receiver dropped the ball. Florida controlled the game thereafter.

Perhaps the most gut-wrenching game of the year was a 17-13 win over Georgia in Auburn. An earlier win over Mississippi State had improved Auburn's record to 8-1 and boosted Auburn to number seven in the nation.

A courageous defensive effort included goal line stands at the end of the first half and at the end of the game. Georgia had first and goal on the two shortly before intermission, but had to settle for a field goal. Then late in the game, with Auburn ahead by four points, Georgia had first and ten on the fourteen. Georgia gained eight yards in three plays and attempted a quarterback sneak on fourth down. But Auburn stiffened to preserve the victory. Gargis had one of his greatest days at quarterback, rushing for 160 yards on twenty-four carries. McIntyre gained 112 yards on nineteen carries. They both scored touchdowns. Chris Wilson kicked a 36-yard field goal for Auburn.

Auburn, bound for the Gator Bowl, remained number seven as it went into battle with Alabama, which for the second year in a row brought a 10-0 record, a number-one ranking and a major bowl date with Notre Dame into the game. Auburn played its heart out but lost a tough one, 17-13. Auburn threatened to pull it out late as it scored with 2:47 left to make the score 17-13, and then got the ball back at midfield with 1:07 remaining. But an Alabama defender got in the way of an end-around handoff from Gargis to tight end Dan Nugent. Alabama recovered the fumble and ruined Auburn's night. McIntyre led Auburn with ninety-nine yards rushing and scored Auburn's first touchdown. Gargis scored from the two for the second touchdown. Jackson added sixty-nine yards rushing. Tackle Rick Telhiard stood out on Auburn's defense.

The key play of the game, and one of the most remembered plays in the Auburn-Alabama series, came in the third quarter when Gargis connected on a 41-yard pass to Gossom for an apparent touchdown. But as the specialty teams ran on the field for the extra point attempt, an official said Gossom had stepped out of bounds before catching the ball, which was illegal at that time. Officials returned the ball to the original line of scrimmage and Auburn didn't regain its wind until late in the game.

The pass play was designed to trick Alabama's defensive back into committing too soon on Gossom. With the ball snapped on the right hash mark, Gossom ran several yards downfield and cut right to the sidelines. Gargis pumped once, Gossom turned and sprinted long and Gargis laid in the pass before the safety could get over. Gossom sidestepped a tackle and ran into the end zone. But back upfield an official pointed to where Gossom's foot had touched the out-of-bounds line. When Gossom had broken long the defensive back got a piece of him on the sidelines and Gossom had to plant a foot to keep his balance.

"It was very, very close," Gossom said. "The people on television said my top three toes came down on the line."

After scoring, Gossom ran to the sideline and the extra point team came out and lined up. "All of a sudden there was this confusion," Gossom said. "Coach Jordan went berserk." The NCAA later changed the rule to allow players to step out of bounds and return to the action.

Following the game Jordan offered one of his more memorable lines: "If Alabama is number one, then we're number one-and-a-half."

Jordan didn't allow the heartbreaking defeat to affect preparations for the Gator Bowl match with Texas. Auburn battered Darrell Royal's Longhorns, 27-3. McIntyre again led the team in rushing with eighty-nine yards. Jackson gained sixty-four yards and scored a touchdown. Gargis received most valuable player honors as he rushed for fifty-one yards and threw for sixty yards on six completions, two of them for touchdowns to Ed Butler. Freshman fullback Earl Campbell rushed for ninety-one yards for Texas.

The Gator Bowl victory stationed Auburn at number eight in the nation behind a stream of great teams including number-one Oklahoma, Southern Cal, Michigan, Ohio State, Alabama, Notre Dame and Penn State. Auburn sat a spot above Nebraska. Once again Auburn mixed with the best teams in the country.

Jordan seemed to be getting better with age as a head coach. His past seven teams had played in bowl games. In the last six seasons, counting bowl games, his teams had won fifty-two of sixty-eight games, with six of the losses coming in one season. Three of his past five teams had finished in the top ten.

Now his twenty-fifth season as Auburn's head coach and his sixty-fifth birthday stared him in the face.

Beautiful numbers, Jordan thought, to retire on.

22

"They lived and died for Auburn"

In mid-December 1974, before the Gator Bowl, Jordan told athletic director Hayley he planned to resign. During the Gator Bowl victory celebration Jordan discussed the resignation with President Philpott, and said he planned to announce it before the 1975 football season. It would give him twenty-five years as Auburn's head coach.

Jordan thought of twenty-five as a magical number. He had also accomplished all there was to accomplish as a head coach: National and SEC Coach of the Year honors, a national championship, a conference title, a Heisman Trophy winner, an Outland Trophy winner, twenty-two All-American players, and scores of all-conference performers. He was ready to wake up on a Saturday morning in the fall without a knot in his stomach, and to spend time with his wife and children and grandchildren.

Of course he would miss coaching, and time would tell just how much. But Jordan saw that the college game was evolving rapidly into something bigger and more complex. He had participated in enough new eras during his fifty years as a player and coach. The time had come, in his words, to put on his hat and walk out.

One reason Jordan wanted to make the announcement before the season was that he wanted his team and himself to go out in a blaze of glory. His preseason announcement would lend drama to the season and hopefully lift his team to even loftier heights than anticipated by preseason forecasters.

"It would be nice to go out with a bang," Jordan said. "We have the talent and the determination to make it a special year. I want it to be the kind of thing I can remember for a long, long time."

Jordan had watched how Nebraska's Bob Devaney withdrew from the sidelines. Devaney announced his forthcoming retirement in January 1972. The Cornhuskers rose to the occasion and finished number four in the nation that year. In Devaney's final game as head coach, on New Year's Day 1973, Nebraska blasted Notre Dame 40-6 in the Orange Bowl. Jordan liked that.

Another reason Jordan preferred a preseason announcement was that the Auburn Board of Trustees, in its search for a head coach, would be less likely to go outside of the existing coaching staff with Jordan still the head coach and emphatic that his successor be promoted from within.

Assistant head coach Paul Davis said Jordan spoke to him about his retirement plans early in the 1974 season. According to Davis, Jordan said, "I'm going to recommend you for the job. I'll let you know when you need to go talk to the Board of Trustees."

Many Auburn people expected Davis to succeed Jordan. Davis had served as assistant head coach since coming to Auburn in 1967. Jordan had leaned on him heavily at times to serve as head coach, such as during Jordan's bout with prostate cancer. Davis had also assumed the role of head coach when Jordan missed the Gator Bowl in 1970 due to an appendectomy. Davis had five years of head coaching experience at Mississippi State, though it ended sourly. Finally, Davis was a defensive coach and Jordan's coaching philosophy began with keeping the other team out of the end zone. The only negative mark on paper against Davis may have been his age: fifty-three.

Others thought offensive coach Gene Lorendo might be in line. Lorendo had played at Georgia when Jordan assisted there in the 1940s, and had followed Jordan to Auburn as one of his original assistants in 1951. Lorendo had stood at Jordan's side for the duration and was greatly responsible for bringing the passing game into the offense in the late 1960s when Jordan's conservative attack had run its course.

Despite the excellent credentials of both Davis and Lorendo, a source close to the situation may have hit the nail on the head when he said the Auburn administration would never have allowed Davis or Lorendo to get the job because Davis "liked to party too much" and Lorendo "cussed and chewed tobacco."

While Jordan leaned initially to Davis, the administration found a fair-haired child during the 1974 season in Doug Barfield. Jordan had promoted Barfield to offensive coordinator from JV coach prior to the season and Barfield's veer offense chewed up major yardage game after game. The Birmingham Touchdown Club named Barfield the SEC Working Coach of the Year in 1974. When Auburn ripped Texas 27-3 in the Gator Bowl, Barfield became the leading candidate to succeed Jordan. He was only thirty-nine years old.

During the Gator Bowl, an Auburn trustee attempted to introduce Barfield at a hotel hospitality gathering as "Auburn's next head football coach."

"I said, 'Wait a minute, hold on,'" Barfield recalled. "'Don't be saying those things.'" Barfield didn't know of Jordan's definite plans to retire. "I thought it was just a few folks who liked what I was doing," Barfield said.

Barfield spoke frequently with Jordan during this period about the older man's coaching philosophies and feelings about Auburn. "He had a grasp of the whole situation and of Auburn people better than anyone," Barfield said. "He had weathered some tough times. He was able to do that because of his temperament and personality and his relationship to Auburn people. We became pretty close. I valued his opinion and assessment."

Barfield said Jordan never spoke to him about becoming the next head coach until it happened. Jordan never brought up the subject with Davis again either, until after the decision. In the end, Jordan recognized that his influence was limited with regard to the selection of either Barfield or Davis; instead he focused on the importance of promoting a man from his staff, and he considered both Davis and Barfield very capable of succeeding him. "I was fighting, like all get-out, to make sure as best I could that somebody on the present

Auburn staff became the new head coach," Jordan said.

The Board of Trustees met in Montgomery on Monday, April 7 to discuss the hiring of a new head coach. They debated whether or not to form a search committee. The majority decided against it. Barfield had the votes going in, including the support of trustee Henry Steagall, who was executive secretary to Governor Wallace.

"The majority of the board felt we should go ahead and name one of the two (Barfield or Davis) that Coach Jordan had recommended," Philpott said. "The ultimate decision — and this decision was made by the board, and Coach Hayley and I were in concurrence on their decision — was that Coach Barfield be appointed."

Philpott said the plan was for Jordan to talk with Davis and Barfield the next morning about the decision, then for Philpott, Hayley and Jordan to officially offer the job to Barfield, and then hold a press conference in the afternoon announcing Jordan's retirement and Barfield's hiring. But early that evening following the board meeting, a board member leaked the developments to a reporter in Mobile.

Davis walked in his house that night and the phone rang. A reporter wanted to verify the story that Jordan was retiring. Davis said he didn't know anything about it and immediately called Jordan.

"I called Coach Jordan and said, 'You have a rumor out that you're going to resign,'" Davis recalled. "He blew his top."

Jordan didn't offer an explanation and said he would call back, which he did a short time later. He asked Davis to come to his house.

"I went over there and he told me they had hired Doug as head coach," Davis said. "That just hit me cold. I couldn't believe it."

Davis was hurt because he hadn't been kept informed of the developments. He felt out-politicked. The turn of events would always puzzle Davis. "I never held any animosity toward Jordan. We remained friends. I never was a politician. I didn't know all of the board of trustee members. I was a football coach."

Davis said the board member who leaked the news phoned him the next day and apologized.

Barfield also walked into his house that evening with the telephone ringing. He heard of his good fortune from two callers. Barfield denied it because he hadn't heard the official word. But he was aware of the ongoing speculation over when Jordan would retire and he felt he would be considered for the job. "Where there was so much smoke, there might be some fire," Barfield said of the phone calls.

The third call of the evening came from Philpott, who asked Barfield to come to the President's home. Philpott, Hayley and Jordan awaited Barfield. They offered him the job around eight p.m. and Barfield accepted. "I would have taken it for groceries at the time," Barfield said.

Barfield understood Davis's disappointment. "Paul was one of the greatest on-the-field coaches I've ever seen," Barfield said. "He thought possibly he was going to get the thing. I never felt there was any vying among us. I was just coaching as hard as I could."

Auburn called a press conference for eleven a.m. on Tuesday, April 8, one week before the beginning of spring football practice. Mrs. Jordan accompanied her husband. Others in the room included Buck Bradberry, Kenny Howard, Gene Lorendo, Shot Senn, Joe Connally, Jordan's long-time secretary Emily Foster and Bill Beckwith.

Jordan didn't hide his displeasure about the leak. He felt stabbed in the back at a time when he should have been feeling great pride over taking one of the most important steps of his life. He would be making a number of phone calls to friends in the following days to apologize for how the news had reached them.

"I'm terribly upset with the way the story broke," Jordan said. "The rug was pulled out from under me. The most disappointing thing is I haven't had a chance to talk to the players. Whoever broke the story to the media has done irreparable harm to Auburn. This is just not Auburn's way of doing things."

Jordan indicated he had no hard plans for the future. "I'm not a wealthy man, just sort of comfortable," he said. Jordan's salary just topped $44,000, compared to the $12,500 paid him his first season in 1951. "I'm not tired of coaching. I just wanted to get out when I was ahead. I don't feel like I'm a legend."

Jordan said Barfield possessed qualities which would attract attention. "He is a leader, has a high moral character and interacts with people well," Jordan said.

Recognizing the possibility of a conflict between Barfield and Davis supporters going into the season, Jordan quoted Winston Churchill: "If the past and present fight, bicker and quarrel, we will surely lose the battle of the future." He then added, "Let the past and present unite behind our new head coach and let's win the battle of the future."

In Tuscaloosa Bear Bryant said Jordan's announcement caught him by surprise. "I hate to see him go," Bryant said. "Coach Jordan has meant an awful lot to the Southeastern Conference."

Bobby Dodd, Georgia Tech athletic director and former head football coach and Jordan rival, commented, "One of the distinguishing features about Coach Jordan's teams was morale. They came to whip you and they lived and died for good old Auburn."

Jordan's companion from Montgomery, Billy Thames, said, "His retirement is the biggest loss Auburn has ever suffered in any position." Thames was still bitter that his friend wasn't the athletic director.

Jordan was on his way out as head football coach, but his service to Auburn University would continue. On May 24, 1975, six weeks after the press conference, Governor Wallace appointed Jordan to fill a vacancy on the Auburn University Board of Trustees. Jordan had made it known that he very much wanted the position. Jordan's appointment became effective upon his retirement the following year.

A busy spring practice kept Jordan from thinking too much about his now-official pending retirement. But it hit him during the summer and he grew anxious. "I don't want the season to start because I know it will come to an end," he said. He was concerned that his edginess would spill over to the players. "I've got to be careful or I will spoil the whole thing."

In July, a development in the Jordan family temporarily relieved him of the mental taxation. A grandson, James Ralph Jordan III, was born. On August 31, the Reverend Bill McLemore of Holy Trinity Episcopal Church baptized Shug's grandson. Prior to the ceremony, while speaking with the family, McLemore referred to "the River Jordan."

"That's JUR-den, preacher," the proud grandfather laughed, making light of his old Selma accent.

Going into fall practice only two starters returned on defense — tackle Rick Telhiard and end Liston Eddins. Jordan expected to field a solid team, but he knew that so few proven bodies on defense was dangerous. The offense returned the starting backfield of Gargis, McIntyre and Jackson, and excellent linemen in Lynn Johnson, Dave Ostrowski and Chuck Fletcher. Preseason forecasts said Jordan's retirement would have a positive impact on the team. The Associated Press picked Auburn number seven in the nation.

The lineup of SEC head coaches going into Jordan's final year included Alabama's Bryant, Doug Dickey at Florida, Vince Dooley at Georgia, Fran Curci at Kentucky, Charlie McClendon at LSU, Ken Cooper at Ole Miss, Bob Tyler at Mississippi State, Bill Battle at Tennessee and Fred Pancoast at Vanderbilt.

It was almost as if the disappointment and hurt feelings that resulted from the story leak in April formed a cloud that never went away. Auburn won three, lost six and tied two in Jordan's final season as head coach, only his third losing season in twenty-five years. The coaching staff experienced fragmentation due to Barfield's hiring, and also some uncertainty as coaches wondered what Barfield intended to do when he became head coach.

But the poor record stemmed mainly from the tremendous loss of personnel on defense after the 1974 season, a rash of injuries to both the offense and defense throughout the 1975 season, and simply too many turnovers. Jordan's pending retirement probably worked against the team.

"Sometimes you can try harder and it hurts you," Gargis said. But the bottom line was that the talent just wasn't there on most Saturdays and the team's confidence drained. "We got in the hole a couple of times and couldn't overcome it," Gargis said. "We lost that feeling that we could win."

As two-a-day practices began Jordan fretted about his squad being a week behind Memphis State and Baylor, the first two opponents of the season. Those teams would play their first games a week before Auburn opened its season.

Off the field an issue involving the NCAA concerned Jordan and revealed his growing disgruntlement over the game's governing body. The latest NCAA rule said visiting teams could only dress forty-eight players, while the home team dressed sixty.

"I have enough states rights in me to resent being told how many people you can dress out," Jordan said. "From time immemorial we've been able to dress out kids that we knew weren't going to play. To give them the chance to run out on the field before their mothers and fathers and grandparents and girl friends...it doesn't cost anything or hurt the economy of football which seems to be the reason for some of these asinine, silly rules."

Two of the many injuries that would plague the 1975 team occurred two weeks before the opening game. Running back McIntyre, hoping to build on his great sophomore year, aggravated a hamstring. He would miss the opening game and be hampered by the problem most of the season. Jeff Gilligan, starting split end, separated a shoulder.

Before the home crowd, Auburn, a twenty-point favorite, lost its opener to Memphis State, 31-20. Mitzi Jackson rushed for 177 yards and Auburn gained 290 yards on the ground, but turnovers burned Auburn the entire game. Auburn fought back from a 24-0 deficit to 24-14 and threatened to score again early in the final period. But a fumble gave the ball to Memphis State, which then drove over the inexperienced defense for the clinching score.

"This has to be one of the most disappointing afternoons in the twenty-five years I have coached at Auburn," Jordan said. "I don't think they were a well-coached football team. So that's my fault. I had the impression at times that some people didn't even know they were supposed to be in the ballgame."

Jordan's agony and frustration multiplied. Auburn tied Baylor 10-10 the following game.

The week before the Tennessee game in Knoxville, Jordan said, "I'm somehow glad to be getting out of the intercollegiate scene. I find myself so incompatible with the whole structure of intercollegiate athletics that I would be better off from a mental standpoint and be free of the annoyance. The rules are just becoming more ridiculous each year. If all of the presidents that are now running the NCAA with the assistance of faculty chairmen continue, I think the intercollegiate scene is going to be in shambles. There are so many people voting on intercollegiate athletics who don't know anything about athletics."

The trip to Knoxville was a sentimental one for Jordan. The game broke Jordan's heart. Auburn led in the final quarter, 17-14, but Tennessee drove eighty yards for a touchdown and won the game, 21-17.

Auburn went 0-3-1 on the season when it lost at home to lowly Virginia Tech, 23-16. "To come right into our own backyard and find ourselves out-coached, out-fought and out-everything was just a little bit too much," Jordan said.

Auburn rebounded with a 15-9 win over Kentucky, and came back from a 27-10 deficit to beat Georgia Tech in Atlanta, 31-27. The victory over Jordan's long-time rival pleased him to no end. He called it one of the tremendous accomplishments in his twenty-five years and it was certainly the highlight of his final season.

A narrow 17-14 victory over Florida State evened Auburn's record at 3-3-1, and Jordan felt a strong finish could push his team into a minor bowl game. But Jordan had won his last game as a head coach. A season-ending knee injury during practice to offensive tackle Chuck Fletcher set the tone for the upcoming Florida game. The Gators won, 31-14.

Jordan appeared as head coach on the home field for the final time against Mississippi State on November 8, 1975. He received a thunderous, emotional, standing ovation from a homecoming crowd of 64,796 as he came on the field before the kickoff. He wore his traditional light jacket and khaki pants. His players, who had run on the field ahead of him, huddled and applauded him as he walked along the sidelines. Tight-lipped and with his head bowed, Jordan lifted his right hand to acknowledge the crowd. Then he broke into a trot. When he reached his players he spread his arms and hugged those in front. The remainder of the team closed in around him. Shortly after the kickoff Jordan wiped tears from his eyes. He received a similar ovation prior to the second half kickoff.

"Such a flattering thing, such an overwhelming thing, such an awesome thing to have 65,000 people stand on two occasions and give me a standing ovation," Jordan said. "They made it all worthwhile. Baseball players tip their cap. I didn't have a cap on so I couldn't do that. Cassius Clay would have danced around the ring or shaken hands with himself. I'm no Cassius Clay. The only thing I could think to do was run. And I don't do a very good job of that, but my arm action was pretty good."

The game, like the season, was a disappointment. It ended in a 21-21 tie. Auburn was in position to win it with a late field goal, but fumbled on a simple running play deep in State territory while attempting to use some clock and set up the field goal. The injury list expanded. Running back Mitzi Jackson broke his leg. Offensive lineman Lynn Johnson hurt his knee.

"There's been something wrong with this ill-fated season from the very beginning," Jordan said.

The tie with State gave Jordan an 88-15-2 record on the home turf, though Jordan and Auburn were later credited with a victory over State when an NCAA penalty forced State to forfeit the 1975 game.

Auburn lost its next one to Georgia, 28-13, in Athens. Following the game Jordan and one of his former players and assistant coaches, Vince Dooley, met for the final time in the middle of the field. Their teams had played twelve times and each had won six since Dooley departed Auburn to become head coach at Georgia in 1964. Dooley said only twice in his career did his emotions get the best of him when he met the opposing coach following a game. One was when the opposing coach was his brother, Bill Dooley. The other encounter was with Jordan following their last game.

"This was my coach," Dooley said. "This was the one who gave me a start. To see him come out to congratulate me in a very graceful, gentlemanly way...my emotions took over. I hugged him. I have never meant anything more sincerely in my life. It was an outburst of love."

And so there was one game to go. Jordan had tangled with Bear Bryant seventeen times since Bryant took the Tide post in 1958. Jordan's teams had won five (1958, 1963, 1969, 1970, 1972) and lost twelve. No other coach had beaten Bryant more times. Alabama came into the game with a 9-1 record and bound for the Sugar Bowl. Auburn came in 3-5-2 with only four players who had started in the previous year's Alabama game: Telhiard, Gargis, McIntyre and Ostrowski. Despite the difficult season, Jordan admired his players for holding together and working hard until the end.

Jordan dressed in a suit and tie for his final game. Before the kickoff Bryant approached Jordan, removed his houndstooth hat and shook Jordan's hand.

Gargis recalled Jordan's address to the team before the game. "He said, 'If you can walk off the field after the game and feel like you did your best, then I'm satisfied. If you win, you win, if you lose, you lose. But you will always feel good about yourself knowing you did everything you could to win.'"

There was no magic for a retiring coach this time. It went as expected, with Alabama winning 28-0. Auburn played Alabama close for the first half and trailed only 7-0 at intermission. But Alabama quarterback Richard Todd, who had thrown a seventeen-yard pass for a Tide touchdown in the first quarter, scored two touchdowns on 33-yard and fourteen-yard runs in the third quarter, and threw a 24-yard touchdown pass to Ozzie Newsome in the final period.

"This season will stay with me as long as I'm alive," Jordan said in a downcast locker room following the game. "I'd like to have another time at bat. But it just can't happen. I'm sitting here right now wishing I could come back another year."

The Sunday after the Alabama game Jordan taped his final "Auburn Football Review" in Montgomery. The television station, WSFA, hosted a small party for Jordan. Officials came from South Central Bell, the show's sponsor. Former players dropped by, including Bill Newton and David Langner of blocked-punt fame. The Monday morning after the show Jordan preferred not to labor over the disappointing season or the recent loss to Alabama, but instead reflected on the 17-16 win over Alabama in 1972.

"An oft-forgotten young man was not present yesterday at the broadcast," Jordan said. "Sort of like when the astronauts go to the moon, two get off and walk around on the moon and one flies that machine up there waiting on them. And he's oft-times forgotten. And Gardner Jett will always be the forgotten man, but not by his coach. He's the guy that kicked the field goal when everybody said we shouldn't go for a field goal. And somebody had to kick the extra points after those two blocked kicks. We could have lost the ballgame. Except for Gardner Jett."

Defensive tackle Telhiard and punter Clyde Baumgartner made first team All-SEC from Jordan's final squad.

Jordan appeared as a head coach one last time in the American Bowl in Tampa, Florida on January 10, 1976. His South team fell to the North, 21-14. Barfield served as his offensive coordinator. As with Auburn's season, turnovers stalled the South throughout the game.

"There comes a time to quit and this is it," Jordan said. "I'm going on sixty-six, and with the Lord's permission I have a lot of living to do."

Twenty-five years. The Jordan era had ended.

23

"He was at peace with himself"
●●●●●●●●●●●●●●●●●●●●●●●●●●●●●●●●

In late September 1979 Shug Jordan sat in his Memorial Coliseum office, freely offering his opinions about the state of college football to a young sportswriter. Jordan was enjoying it immensely as it allowed him to escape briefly the more pressing business at hand, which was finding a replacement for President Philpott, who had announced his retirement earlier in the month.

The search for a president was one of Jordan's two most important duties as a member of Auburn's Board of Trustees; the other was successfully leading the drive to expand Jordan-Hare Stadium. On this overcast September morning construction was ongoing at the stadium. The work would continue through 1979 and be completed for the 1980 season. But Jordan would never see the Tigers play in the enlarged arena; he died the next summer.

Retirement began well for Jordan following the 1975 football season. On March 26, 1976, his hometown of Selma held "Shug Jordan Day."

Jordan said, "To be honored by your hometown, when people who have known you all of your life see fit to call you back and say nice things about you, this is the greatest honor a man can obtain."

Jordan was not one to push himself in retirement to make himself feel useful. He enjoyed taking it easy. He didn't have any serious hobbies. A wicked slice dominated his golf game. He wasn't mechanically inclined. He liked to cut the grass and would fiddle around in the yard, but his wife was the one with the green thumb.

He would get up some mornings and walk with his wife and dog, but even then he only liked a brief stroll.

He loved being with his four grandchildren, although this reminded him of how little time he had spent with his own three kids. "I was always off at an alumni meeting, on a recruiting trip or tied up with football in some way," he said. "I'm trying to make up for lost time, but I will never be able to retrieve some of those days when Ralph and I should have been out there fishing."

His son, Ralph Jr., said, "Our best time was as I got older, went through college, married and began to develop my household. As I began to encounter some of life's problems and some of the stress and strain, I had the benefit of his experience and his willingness to provide advice and counsel, whether it be finances or which job to take or how to approach something. He was not one to burden you with his advice. He really appreciated you asking him. You could tell it was advice he had picked up the hard way. It was built on years of experience, years of dealing with other people my age."

Jordan continued to address the old familiar alumni groups. He also spoke before some not-so-familiar organizations. Once he received a request to speak before the Scott County Alumni Association in Oneida, Tennessee, in the northeast part of the state. He hadn't heard of an Auburn club there so he called his son, who lived in nearby Norris. His son wasn't aware of a major outpouring of affection for Auburn in the heart of Big Orange country, either. They found out that Scott County High School had its own alumni group that met once a year and invited a guest speaker. Jordan traveled up and gave the talk.

Traveling was not high on Jordan's retirement list of things to do. In the fall of 1979 he and Evelyn and a group flew to Istanbul in Turkey and toured the Black Sea countries. The expedition wore out Jordan. He swore he would never leave the U.S. again.

"His idea of traveling was to go to Montgomery to see Billy Thames for lunch," Jordan's son said. "He would rather go uptown and sit in the barber chair than go anywhere."

What Jordan enjoyed most during his retirement was simply

maintaining his contacts. He spent hours and hours on the phone at home and at his office.

Doug Barfield, who had the unenviable task of succeeding Jordan as head coach, recalled that Jordan's office was just down the hall from his own. "You were very aware of the man and his presence," Barfield said. Jordan purposely stayed out of Barfield's hair.

"I don't know what an old retired football coach could do anyway," Jordan said.

Jordan attended most of the home games and attended the Alabama game in Birmingham. Billy Thames said that in the first couple of years of Jordan's retirement, the coach greatly missed being around his boys, hard-nosed scrimmages and Saturday game days. Pat Sullivan said Jordan certainly missed specific moments such as when the players reported back for fall practice. "That's a special time," Sullivan said. "It's a new year, a new beginning. The anxiety, the bond, the love, the relationships. I'm sure Coach Jordan never got that out of his system."

But generally Jordan was content to be off the sidelines. He took great pride in serving on the Board of Trustees and took his work there seriously. Kenny Howard said Jordan considered his title of trustee as one of the high water marks of his career, if not the highest. Jordan's son said his father was ecstatic about being a member of the board.

The most controversial issue during Jordan's years as a trustee was whether or not to expand Jordan-Hare Stadium. On January 12, 1978 the board approved a feasibility study of the expansion. Discussions continued nearly all year. Jordan was the leading proponent of the expansion movement. The plan called for adding an upper deck on the west side, VIP seating, rebuilding the press box and installing lights. Seating capacity would increase from 61,261 to 72,169.

Those opposed to the plan suggested that the stadium expansion money — several million dollars — should be channeled instead into the school's academic programs. They questioned the wisdom and appearance of spending money on a football program that was currently under investigation by the NCAA. Also, most current home games failed to fill up the existing capacity. Average attendance in 1977 had fallen below fifty thousand. And athletic director Hayley and head coach Barfield were quickly losing the support of the Auburn masses.

The plan nearly fell by the wayside when the original project estimate of three-million dollars was more than doubled. Jordan pushed it nevertheless. "Auburn is going to have a good football team in the future," he said. "With the proper type of football team in Auburn and an attractive schedule, we can have 72,000 in Auburn to see football, and consistently."

On November 29, 1978, the Board of Trustees voted 4-3 in favor of the expansion. Jordan, Walston Hester, Red Bamberg and John Pace voted for it. Henry Steagall, Sue Fincher and Congressman Bill Nichols voted against it. Four trustees didn't vote. One of those opposed, Steagall, later said Jordan showed tremendous vision in pushing the project through. Steagall, of course, was so right.

Auburn football in the 1980s, under head coach Pat Dye, filled up Jordan-Hare to the point that another stadium expansion was executed. Auburn added an upper deck on the east side and increased seating to 85,214 for the 1987 season. Auburn sold 75,000 season tickets a year during the later Dye years. The program's greatest hour came on December 2, 1989 when Auburn hosted the University of Alabama in Jordan-Hare Stadium before 85,319 fans. Jordan had visualized the Auburn-Alabama game coming to Auburn from Birmingham. Georgia, Georgia Tech and Tennessee had all eventually found their way to the Plains, and Jordan figured it was just a matter of time before Alabama fell in line. Jordan once told Billy Thames that he would rather play Alabama in Tuscaloosa than in Birmingham when Alabama served as host.

In January 1979 Jordan experienced a proud day when he and Evelyn joined Vince and Barbara Dooley at the inauguration of Fob James as governor of Alabama. Dooley and James had played together on Jordan's early teams and Dooley coached under Jordan for eight years before taking the head job at Georgia in 1964. Now James was reaching the pinnacle of his political career, and Dooley was entering his sixteenth season at Georgia with three SEC titles and four major bowl games under his belt. And he was only two seasons away from a national championship.

"We reminisced about bygone days and looked to the future," Dooley said of what would be his last visit with Jordan. "It was a special day in my life because it gave me the chance to spend the whole day and evening with Coach Jordan. I wish we had other moments like that through our lifetimes, but, of course, it was impossible."

On May 23, 1979, Jordan created a stir with comments he made to the Abbeville Auburn Club. He said the Board of Trustees was "collectively ill-informed" and was merely a "rubber stamp" for the university administration. Jordan said the board's purpose should be to establish policy, while the administration should handle daily operations. Several months later Jordan said his criticism must have hit home because the board was displaying more initiative and leadership.

But Jordan's first love was still football, and on that September morning in 1979, ten months before Jordan's death, the young sportswriter could only count his blessings as Jordan spoke at length about the college game. The great coach pulled no punches.

One of his chief concerns was discipline, or the lack of it. "Discipline is harder to get across and harder to understand on the part of young people," Jordan said. "Not because they're black athletes or white athletes, but just because of their own background and family background. I think you're seeing a slackening of discipline, not only in football, but you see it in major league baseball, you see it in the Army and the Navy. I don't think it's real good. I don't know that I would have had the answer to it if I hadn't gotten out. I might have relaxed my rules and regulations with the times. But I think I would have been wrong and I'd really have to question my approach to discipline if I did that."

The increasing specialization in the game didn't bother Jordan, but he was glad to have sidestepped most of it.

"You have such a specialized game," Jordan said. "I'm sure it allows a lot of people to play and that's good. But I sit up there in the pressbox and half the time I don't know who's in the game. With all these specialized teams, kickoff return, punt return, punt protection, goal line stand, extra point and field goal teams, there's a great influx of people going and coming. It sort of looks like 42nd and Broadway to me."

Jordan had also become aggravated over what he perceived as poor coaching with regard to basic blocking and tackling techniques.

"People used to be taught to block and tackle with their shoulder and in close to the neck where the shoulder and neck join," he said. "We used soft headgear and won a national championship with foam rubber inside and a soft outer shell rather than that plastic type thing they use today. Coaches today are teaching people not to tackle with their shoulder, but they tackle with their head. They stick their head right into the numbers of the man running with the football. Consequently you see most of the big linemen and people that do the tackling walking around with something called a donut around their neck. That's from whiplash I guess. And what a tremendous amount of pressure when you hit with the top of your head. What a tremendous pressure that puts on the spine. I just wonder if there wouldn't be less injuries if we went back to tackling and blocking with our shoulders."

One of the popular college football issues during the fall of 1979 was a playoff system to determine a national championship. Jordan opposed it.

"I never have been for the playoff," Jordan said. "We in the Deep South are subjecting our football players to the hottest months of the year. We find ourselves going out and trying to play football with heavy equipment and headgear on in August. By the time you play a bowl game you have practiced from mid-August to January. That's enough football. I don't think a playoff is going to solve anything. It's just going to lengthen the season. People are tired. What about going to school, what about examinations, or is all that important? I think it is. I think it really is and I would hate to see them go to a national playoff."

Jordan had become especially disillusioned with what he perceived as a win-at-any-cost attitude prevailing in college football.

"I put a lot of stock in doing the very best that you can and playing the game up to the hilt," Jordan said. "We're sorry if we lose and it's disturbing to us and we'll try and do better the next time. But to become absolutely obsessed with winning is wrong. Now I'm not trying to underestimate winning. I think it's vital to a football coach, it's vital to a team, it's vital to a business. But not at any cost."

Related to the subject of winning, Jordan referred to a recent exchange with a reporter from *The New York Times*. The reporter had called Jordan for his input concerning the statement that Bryant, by his own admission, had mellowed with age.

"Do you think he has?" the reporter asked Jordan.

"Hell no, I don't think he's mellowed," Jordan said.

The reporter also said that Bryant had claimed he was more interested in turning out the right kind of people than he was in winning.

"Do you believe that?" the reporter asked.

"Hell no, I don't believe that either," Jordan said.

The following month, October 1979, Governor James appointed Jordan to a five-man search committee for finding a successor to Philpott. "Coach Jordan had a great sense of direction and perception," James recalled of Jordan the trustee. "His presence and stature were such that he was himself, which was plenty."

On March 9, 1980, Dr. Hanly Funderburk, chancellor of Auburn University at Montgomery, and Dr. Steven Sample, vice president of the University of Nebraska, each received six votes from the Board of Trustees. Jordan had voted for Funderburk. On April 6, Sample withdrew his name. On April 7, the board voted 10-1 for Funderburk to assume the presidency. Jordan again voted in favor of Funderburk. This was Jordan's final official contribution to Auburn University.

By now Jordan's health had turned against him. In late February he had received blood treatment for an anemic condition at

Brookwood Medical Center in Birmingham. His family had felt that at Christmas Jordan seemed somewhat lethargic and not as active with the grandchildren as he normally was.

On April 22 Jordan visited his urologist, Dr. Sheridan Shirley, at Brookwood. Ralph Jr., visiting from his home in Tennessee, drove his dad to Birmingham. They expected a brief visit. But Ralph Jr. became concerned as his dad's time with the doctor stretched on. Eventually Dr. Shirley called Ralph Jr. into his office. Shirley wanted to put Jordan in the hospital and run some tests.

"Can you tell me what the problem is?" the son asked.

Shirley rose from his desk, walked to the door and closed it. "Ralph, your father's got cancer," Shirley said.

Shirley said the prognosis was grave.

"Does he know?" the shocked son asked.

"No, and we will find an appropriate time to tell him," Shirley said.

What Jordan had was acute leukemia — a malignancy in which cancer cells from the bone marrow enter into the blood. It had arisen from myelofibrosis, an abnormal condition of the bone marrow, which often results in acute leukemia.

On Friday, April 25, following two days of tests, as Jordan prepared to check out of the hospital, he suffered a heart attack in his room. He immediately received a temporary pacemaker. On Tuesday, April 29, doctors installed a permanent pacemaker in Jordan. During this period the *Birmingham News* reported that Bear Bryant visited Jordan. Bryant would be dead of a heart attack within three years.

On May 2, Jordan was moved from intensive care to a private room. In the days that followed at the hospital and then at his home in Auburn, until his death, those closest to him met with him or phoned him for the last time.

Former running back Terry Henley visited Jordan in the hospital. Henley had written Jordan weeks earlier and asked him to write a letter regarding an employment matter. When Henley walked in the hospital room Jordan was sitting up in bed. Jordan said he had written the letter. Henley thanked him but said it obviously wasn't a priority at the moment. They reminisced and also talked about the current Auburn football team. They both expressed amazement at the speed with which running backs James Brooks and Joe Cribbs could turn the corner.

"What about me turning the corner when I played?" Henley asked his old coach. "What does that make you think of?"

"Slow motion," Jordan replied.

When Pat Sullivan visited Jordan at the hospital their affection for each other was displayed not so much in words as in their eyes, expressions and gestures. Jordan and Sullivan greatly respected and trusted each other. Both were leaders.

"He had that kind of smile on his face like he was happy to see you and everything was going to be all right," Sullivan said. "He was at peace with himself. He didn't want anybody suffering because of him."

Kenny Howard accompanied Mrs. Jordan to Birmingham to bring Jordan back to Auburn. Jordan had grown pale and thin, "but he was just as sharp and alert as I had ever seen him," Howard said.

Jordan asked Howard, "Am I dying, Kenny?"

Howard hesitated briefly and replied, "Well, all of us are dying a little bit every day."

Jordan returned to Auburn to live the final weeks of his life at home. He received blood transfusions at East Alabama Medical Center in Opelika, but his condition deteriorated. He became terribly thin. He knew the end was at hand. His personal physician, Dr. Jim Mathews, administered to Jordan in the coach's home.

Ralph Jr. drove his dad around Auburn on several occasions. The last time the son and father were together outside of the home was when they met athletic director Hayley outside the south end of Jordan-Hare Stadium. Hayley opened the gate and they drove slowly around the field to allow Jordan a look at the nearly-completed construction of the upper deck on the west side. Such glory this man had inspired on this gridiron. Such memories of him.

In the days before his death Jordan received few visitors at his home. Former assistant head coach Paul Davis was one. As they conversed on the sofa, Jordan placed his hand on Davis's hand and patted it.

Doug Barfield sat at Jordan's bedside. Jordan inquired of Barfield's children. "Coach Jordan was not a whiner," Barfield said. "He did not want to talk about his condition. He was still upbeat."

Former assistant coach Buck Bradberry visited his mentor five days before Jordan's death. Bradberry sat in a chair next to the sofa where Jordan stretched out. What Bradberry remembered most from their exchange was their laughter.

Terry Beasley spoke with Jordan over the phone three days before Jordan's death. Jordan told Beasley not to visit him. Jordan didn't want Beasley to see his declining condition. He preferred that Beasley remember him as the vigorous man he was. During their conversation Jordan spoke at length about Auburn football in the 1950s and 1960s, recalling specific practices and talks to his teams.

J.D. Bush, Jordan's football teammate at Auburn, visited Jordan shortly before he died. Bush and Jordan said goodbye to each other. Bush searched for words. "You're here for a while and you've got to go on," Bush said to Jordan. "There's another station down the road."

Billy Thames, one of Jordan's greatest supporters, visited Jordan in the final days. They shook hands, then Jordan kissed Thames's hand and said, "Billy, say goodbye."

Early on Thursday morning, July 17, 1980, with his family at his bedside, Jordan died peacefully and with dignity. He was sixty-nine years old. Auburn and the college football world went into mourning.

The funeral service was held the next day at two p.m. at Holy Trinity Episcopal Church in Auburn. The Reverend Bill McLemore conducted the service. Pat Sullivan, Terry Beasley, Mike Neel, Terry Henley, Rusty Deen and Phil Gargis served as active pallbearers.

"That was the greatest honor I ever had," Beasley said.

A huge crowd packed the 250-seat church, which was just a block from Jordan's home. Mourners overflowed onto the lawn outside on a typically hot summer day. Governor Fob James, Vince Dooley, Lloyd Nix, Ken Rice, George Atkins, James Owens, Dave Beck, Connie Frederick, Danny Sanspree, Mickey Zofko and Thomas Gossom were but a few of the many friends and former players to attend the service. Coaches Bryant, Ken Donahue, Mal Moore and Bill Oliver flew in from the University of Alabama.

A seat was reserved for Bryant at the front of the church, but he preferred to stand near the back. An excited undertaker told McLemore about the situation.

"What should I do?" the undertaker asked McLemore.

"You let Bear Bryant do whatever he wants to do," McLemore replied, recognizing that Bryant didn't want to call attention to himself by walking down the aisle and sitting in front.

Prior to the service reporters from the major networks asked McLemore for a copy of his sermon. He told them there would be no sermon.

"The people gathered here are the sermon for Coach Jordan," McLemore told the congregation.

The service lasted fifteen minutes.

Jordan was buried at Memorial Park in Auburn.

A large part of Auburn University had died with Jordan. Southern culture had suffered a major setback. College football had lost a great coach.

Shug Jordan was gone.

Bibliography

•••••••••••••

Bolton, Clyde. *Unforgettable Days In Southern Football*. Huntsville, AL: The Strode Publishers, 1974.

Bolton, Clyde. *War Eagle, The Story of Auburn Football*. Tomball, TX.: Strode Publishers, 1973.

Bryant, Paul W., with John Underwood. *Bear*. Boston: Little Brown and Company, 1974.

Dooley, Vince, with Loran Smith. *Dooley's Dawgs*. Atlanta: Longstreet Press, 1989.

Dye, Pat, with John Logue. *In The Arena*. Montgomery, AL: The Black Belt Press, 1992.

Edson, James. *War Eagle - A History of Auburn Football 1892-1951*. Nashville: Benson Printing Co.

Fitts, Alston III. *Selma, Queen City of the Black Belt*. Selma, AL: Clairmont Press, 1989.

Grayson, C. C. *Yesterday and Today: Memories of Selma and Its People*. New Orleans: Pelican Press, Inc., 1948.

Hester, Wayne. *Where Tradition Began, The Centennial History of Auburn Football*. Birmingham: Seacoast Publishing/The Birmingham News, 1991.

Housel, David. *from the desk of david housel..., A Collection Of Auburn Stories*. Auburn: The Auburn Network, 1991.

Housel, David. *Saturdays to Remember*. Auburn: The Village Press, 1973.

Jackson, Walter. The *Story of Selma*. Birmingham: The Birmingham Printing Co., 1954.

Koger, Jim. *National Champions*. Columbus, GA.: Atlantic Publishing Company, 1970.

Little, Tom. *Soaring Eagles*. Montgomery: L&M Corporation, 1965.

Morrison, Samuel E. *The Invasion of France and Germany*. Boston: Little, Brown & Company. 1957.

Reeder, Paul. *The Auburn Tigers of 1957, National Champions.* Montgomery: The Brown Printing Company, 1990.

Ryan, Cornelius. *The Longest Day.* New York: Victor Gollancz Ltd.

Smith, Loran, ed. *Between the Hedges.* Atlanta: Longstreet Press, 1992.

Wallace, Francis. *Knute Rockne.* Garden City, NY: Doubleday & Company, Inc. 1960.

Wilkinson, Bud. *Football Winning Offense.* New York: Time, Inc., 1987.

PERIODICALS

Atkins, Leah Rawls, "Ralph 'Shug' Jordan, A Solidier, Engineer As Well As Coach." *The Auburn Alumnews,* November-December 1988.

Donnell, Rich, "Shug Jordan: Gentleman Coach." Alabama Magazine, September 1985.

Hemphill, Paul, "Waaaaar EA-gul." *Atlanta Magazine*

Jenkins, Dan, "...And Auburn Runs The Most." *Sports Illustrated,* September 21, 1964.

Johnson, William, "The Alabama quality of mercy was strained." *Sports Illustrated,* November 18, 1968.

Logue, John, "Auburn's Shug Jordan: Last of the Legends." *Southern Living,* September 1974.

McGowen, Dru, "Home Schedule Godfather." *Inside The Auburn Tigers,* October 1988.

McGowen, Dru, "Marauders Own Colorful History." *Inside The Auburn Tigers,* May 1991.

McGowen, Dru, "The Coach's Wife." *Inside The Auburn Tigers,* January 1990.

Putnam, Pat, "Underneath that 7 is an S." *Sports Illustrated,* November 27, 1971.

"Southeast Conference." *Sports Illustrated,* September 23, 1957.

"Sullivan To Beasley Or...How Auburn Stopped Running And Learned To Love The Bomb." *Sport,* 1971.

REFERENCES

Alabama Football Media Guide, 1989

Auburn Football Game Programs, 1951-1975

Auburn Football Media Guides, 1979, 1992

The 1992 Southeastern Conference Football Guide

MEDICAL CONSULTANT
Dr. Robert M. Donnell, Mobile

PHOTO CONSULTANT
Les King, Auburn University Photographic Services

TRANSCRIPTS
Harry M. Philpott Oral History Transcripts, Transcribed by Alfrieda
    Brummitt, Edited by Dwayne Cox and Kayla Barrett, Auburn Univer-
    sity Archives, January 13, 1992

SHUG JORDAN DIARY OF 1975 SEASON
Auburn University Archives

VIDEOS
100 Years of Auburn Football

OTHER SOURCES
Auburn University *Glomerata*, 1929-1976
Selma High School Yearbook, 1924, 1925, 1927

NEWSPAPERS
Alabama Journal
Auburn Bulletin
Auburn Plainsman
Birmingham Age-Herald
Birmingham News
Birmingham Post-Herald
Montgomery Advertiser
Selma Mirror
Selma Times-Journal
Auburn Alumnews

INSTITUTIONS
State of Alabama Archives and History, Montgomery
Auburn University Archives
Montgomery Public Library

Auburn University at Montgomery Library
Selma Public Library

PUBLIC RELATIONS
Auburn University Sports Information
Florida A&M Sports Information
National Collegiate Athletic Association
University of Alabama Sports Information
University of Georgia Sports Information
University of Notre Dame Sports Information

Interviews
•••••••••••

(Conducted in person and/or by telephone specifically for this project)
Marjorie Moss Anderson
George Atkins
Leah Rawls Atkins
Tim Baker
Doug Barfield
Jeff Beard
Terry Beasley
Buck Bradberry
J.D. Bush
Joe Connally
Paul Davis
Rusty Deen
Vince Dooley
Caroline Draughon
Dr. Ed Dyas
Roswell Falkenberry
Mrs. Roswell Falkenberry
Jimmy Fenton
Tucker Frederickson
Don Fuell
Phil Gargis
Tom Gossom
Sam Hobbs
Terry Henley
Hal Herring
Billy Hitchcock
Jake Hitchcock
Kenny Howard
Fob James
Shug Jordan
Ralph Jordan, Jr.
Mike Kolen
Dr. Woodward D. Lamar
Billy Lapsley
Gene Lorendo
Ken Lott
Buddy McClinton

Dick McGowen
Henry McHarg III
Secdrick McIntyre
Reverend Bill McLemore
Dr. Greer Megginson
Carl Morgan Jr.
Dorothy Neill Moore
Mike Neel
Ralph O'Gwynn
Bill Oliver
Bummie Roton
Bo Russell
Elmer Salter
Joe Sarver
Henry Steagall
Carl Stephens
Pat Sullivan
Sol Tepper
David Thames
Gusty Yearout
(Conducted by author for articles appearing in *Alabama Magazine* and *Inside The Auburn Tigers*, from which material was used for this project)
Jeff Beard
Terry Beasley
Vince Dooley
Mailon Kent
Secdrick McIntyre
Bill Newton
Dr. Lloyd Nix
Jimmy Phillips
Ken Rice
George Rose
Bo Russell
Pat Sullivan
Jack Thornton
Billy Thames
Travis Tidwell